The Dark and Evil World of Arkansas Prisons

Transformed Through Federal Court Intervention

First Edition

Andrew Fulkerson, J.D., Ph.D., Jack Dison, Ph.D.,
and Linda Keena, Ed.D.

cognella®

SAN DIEGO

Bassim Hamadeh, CEO and Publisher
Alisa Munoz, Senior Project Editor
Casey Hands, Production Editor
Emely Villavicencio, Senior Graphic Designer
Greg Isales, Licensing Associate
Natalie Piccotti, Director of Marketing
Kassie Graves, Vice President of Editorial
Jamie Giganti, Director of Academic Publishing

3970 Sorrento Valley Blvd., Ste. 500, San Diego, CA 92121

Contents

Acknowledgments

The authors wish to express their appreciation for the contributions of Southeast Missouri State University graduate assistants, Megan Newman and Crystal Cecil, and University of Mississippi graduate assistants, Maisha Bulaya and Clay Taylor, for their efforts in this book. Arkansas State Representative Jimmy Gazaway and Arkansas Department of Correction Chief of Staff Solomon Graves also provided invaluable assistance. Inmates who suffered from the abusive conditions that were forced on them for decades by an unthinking or uncaring state government, along with the state and prison officials and inmates who had the courage and tenacity to implement the reforms mandated by the federal courts, must also be recognized. Finally, Judges J. Smith Henley and G. Thomas Eisele, along with attorneys for inmates, Chief Justice Jack Holt and Phillip Kaplan, must be honored for their efforts, without which the reforms that brought the Arkansas prison system into the modern age would not have been possible.

Andrew Fulkerson, J.D., Ph.D.
Jack E. Dison, Ph.D.
Linda D. Keena, Ed.D.

1 | Beginnings

Introduction

Arkansas has been a relatively poor state in a relatively affluent nation. That fact and other social, political, and cultural realities of the region and of the nation produced a prison system that deserves historical attention. After early experimentation with an imitation of the Pennsylvania model, followed by extensive use of leasing inmate labor, the state finally settled on a plantation-type farm prison. Although periodically criticized both by reform-minded Arkansans as well as outside observers, the system became strongly woven into the fabric of the state's institutional composition and was not dislodged until the highly visible controversy and the subsequent intervention of the federal courts it produced in the late 1960s.

Beginnings

Governor James Conway signed legislation to create the first prison in Arkansas in 1838, just two years after Arkansas became a state. In requesting the prison in 1836, the governor asked for "a prison to protect society from the ravages of crime and to correct criminal behavior" (Crosley, 1986, p. 11). This prison, built for slightly more than $150,000, began operating in 1841 on land located at the present site of the State Capitol Building in Little Rock.

This first prison was at least partially patterned after the Pennsylvania version of the penitentiary movement, which was pioneering long-term incarceration of serious criminal offenders. The early Pennsylvania system penitentiaries placed convicts in virtual isolation from others to separate offenders from corrupting outside influences, thus giving them an opportunity to ponder their misdeeds. The prisoners were also required to perform labor so as to offset costs of incarceration (Barnes, 1921).

Exactly how this technology was implemented in Arkansas in the early 1840s is unclear. In whatever form, its implementation was short-lived since the main building of the prison was burned in a riot in 1846. Rebuilt with the assistance

FIGURE 1.1. Arkansas state penitentiary, 1892.

of convict labor, the same building was again heavily damaged by fire in 1850 (Bayliss, 1975). Following the 1846 fire, a member of the state board, which directed the penitentiary, expressed total disillusionment with the Pennsylvania model stating, "The Pennsylvania system is not effectual either as a preventative or restorative means to reprove lawlessness or disorder ... indeed our state prison has been a complete failure" (Crosley, 1986, p. 13). Officials speculated whether corporal punishment might offer more promising results.

In the earliest years, state employees operated the penitentiary, but the responsibility shifted to private contractors with the negotiation of a contract in 1853 to build a wall around the penitentiary. Under the supervision of a state inspector the contractor supervised inmates and provided daily upkeep with state subsidies. Thus, the use of inmate labor was first introduced to the general operation of the institution. This arrangement, a very early form of privatization, was clearly designed to relieve the state of the financial burden of prison operations. This continued until the penitentiary was abandoned to federal troops in the Civil War who used it as a military prison (Bayliss, 1975). When federal troops entered Little Rock in 1863 they discovered an empty prison (Ayers, 1984).

The Lease System
With the enactment of the 13th Amendment abolishing slavery, many of the former slaveholding states of the South developed the practice of leasing entire prisons to private contractors who put prisoners to work in farming and other forms of labor. The practice of prisoner leasing in the post–Civil War American South "is commonly attributed to the legacy of slavery, the destruction of southern penitentiary buildings during the Civil War; postwar fiscal retrenchment,

FIGURE 1.2. Arkansas State Penitentiary, main entrance and guard house, 1920s.

political corruption, and a general lack of concern for convicts, most of whom were [B]lack" (Lichtenstein, 1996, p. 3).

These conditions were all present in Arkansas. Following the Civil War, the state prison was in need of major repairs. In order to operate a prison at minimal state expense, Arkansas turned to a creative leasing arrangement. A contract was let for a 15-year lease, which subsidized the lessee to establish a convict lease system. Inmate labor first was to be used to repair the penitentiary while subsequent profit from leasing convict laborers would reimburse the state for all expenses incurred (Bayliss, 1975). Although the arrangement did not work as well as planners expected, it was clear from the state's decision that officials had identified leasing as the way to dispose of the management of convicts with minimal effort and expense.

In 1867, the chairman of the Legislative Committee on Prisons spoke words that represent much of the essence of the correctional philosophy that was to be pursued for many decades: "Punishment is the only preventative of crime and the fear of it the only restraint upon the passions and wicked hearts of evil men. ... [Let us] place the penitentiary upon such a footing as would render it of no expense to the state, and the State penitentiary would become a source of material revenue" (Crosley, 1986, p. 19). Policy makers were convinced that prisons must be severely punishing and at the same time managed in such a way to contribute revenue to the state rather than being a continuing expense.

The idea of leasing became increasingly accepted and was further institutionalized by law in 1873, which created 10-year leases at no cost to the state, even for the care of the inmates. Few restrictions were placed on the lessee regarding convict treatment, and reports circulated that those who obtained the contract could make a "handsome fortune" (as cited in Bayliss, 1975, p. 198). Making a profit was easy for contractors as the number of inmates was increasing rapidly. The number of inmates doubled between 1874 and 1876. Sentences were made more severe during this period. The punishment for stealing anything over $2 in value was considered grand larceny and punishable by up to 5 years in prison. During this period, the bulk of the new convicts were Black (Bayliss, 1975).

Occasionally, attention was directed to abuses in the lease system. In response to accusations by the press of mistreatment by the contractor regarding food, clothing, overwork, beatings, and killings, the Board of Penitentiary Commissioners conducted an investigation in 1875. Although the commissioners found no violations of the contract, they did report the use of excessive force in punishment, as well as poor and unsuitable living conditions. The commissioner referred one cruel and possible criminal killing to a grand jury. A legislative committee noted the "dreadful mortality" rate in 1880 when 20% of the prisoners died. The committee described the lease system as "cruel, barbarous, inhuman, and totally at variance with the civilization of the age," but nevertheless recommended no remedy, given the financial conditions of the state (as cited in Bayliss, 1975, p. 202). The conditions under which leased prisoners in post–Civil War Arkansas and other states were viewed to be worse than that of slaves prior to abolition because slave owners at least had a property incentive to keep slaves alive and well enough to work. The live slave had a significant value that was lost if the slave died. The holder of a prisoner lease had no such financial incentive (Oshinsky, 1996).

Although leasing became the selected method of choice, there was some debate regarding its application. Few objected to inmates working inside the walls of the prison, but inmates working outside the walls proved controversial. The lease law of 1873 prohibited inmates from working in Little Rock except on

FIGURE 1.3. Saw mill scene, state farm, Cummins, Arkansas, date unknown.

FIGURE 1.4. Possibly Pulaski County Prison Farm, date unknown.

"public improvements." According to Bayliss (1975), the objections to outside use of labor were not so much determined by concern for abuse of inmates, but rather the fear of the inmates themselves and competition with free labor for scarce jobs. Those who worked outside the walls were typically used to make bricks, mine coal, farm, construct railroads, and conduct similar activities.

The new law of 1881 placed almost no restrictions on where leased inmates could work and further required that contracts must not only be free of cost to the state but that they must provide a net gain to the state's treasury. The terms of one successful bid paid the state $3.75 a month per inmate, paid all mainte-nance costs for those confined, provided transportation of prisoners, and paid the salary of a physician and chaplain (Bayliss, 1975).

The following is a description of living conditions at work sites where prisoners were leased:

> In the lease camps, railroad cars and single-story wooden huts housed convicts who slept on cots set from wall to wall. The danger of escape compelled the authorities to shut up the dwellings at night, leaving the air indescribably foul. Water was usually so scarce that bathing became almost impossible. Other sanitary arrangements were invariably crude. Disease was rampant. Food was either as plentiful or scarce as the economy of the leaseholder determined. The coarse nature and wretched preparation of what foods were provided was a hardship to the victims who ate it and brought

no pride to the state, which paid for it. Heat was usually lacking, although rickety stoves or open fires sometimes added smoke to the increasing discomfort of the prisoners who experienced little attendant warmth on cold winter nights.

Fear of prisoners escaping was the determining factor of prison discipline. Various devices for restraining the prisoners were tried from shackling their feet to adding heavy iron balls to the chains in desperate cases. Striped garments were used everywhere. The convicts had "no picayune tastes regarding their footwear—they were glad to get any at all" (Crosley, 1986, pp. 21–22, internal citations omitted).

Little attention was given to monitoring and enforcing the few regulations that were in place to control leasing. Governor James Berry took exception to the trend by insisting the penitentiary commission conduct inspections and enforce compliance. On a tour of leased convict work sites, he and his fellow commissioners discovered filthy and unsanitary living conditions, failure to separate those who were sick, and the lack of proper inquest procedures in the event of violent deaths. Leased convicts were beaten with impunity, over-worked, and not provided proper food, clothing, and shelter. Some inmates were described as being in "wretched" condition and seemingly had been provided "inhuman" treatment (Bayliss, 1975). As a result of the criticisms raised and the expectations for compliance, the leasees subsequently sold the contract. Again, although limitations of the system were recognized, it remained firmly in place.

There was little basis on which prison reform could proceed in these early years. There was virtually no popular support for reform among the citizens, the politically powerful, or even the press. The objective of protests was to moderate major abuses of prisoners, but no suggestions were offered for change. It seemed to be commonly understood that even if there were better ways to operate a correctional system it would cost money, and spending money on prisons was becoming unthinkable. Clyde Crosley (1986) referred to the voices of reform in this period as "criers in the wilderness" who were heard only faintly, if at all, among the much louder voices singing the praises of a prison, which made money and provided cheap labor for the economically struggling state.

One set of incidents that did capture political, public, and press attention was the Coal Hill "horrors." March 1888 issues of the *Arkansas Gazette* gave front page coverage to mistreatment of convicts leased for coal mining at the Quita Coal Company in Johnson County. Headlines reported "Unequaled Brutality," and "A Hell in Arkansas." Rumors of brutality had circulated for some time, eventually resulting in an official investigation.

The findings were that the "wardens" in charge of the convicts beat men to death, forced them to fight each other (sometimes until one died), and failed to provide clothing, adequate food, and medical treatment. Convicts worked all winter with no shoes or socks, were frequently ill due to unsanitary conditions, were forced to work while ill, and lived in fear of death if they complained or reported their situation to authorities. The convict camp was closed to the outside world. Even the coroner was denied access to investigate violent deaths. There seemed to be no limit to the discretion exercised by contractors in the treatment of convicts. The following is one example:

> Last summer a warden whose name was Hudson had a negro chained to the post and stripped. Hudson hit him 150 licks making the back raw and causing the negro to yell so that his shrieks were heard at Coal Hill more than a mile away. When he had whipped the man that way, he then took salt and water and threw on the lacerated and bleeding back. He then left the negro standing in the hot sun while he went downtown and attended to some business. He then came back and whipped the negro until he died. …
>
> There are 140 men in the camp. … The men sleep in a building ninety feet long, eighteen feet wide, and twelve feet high … sick and well and crippled all sleep alongside each other. … The men sleep on beds made of shucks and straw, which have not been changed, so witnesses say, but once in the last fifteen months … a sickening stench arises from the men, and many of them are covered with vermin.
>
> Mr. Blythe (the coroner) had the body exhumed … it could be seen that he died from injuries inflicted by the prison authorities. … On the back were thirty four gashes, in any one of which a man's two fingers could be placed" (*Arkansas Gazette*, 1888).

Convict labor, exposed by the press and much discussed, eventually became a major political issue. In Governor Hughes's unsuccessful 1888 campaign for reelection, charges about lease system abuses were used against him. In the 1889 poll of state legislators' list of priorities while in office, the highest priority was to change the management of convict labor. The subsequent legislation required proper inquests of deaths, established time off for good behavior, and created the position of the inspector to visit all convict labor sites and report periodically to the penitentiary commissioners. Nevertheless, it must be noted that Arkansas's convict leasing system remained essentially intact. Thus far it had weathered the storm of public indignation and political controversy (Bayliss, 1975).

Having surfaced as a public issue, the convict leasing system continued to receive explicit political attention in the late 1800s. In 1888, the Union Labor Party announced its opposition to the leasing system and proposed that all prisoners be employed inside the walls of the penitentiary (Crosley, 1986). Similarly, the populist movement strongly criticized the use of convict labor and fought for its abolition. In 1892 the Democratic party platform called for the abolition of the convict lease arrangement, suggesting instead "a system adopted for the treatment of convicts more consistent with the better instincts and more improved methods of our age" (Crosley, 1986, p. 29). The People's Party called for a reformatory for young offenders and a prison farm where all inmates could work productively to support the whole system.

Under the leadership of Democratic Governor James Engle, steps were taken to move away from leasing toward an Auburn system in which all inmates would be housed in and work gainfully inside the state penitentiary. A physician was to be employed to ensure the humane treatment and general health of the prison population, and a chaplain was to give religious services and to operate a night school for young offenders. Although based on good intentions, the bill was of little influence due to the lack of financial appropriation for implementing the plan. The bill contained a provision to "temporarily" contract prisoners out to private interests until they could be accommodated inside the prison walls. Thus, the leasing system continued (Bayliss, 1975).

In 1899 the legislature decided to destroy the old penitentiary in order to make a site for the state capital building. Bricks taken from the dismantled old prison were laid by inmate labor as part of the walls of the basement of the present state capitol building. The new penitentiary was built five miles south of Little Rock (Crosley, 1986).

By the turn of the century, some progress was visible. Inmate death rates apparently had declined due to increased inspection and monitoring of leased inmates. Late century reports bragged about improvements in food, clothing, and health care. Nevertheless, there was considerable discontent with the state's manner of dealing with its convicted felons. Even the Board of Penitentiary Commissioners complained that "dictates of humanity demand that the present system be modified as to relieve it of much of its harshness and cruelty" (as cited in Bayliss, 1975, pp. 209–210). Reports in 1901 indicated that the system was in "deplorable condition," referring to fraud, illegal transactions, and prisoners' working and living conditions (Bayliss, 1975, p. 212).

In the early 1900s, Arkansas began moving to another method of dealing with persons convicted of a crime. It was several years, however, until the lease system was thoroughly uprooted. Governor Jefferson Davis was direct and forceful in his 1903 attacks on the lease system and its supporters: "There is a crowd of leeches and blood suckers that is trying to build up a penitentiary dynasty and political penitentiary ring, the object and purpose of which is to control the politics of Arkansas, and incidentally to loot the state treasury while doing it" (Crosley, 1986, p. 34).

In the administration of Governor George Donaghey, dramatic progress was made in challenging and uprooting the lease system. In spite of public opinion, political platforms, and even bills passed by the legislature to the contrary, the practice of contracting with private citizens and businesses for inmate labor still managed to survive. Having fought both the idea of leasing and the political functionaries who controlled it without success for 3 years, Governor Donaghey became frustrated. In a bold frontal attack on the system, the governor pardoned 360 inmates on December 27, 1912. In 1913, the legislature passed a bill officially ending convict leasing (Crosley, 1986).

Prison Farms

As the use of leasing faded, the state began to implement an alternative method of managing its inmate population. That new method was the prison plantation or prison farm.

Many Arkansas prisoners had worked on Arkansas farms acquiring agricultural skills. It seemed logical to use inmate labor on state farms as an alternative to leasing them to private contractors. Criminals were still put at hard labor on state-operated prison plantations, a practice commonly regarded as appropriate punishment for a criminal conviction. Many Arkansans were not familiar with industrial labor and production, but they understood farming and believed in the value of farm labor. Through farming, the penal system could still produce enough income both to support itself and to make generous contributions to the state treasury. What was missing was the need to share these financial benefits with "middlemen" private contractors. Also, by managing its own farming operations, the state would have better control of the living and working conditions of inmates. Thus, it was argued, there would be less possibility of inmate abuse scandals, which had become so problematic to the state under the leasing system. Indeed, the idea of prison farms was an idea whose time had come.

In order to have publicly controlled prison farms, it was necessary to acquire farmland. This objective was first accomplished by leasing land. A 1901 report indicated that the state had spent $300,000 in the previous 7 years for land rent (Bayliss, 1975). Considering it prudent to buy rather than lease land, the legislature in 1902 entered an agreement to purchase two plantations in Lincoln County (Crosley, 1986). Thus, Arkansas began its long-term commitment to prison farms as the means to respond to persons convicted of serious crimes.

The two plantations purchased in Lincoln County were the adjacent Cummins and Maple Grove Plantations. The plantations, which together totaled about 5,500 acres, were purchased for $140,000. When this property was acquired it was announced that the property would be paid for by the "labor of the convicts" (Crosley, 1986, p. 34).

In 1909, a few years before leasing was banned, the General Assembly authorized another form of state-controlled inmate labor, the road crews. Counties or groups of counties could form convict road districts. The counties agreed to house, feed, and otherwise care for inmates in exchange for the use of their labor in building and maintaining roads. The Department of State Lands, Highways, and Improvement determined the nature of the work to be done while state employees appointed by the prison board did the supervision of convicts. These chain gang road operations reportedly produced living, working, and general treatment conditions which were as harsh and corrupt as the leasing arrangement had been (Crosley, 1986). The use of road crews was not widely embraced by the counties, perhaps because it was considered to be troublesome to administer and ineffective.

In 1911, the legislature authorized the prison board to purchase additional farmlands for incarcerating state prisoners. Cummins Farm was being used exclusively for Black prisoners and need was being expressed for a similar facility for White convicts. Funds were made available in 1916 to buy a new penal farm for Whites, the Tucker Farm, which was to be developed by and for White convict labor. Both Cummins and Tucker were acquired as farmlands suitable for cotton production (Crosley, 1986).

Farming operations became predominant in the prison system in the first 3 decades of the 20th century. In 1933, the prison at Little Rock was sold to the Highway Department. The proceeds from this sale were used in part to construct an electric chair facility at Tucker. The headquarters for the state prisons was moved to the Tucker Farm. In that same year, a new penal board was given responsibility not only for the prison farm system but also to act as a parole board. Bookkeeping and auditing were established for the first time as part of the system (Crosley, 1986).

In 1934, a highly publicized controversy emerged in the prison farms. A shortage of mules, as well as funds to replace them, was hindering farming operations at Tucker. Men were used instead of mules to pull various farm implements such as planters. News stories exposed and criticized the use of men instead of mules. Farm superintendents along with the chairman of the penal board defended the practice, contending that the work involved was no more demanding than other tasks. The governor, under pressure from the public, ordered that men no longer be required to fill in for mules (Crosley, 1978). Stories written about men for mules also gave attention to the practice of inmates serving as "trusty" guards, a topic that also raised questions and controversy (Crosley, 1978).

The Inmate Trusty System

The essence of the prison farm operation was the "trusty" system. The trusty system made it possible to work large numbers of inmates in the farming operations at minimal cost to the state. This organizational scheme used inmates (trusties) to guard other inmates and to perform virtually every task necessary to maintain the prison and run its day-to-day operations. The trusty system remained intact with minor modifications from the inception of the prison farms until the mid 1960s. This section describes the trusty system, as it existed in the 1930s, based primarily on the writings of and interviews with Clyde Crosley, an inmate in the prison system in the 1930s, along with other accounts of the trusty system.

In 1935, there were 1,671 inmates at the seven camps of the two Arkansas state prison farms. Slightly more than 200 of these were on trusty status, 162 were categorized as "inmate guards," and the remaining 43 were "riders" or supervisors. At this time Arkansas relied on the services of 12 state employees to run the entire prison system. There was one superintendent, two wardens, a transfer warden, a bookkeeper, and a deputy warden for each of the seven camps (Robinson, 1936).

Each of the several "camps" had a barracks building as living quarters for inmates, a residence for the deputy warden, barns and other buildings for farming equipment, animals, and so on, and a few small "shotgun" houses for top ranking trusty inmates (Crosley, 1986).

Those in the lowest stratum of the prisoner social system were known as rank men. These were ordinary inmates who were not trusties. Rank men had virtually no power in the system. They did the hardest and most undesirable jobs, had the fewest privileges, and always lived under the whip and under the threat of death (House, 1987). Clyde Crosley describes his initial experiences as a rank man in his book *Men or Mules* in the following way:

> About the time Ray and the other two young convicts were being told to follow the crowd when the dining room door opened, they heard from the front picket a sound like a pistol shot, then a scream of pain, anguish and misery. The barber seemed undisturbed, "You short-hairs will get used to that sound. You'll hear and see what causes it morning, noon, night, and all day in the fields. That's the 'bullhide.' The warden is tearing the ass off a night guard that went to sleep on the job last night. He was a trusty guard, but not anymore. You don't really have to do anything to get your ass torn off, you get it just because you came. If you don't like it, you can go home" (Crosley 1978, pp. 21–22).

Between rank men and trusties was a stratum of the system known as "half-trusty." The half-trusty was not under guard during the day, had a better job than rank men, and had freedom of movement during the day in a given area. Half-trusties, also known as "do pops," generally had work responsibilities for cleaning buildings, cooking, waiting tables, caring for animals, or similar tasks. The "do-pops" name was derived from the fact that "they [we]re supposed to pop doors open for superiors" (Murton & Hymes, 1969, p. 23). They were not permitted to have firearms as were many trusties, and they slept in the same area as the rank men. To be a half-trusty provided some relief from the harshness of the way of life required of rank men and also could be a stepping stone to becoming a full trusty (Crosley, 1986).

Among trusties there were three basic levels or ranks. The lowest were "shot-gun men" who stood close by rank men to guard them while they performed various agricultural field tasks such as hoeing and picking cotton. This task was regarded as relatively undesirable in that it involved walking all day every day and being exposed to the weather. Other trusty positions such as night guard, which had nothing to do with field work, were of similar rank with shotgun men (Crosley, 1986).

The middle rank of trusties was typified by the "high power." In the field the high power was on horseback, carried a rifle such as a 30-30, and followed the field crews and hoe squads at some distance. The responsibility of the high power was to provide secondary security of the inmates working in the field, as a backup to the primary security given by the shotgun men. In the event that a rank man overpowered a shotgun man and took his weapon, or even if all the shotgun men guarding a work squad were overpowered, the chance of further taking advantage of the situation would be checked by the highpower mounted just out of the effective range of a shotgun (Crosley, 1986).

The highest ranking trusties were the supervisors, referred to as "riders." It was the responsibility of the rider to see that the work got done and who was going to do it. The highest ranking rider in a camp was the rider for the long line. The authority of this rider on a day-to-day basis rested on his ability to impose sanctions. The rider determined who was to be whipped by the bullhide, although the deputy warden did the actual whipping. Ultimately, the long line rider determined unilaterally whom on the long line would live and who would die. An example of such authority is provided and depicts a man being killed by first being repeatedly whipped and subsequently being worked in the field until he died:

> As Wisconsin hurried toward the squad, blood oozed through the rear of his pants ... but he knew he must keep working, working, working. ... Slim tied him on the water cart and took him to the stockade, moaning and groaning with high fever. Everyone in the line "dummied up." They were unusually quiet, tired, disgusted, and fearful. They had just witnessed another prisoner murdered. They kept quiet, obeyed and lived another day (Crosley, 1978, p. 40).

Other riders in the camp did not have nearly so much responsibility, nor as much authority as the long-line rider. There were riders who supervised much smaller groups of men, such as the riders over the plow squad, the wagon squad, the kitchen, the yard, and the garden.

Being selected to rise to a more privileged position in the social structure, whether to a more desirable job as rank man, to a half-trusty position, or to the position of trusty, took place on a very informal basis. The key was to have or develop contacts among persons of power. "Someone needs to go to bat for you to help you get into a better position." Such contacts may be on the outside of the prison itself, including judges, law enforcement officers, or other persons of influence who could contact prison administrators and urge them to take care of a given inmate (Crosley, 1986).

More often the selection process involved developing informal relations in the institution with inmates who were in a position to influence both the wardens and the other inmates. Much of the determination of upward mobility rested simply on who knew you and what they thought of you. Those in a position to assist in selection were not at all hesitant to ask, "What's in it for me?" Such an economy of selection and maintenance in higher positions included such commodities as direct cash payments, sexual favors, protection, better food, better clothing, or other amenities. An example of the dynamics of the selection process from Crosley's writing in *Men or Mules* is the following:

> The cost of joining the plow squad was a one-time fee of one dollar. Only "hustlers" were asked to join, and they agreed to help the group hustle food (Crosley, 1978, p. 73).

In selecting a person for becoming a trusty, of prime importance was whether the person could be trusted to play the game by the traditionally established rules. If a rider recommended someone to be a shotgun guard, he was invariably asked, "Are you willing to put your ass up for him?" This meant that the trusty making the recommendation would be held responsible should the new trusty violate the norms. The convict's word was one of the few items with which he could bargain. If a major violation occurred, such as escape, the recommender would, himself, be whipped with the bullhide and immediately become a rank man. The ever-present possibility of such downward mobility and its consequences was a major motivation to maintain the system (Dison, 1987).

The actual approval for being moved from one position to another had to go through the wardens. For example, if someone was being considered for trusty status, the trusties (generally riders) discussed it with the deputy warden, who talked with the warden, who was responsible for either Tucker or Cummins Prison Farm, and then with the superintendent who has responsibility for both Cummins and Tucker. The chain of command was strictly followed. Trusties communicated with deputy wardens, who communicated with wardens, and so on, up the line. It was traditional among wardens to avoid persons who were wanted in another jurisdiction and to favor those with long sentences. The latter criterion was justified by reducing turnover, although it had the effect of ensuring that those inmates with more severe offenses had a greater probability of becoming a trusty and ensuring that those with less severe sentences did not have an opportunity to become trusties (Crosley, 1985).

Although the deputy wardens officially approved one's becoming a trusty, often the deputy warden was highly influenced by the trusty inmates. This influence might have come in the form of direct recommendations and persuasion, but the influence was generally subtler. The deputy warden was consciously manipulated and "programmed" by the trusties. In their conversations with the deputy warden one would allude to a problem or potential problem and others would, without connecting the two, plant the idea for solving the problem. Others would, in a subtle way, reinforce points made by others. At some point the deputy warden would "make the connection" and assume the idea was his. Such manipulation was by no means limited to selecting trusties, although this was one of its principle uses.

Although the trusties had enormous discretion over the fate of rank men and not infrequently abused that discretion, the general relationship between trusties and rank men was generally neither hostile nor antagonistic. There were two readily apparent explanations for this. Many among the rank men had aspirations for becoming trusties. Becoming a trusty was viewed to be perhaps the only way to survive a stay, particularly a long stay, in the Arkansas prison system. Not only could one survive, but also one could have access to a quality of life never before experienced: good food, money, booze, and women. Therefore, the rank men who wished to become trusties legitimated the system in the hope that they too would someday be protected by it. Those who had no aspiration of becoming trusties were simply ignored and had little if any influence on others. Should the latter seek to make trouble, they, without delay, were brutalized or even killed (Crosley, 1986).

Another explanation for the lack of antagonism between rank men and trusties was that the trusties realized that at any time it was possible for them to be ranked (i.e., to become rank men again). The trusty did not want to be in a totally hostile environment and, therefore, cultivated relationships that provided insurance should he again become a peer with the rank men. Also, the pool for selecting new trusties was the rank men. It could and did happen that a person who was once supervised by you at a later time became your supervisor (Crosley, 1986).

One method used by the administration to reduce the probability of trouble was to discourage inmates congregating in groups. This practice, called "syndicating," was not permitted. Ostensibly, this practice kept inmates from organizing themselves for any purpose and was essentially an expression of "divide and conquer." This did not extend to a full rule of silence, but simply discouraged assembly of inmates (Dison, 1987).

Interestingly, the trusty inmates who were charged with the responsibility of keeping inmates from syndicating themselves had an organization that they called "the Syndicate." This organization was under the control of the most powerful trusty and was operated for the purpose of mutual aid and protection. A key protection was the protecting of one's territorial right to a given hustle (means of making money). The Syndicate also met periodically to plan strategy, decide who was going to be "turned out" (become a trusty), who would be paroled, how the administration could be controlled, and other related matters. The Syndicate was also a communication network both for sending and gathering information. It was generally at Syndicate meetings that plans were made to plant information for the deputy warden so that he would "make up his mind" the way they wanted him to (Crosley, 1986).

The inmates who made up the Syndicate organization controlled the camp and ruled it with an iron fist. For themselves they made life easier, for the other convicts they made life harder, and for the wardens they planted, cultivated, and harvested a crop for the politicians to "appreciate" (Crosley, 1978).

An example of the control exerted by the Syndicate on a daily basis was found in an incident involving an inmate named Cowboy, who intended to report to the deputy warden that the rider was going to steal some calves by not reporting the births. Members of the Syndicate worked for the deputy warden and could control who had access to him. They stopped Cowboy from meeting with the deputy warden and informed the rider what was taking place. The rider and other members of the Syndicate seized Cowboy, tied him up, gagged him, put a rope around his neck, led him to the banks of the Arkansas River, and repeatedly threatened him with death. Ultimately, Cowboy begged for his life to be saved, which was granted in the form of his being permitted (actually required) to escape. In this manner, the Syndicate efficiently disposed of a troublemaker (Crosley, 1978).

The Syndicate was not the only element that controlled persons in the prison. The entire system was designed or emerged in such a way that it controlled behavior. The rank men had little choice in the matter. Living and working constantly under the whip and the gun, they either conformed or they suffered pain and/or death. The only other possibility was an escape, which was exceedingly remote. The overwhelming majority of those who tried to escape were shot and killed. As previously mentioned, many of the rank men supported this system and complied with its requirements in the hope that they too could be promoted to trusty and enjoy a relatively good life.

The trusties and half-trusties conformed to the expectations placed on them in large part due to the freedoms and privileges extended to them as trusties. Trusties had much better food, clothing, working conditions, medical care, means of securing money, access to alcohol, women, freedom of movement, and so on. It is certainly possible that the trusties knew what they had going for them and they "did not want to spoil a good thing." It was essentially a trade off between the State of Arkansas through its representatives, the wardens, and the inmates selected as trusties. The state asks the trusties to maintain security and order to see that the work gets done, to make certain that convicts are properly punished, and to ensure that this takes place in a way that was economically advantageous to the state. In return, the state offers the trusties relief from virtually all of the "pains of imprisonment" described in the correctional literature by Gresham Sykes (1971) and others. However, should the trusty violate the trust given to him, the pains of imprisonment would return with a vengeance (Dison, 1987)

From the 1930s Through the 1960s

The years of the Great Depression brought greater austerity to an already impoverished Arkansas. The prison system was not a high priority in state business in those years. Officials expected the system to support itself and otherwise take care of itself and to send dollars to the state treasury.

As part of the New Deal, the federal government created the Prison Industries Reorganization Authority to restructure prison industries in state systems. They conducted a survey of the prison system in Arkansas in the mid 1930s. They reported on a system that emphasized "punishment, hard work, and profits" and that had "practically no development of activities which seek to recondition and redirect the criminal by providing opportunities for self-improvement" (Robinson, 1936, p. 16). The report indicated that housing, sanitary, and other life maintenance resources were woefully lacking in the Arkansas prison farms, as were minimal administrative supports. The survey recommended major changes in probation, parole, industrial production, and farm production (Robinson, 1936).

Upon assuming the office of governor in 1937, Carl Bailey remarked that the prison system was a "social cancer and a relic of barbarism, vengeful, punitive; in no sense corrective or curative" (as cited in Crosley, 1986, p. 60). Although he was unable to make enormous changes in the system, he did use inmate labor to assist with a major flood on the Mississippi River (Crosley, 1986).

Although legal provisions for parole were established in 1907, it was not until 1937 that persons were hired for the position of parole officers. Prior to that, persons on parole were entirely unsupervised. A tradition had developed with the establishment of the prison farms to allow Christmas furloughs to selected inmates. For example, in 1940, 77 inmates were granted holiday furloughs. All returned without incident (Crosley, 1986).

The trusty system was remarkably effective in controlling inmates sent to the Arkansas prison farms. In the entire history of using trusty guards at the prison farms, there was only one major escape incident (Crosley, 1978). On Labor Day, September 2, 1940, the convicts went to the fields to work as usual on the long line. Two highpowers overpowered and disarmed the remaining highpower and the rider. Some of the shotguns cooperated with the prison break, but the others were quickly overpowered. In the field, one inmate guard was killed while resisting the break and another was slightly injured. In all, 36 inmates became involved in the escape using the few mules and horses to transport them to the nearest highway where they commandeered automobiles to make good their escape. Within a few days, the majority of the escapees had been captured or killed. Within a year all of the escaping inmates had been similarly accounted for (Crosley, 1978).

Promptly after the prison break, the Arkansas Board of Pardons and Parole conducted an investigation and later issued a report on the prison break incident. The report defended the Arkansas prison system as it was operated, with particular praise for the use of trusty guards (Crosley, 1986). Governor Bailey also defended the prison operation and its system of trusty guards. To change such a system because of a single prison break he regarded as "absurd" (as cited in Crosley, 1978, p. 198).

Descriptions of the prison farms in the 1950s and 1960s are remarkably similar to those of the 1930s. The trusty system, the general living conditions, the type of work done, and the working conditions had apparently become institutionalized and were passed down from one generation of inmates and state employees to another. The barracks system of housing was unchanged. At the Cummins Farm, barracks

> consisted of one large, open space, packed virtually solid with double-decker beds. There were eight such barracks: one for [W]hite trusties, one for [B]lack trusties, and the remainder for the other prisoners, further divided into "rankers" and "do-pops," as well as being segregated by race (Feeley & Rubin, 1998, p. 54).

The chief means of discipline was the bull hide, administered in the same ritualistic fashion it had been for many years, with the inmate forced to lie down and take the lashes from a whip, crying out the count and other submissive phrases as the beating was being administered (House, 1987).

> The captain looked like a giant standing there with his shirt off and sweat pouring down his chest. He took a mighty swing and the first lash took the right pocket off the man's pants. The man begged the Captain not to hurt him anymore, but the big Captain kept on swinging until blood ran through the white pants (House, 1987, p. 82).

Little is written about the Arkansas prisons in the 1950s and early 1960s. But, the following is a descriptive account:

> The convicts were expected to build their own housing, produce their own food by working in the fields, and even guard each other.

FIGURE 1.5. Picking cotton, state farm, Cummins, Arkansas, date unknown.

> The limited funds that were needed for running the farms were to be generated by selling cash crops, mainly cotton, on the open market. To realize economies, prisoners were housed in cheap, unventilated, overcrowded barracks; food, medical, mental health, and vocational training services were provided at a minimum level, if at all. Of the convicts who survived, many did so only because their families bribed the convict guards, or "trusties," to provide them with the necessities of life (Feeley & Rubin, 1998, p. 52).

This is perhaps a testimony both to the fact that the system and its operation had become familiar and routinized to those aware of it and to the fact that it remained rather hidden from much of the public. Additionally, it was during these years that much attention in political and news media arenas had become focused on the issue of civil rights and racial desegregation. The prison system would have to wait a few years to be in the spotlight.

Conclusion

Many people were surprised by the revelations of the Arkansas prison system, which began in the mid 1960s. As can be seen, these events did not take place in isolation. The context, the form, and the content of the prison system had been constructed and maintained for decades before prison reform finally began to come to Arkansas.

Perhaps the single most predominant theme in the history of Arkansas prisons is the expectation that the system be a minimal economic burden on the state. Correctional philosophy, goals of incarceration, law, policy, and human rights were all secondary considerations relative to costs. It is likely that the early Pennsylvania system was abandoned due in large part to prohibitive costs. The lease system was an appealing option because of its cost efficiency. When the lease system was exposed to public scrutiny and found unacceptable, the search for an alternative was the search for another means to maintain prisoners in a way that would be financially beneficial to the state. The means selected was an enormous farming operation, which maneuvered around objections raised about the lease system and industrial production. Let the other states do as they please, but Arkansas had found a way to deal with its convicts in a way that was beneficial to the state's finances.

Another theme in the state's history was the selection of punishment as a means of responding to persons convicted of crime. Little, if any, consideration was given to educate, rehabilitate, or otherwise provide a positive influence on prisoners. Not only was the emphasis exclusively on punishment, but also the methods and degrees of punishment were virtually without limits, including torture, killing, brutality, exploitation, abuse, as well as inadequate food, clothing, shelter, and medical treatment.

The prison system was given two mandates: bring in money to the state and provide a punishing experience for inmates. It could claim success on both counts.

REFERENCES

Ayers, E. L. (1984). *Vengeance & justice: Crime and punishment in the 19th-century American South*. Oxford University Press.

Arkansas Board of Penitentiary Commissioners. (1891). *Biennial report*. Author.

Barnes, H. E. (1921). Historical origin of the prison system in America. *Journal of Criminal Law and Criminology, 12*(1), 35–60.

Bayliss, G. E. (1975). The Arkansas State Penitentiary under Democratic control, 1874–1896. *Arkansas Historical Quarterly, 34*(3), 195–213. https://doi.org/10.2307/40027657

Crosley, C. (1978). *Men or mules*. Crosley.

Crosley, C. (1986). *Unfolding misconceptions: A study of the Arkansas prison system*. Liberal Arts Press.

Dison, J. E. (1987). *A sociological interpretation of the Arkansas prison system in the 1930s*. Paper presented at Arkansas Sociological Association, Little Rock, AR.

Feeley, M. M., & Rubin, E. L. (1998). *Judicial policy making and the modern state: How the courts reformed America's prisons*. Cambridge University Press.

House, L. (1987, January). A dark and evil world. *Arkansas Times*, 26–29, 80–88.

Murton, T. O., & Hyams, J. (1969). *Accomplices to the crime*. Grove Press.

Lichtenstein, A. (1996). *Twice the work of free labor: The political economy of convict labor in the New South*. Verso.

Oshinsky, D. M. (1996). *"Worse than slavery": Parchman Farm and the ordeal of Jim Crow justice*. Free Press.

Robinson, L. N. (1936). *The prison labor problem in Arkansas: A survey by the Prison Industries Reorganization Administration*. Prison Industries Reorganization Administration.

Sykes, G. M. (1971). *The society of captives: A study of a maximum security prison*. Princeton University Press.

Woodcock, D. (1958). *Ruled by the whip: Hell behind bars in America's Devil's Island, the Arkansas State Penitentiary*. Exposition Press.

KEY TERMS

Great Depression

Lease system

Prison Industries Reorganization Authority

Rank men

Trusty system

QUESTIONS

1. Despite the enactment of the 13th Amendment abolishing slavery, how did the Arkansas prison system compare to slavery?

2. What was the leasing system? Why do you believe the prison system shifted to this method of privatization?

3. Describe living conditions during the leasing system.

4. One essential concept of the prison farm was the trusty system. Describe the three basic levels or ranks under this system. How did living conditions and responsibilities differ between rank men and trusties?

5. Historically, Arkansas prisons were expected to be a minimal economic burden on the state. How did this goal affect incarceration conditions, laws, policies, and human rights?

FIGURE CREDITS

2 | Early Reforms in Arkansas, 1966–1967

Introduction

The mid-1960s marked the beginning of an era of great social changes in American society. Changes included cultural norms, civil rights, criminal procedure, and prisoners' rights. This chapter will address the explosive news media coverage and early federal court cases that arose from reports of abusive conditions of confinement and treatment of prisoners in the two Arkansas prison farms. While Arkansas was not alone in a historical lack of concern and oversight of prison operations, it lagged far behind the rest of the nation in prison reform and implementation of modern correctional practices. Where other states had abolished corporal punishment as a disciplinary tool in prisons, the Arkansas prisons were found to still use the strap for whipping and other barbaric forms of torture as a means of maintaining control of prisoners' behavior. The state further managed to earn a profit from its prison system with an abusive system of inmate "trusty" guards that allowed the prisons to function with only a handful of free-world employees at each prison.

"Hands Off" Evolves to "Hands On"

The summer of 1966 found Arkansas in the last months of the administration of Governor Orval Faubus. Faubus, an extremely popular governor, had been elected to six terms as governor for a total of 12 successive years in office. Faubus had become a national figure in his struggle with the federal government over desegregation of Little Rock Central High School in 1957. The prisons in the early years of the Faubus administration before the Central High School event, and indeed in all of Arkansas history up to this time, attracted little attention.

In the mid 1960s, however, the American press and public rediscovered prisons as a social problem and pondered the question of whether prisoners were human beings who could be restored to a legitimate and productive life. There was much talk, if not action, regarding the ineffectiveness of punishment and the promise of rehabilitation. Federal courts began to reverse their position that inmates had sacrificed constitutional protections as a consequence of being guilty of a crime. Previously, courts imposed the "hands-off" policy in which virtually every inmate claim was routinely dismissed. This approach began to change following *Cooper v. Pate* (1964) when the United States Supreme Court ruled that a state prisoner could sue correctional officers in federal court for alleged violations of constitutional rights under the Civil Rights Act of 1871. *Cooper v. Pate* and most other prisoners' lawsuits that followed were filed under Title 42 U.S. Code § 1983. This law is the current codification of the Civil Rights Act of 1871 that was initially enacted to provide a method for allowing the recently freed slaves to sue state officials in federal courts for violation of civil rights. While Section 1983 was virtually dormant for nearly a century, the U.S. Supreme Court in *Cooper v. Pate* (1964) held that a state prisoner could use this law as the mechanism for seeking relief against state correctional officers. Courts then began to hear a trickle of cases that was soon an avalanche of "hands-on" activity for court participation in prison issues.

Some of this new thinking about corrections had spilled over into Arkansas. Through the rather amazing inmate communication networks, which exist not only within but also between American prisons, Arkansas inmates had become aware of the courts' developing receptivity to cases involving inmates' rights. They were understandably interested in the possibility of legal remedies to their circumstances. The time had come to test the water.

In the mid-1960s, the Arkansas prison system was under the supervision of the State Penitentiary Board, which was a five-man commission appointed by the governor. Operations were under the control of the superintendent and 25 paid free-world employees. This group of individuals had the responsibility for the care and control of more than 1,600 inmates at the 15,500-acre Cummins Farm and 250 inmates at the 4,500-acre Tucker Farm (*Jackson v. Bishop*, 1968).

In October 1965, three inmates were given hearings in federal court based on allegations of mistreatment and requests that corporal punishment in the form of the strap be discontinued. The punishment by whipping was described as follows:

> [The] punishment consists of blows with a leather strap five feet in length, four inches wide, and about one-fourth inch thick, attached to a wooden handle or shaft about six inches long. Ordinarily, the Assistant Warden having in his charge the inmate to be punished inflicts the punishment. A prisoner who is to be whipped is required to lie down on the ground fully clothed, and the blows are inflicted on his buttocks (*Talley v. Stephens*, 1965, p. 687).

The cases were heard by U.S. District Court Judge J. Smith Henley. The petitioners sought relief for alleged violations of the Eighth and 14th Amendments to the U.S. Constitution under Title 42 U.S. Code § 1983. Winston Talley testified that he had been lashed with the leather strap at least 75 times since he had been at the prison farms. Most of the whippings, he said, were for not picking his quota of cotton. Although his claims in regard to number and other details of the whippings were disputed, the court ruled in his favor. It did not go so far as abolishing the whip but established clear limits on its use through state policy. The other two inmates complained of inadequate medical treatment and conditions that threatened their health. The state made no effort to contest these two allegations (*Talley v. Stephens*, 1965).

At that time Dan Stephens was the superintendent of Arkansas prisons. He defended the use of the strap both in the federal court case and to the state prison board. One year prior to the *Talley* case it had been suggested by the governor

FIGURE 2.1. Tucker unit strap.

and by the board that the use of the whip be discontinued. After a brief suspension of its use, the strap was reinstated because, according to Stephens, "without some form of discipline proper order could not be maintained" ("Prison Chief Resigns," 1965). Following the hearings, Dan Stephens resigned as superintendent ("Prison Chief Resigns," 1965).

Faubus was infuriated by this turn of events. He felt that Stephens, an excellent prison superintendent, had been caught in a political crossfire, and that both Stephens and the prison system were being maligned as part of a conspiracy to discredit his administration. Stephens, in his letter of resignation, refers to "a premeditated and consistent harassment of prison authority ... by certain groups for their own particular reasons." Faubus could not prove who was behind this "concerted attack" but was not reluctant to speculate:

> But I do know practically everyone in my organization was convinced that Rockefeller forces and my newspaper critics were behind the efforts to disrupt the prison operations and bring as much discredit as possible to the administration. None of these people, I am led to believe, had any ill feelings toward Stephens, whom everyone regarded as a fine man doing a fine job as prison superintendent (Faubus, 1991, p. 378).

FIGURE 2.2. Tucker unit entrance, 1937.

Tucker State Farm opened in 1916 picture taken in the 1937.

Trouble at Tucker

In the summer of 1966, information began coming together that all was not right at the Tucker prison farm. At this time, the Arkansas prison farms were segregated, with White prisoners housed at Tucker and primarily Black prisoners housed at Cummins. Prisoners under a death sentence were housed at Tucker regardless of race. Some of the more troublesome White prisoners were also placed at Cummins (*Holt v. Sarver*, 1970). There were, however, both White and Black trusties at Cummins (Feeley & Rubin, 1998). Letters from inmates had been smuggled out, describing abuses and violations that went far beyond acceptable standards and even beyond newly developing prison rules for Arkansas. Larry Fugate, then a reporter for the *Pine Bluff Commercial*, noticed a consistency to the allegations in these letters from Tucker which, in his view, gave them more credibility than the gripes that normally flowed from the prison (Murton & Hyams, 1969). Superintendent Bishop also began hearing rumors of problems, but the information was not sufficiently substantiated to warrant action. Bishop's office was located some distance from Tucker at Cummins Farm, where most of the Arkansas inmates were housed, and thus where most of the administrative attention, limited as it was, was focused.

In early August, Jim Bruton, assistant superintendent at Tucker, submitted his resignation after 12 years in that position. This brought about a routine audit that showed discrepancies (Donald, 1966). Larry Fugate contacted the governor's office with what he had discovered in his journalistic investigation, as did Bishop with the results of the Tucker audit. With information continuing to mount, some of which was substantiated and much of which contained possible criminal infractions, Governor Faubus and his staff decided it was time for a formal investigation. They requested that the Criminal Investigation Division (CID) of the Arkansas State Police open a case and proceed to Tucker to gather evidence.

Arkansas State Police CID Investigation

From August 19 through September 7, 1966, Arkansas State Police CID investigator H.H. (Duke) Atkinson, later with the assistance of Investigators Jim Beach and Bill Skipper, interviewed inmates and staff at Tucker, observed and recorded descriptions of prison conditions, and gathered physical evidence (Arkansas State Police, 1966). Although it was months before the final report was submitted and subsequently made public, an aide gave a preliminary report to Governor Faubus while the investigation was still under way.

Faubus's response was swift and decisive. Based on the CID findings, he announced his firing of all three wardens at Tucker, along with the resignation of Assistant Superintendent Bruton, who Faubus said was implicated in the misconduct (Douthit, 1966a). He also demoted most inmate trusties to rank status and had them physically removed from Tucker farm (Donald, 1966). Being "ranked" meant that the trusties had been fired and were returned to hard labor in the "long lines" of the prison farms. Some of the trusties, aware that demotions were underway, handed over their weapons and said, "I don't want to be a trusty anymore." Two wardens and six trusties were brought in from Cummins to assist in the transition (Donald, 1966).

The results of the CID investigation greatly troubled Governor Faubus and prompted him to act with such swiftness that he failed even to consult with the prison board (Donald, 1966; Trimble & Valachovic, 1966). The investigation results were summarized at this time in the following terms:

> Extortion of money from the convicts by prison personnel often through the use of trusties.
> Failure to observe the new rules and regulations for the punishment of prisoners as laid down by the superintendent and prison board.
> The punishment of prisoners in violation of the prison rules.
> Failure to maintain proper security measures.
> Some cases of drunkenness because liquor was permitted to reach the prisoners—a violation of law and prison regulations (Donald, 1966).

As Governor Faubus held his news conference to announce the preliminary findings and the firings, the wardens and their belongings were being removed from Tucker. One of the fired wardens, E.G. Mays, who had been employed at Tucker for less than 3 months, publicly objected to his dismissal. The former barber and deputy sheriff claimed that he was assisting with the CID investigation:

"They have nothing on me. ... I was framed." State police officials offered no support for Mays's claim (Fugate, 1966). The other fired wardens left Tucker without comment. Neither they nor Assistant Superintendent Bruton sought to defend themselves against the charges that had been made public. In fact one of the wardens, when told that he had been fired, asked, "Can we leave now?" but was in such a rush that he was on his feet and out the door before anyone could respond to him ("Cummins Trusty Shot to Death," 1966).

Gene Hale

Gene Hale, aid to Governor Faubus, was dispatched by the governor when the trouble broke out at Tucker in August 1966 (Faubus, 1967). A few days after Faubus left office the *Pine Bluff Commercial* published a detailed account, authored by Hale, of what had happened at Tucker that summer.

Hale reported that Tucker inmates had designed a plan for a mass escape of virtually all prisoners then at Tucker, including the 12 death row inmates awaiting electrocution. Inmates had keys to the arms room that contained pistols, shotguns, high-powered rifles, and a sub-machine gun, along with ammunition. They also had obtained keys to the barracks and cells that housed the inmates. The inmates controlled the one telephone line over which calls were made to and from the prison.

When the CID investigation began it was of limited scope. Hale commended the work of Duke Atkinson, the principle investigator, for working "far above the call of duty, at risk of his life, to learn first hand of the conditions at this prison" (Hale, 1967). As evidence of broad misconduct unfolded, additional state police investigators were sent into the prison. Wardens were "beginning to feel the squeeze" as the veil of secrecy that had enabled them to act with impunity was being lifted. The wardens unsuccessfully urged the state police to leave. The inmates, armed with all sorts of crude but lethal weapons (quite apart from access to weapons in the arms room), also were becoming more anxious. It was no mystery to them how and against whom the wardens typically released their anger and frustration.

It was in this setting that Gene Hale agreed to communicate with the inmates. Although the inmates had been told that the wardens were placed on inactive status, tension remained. Armed with a directive from the governor for Hale and Superintendent Bishop to fire the wardens outright and to instruct the state police to conduct a full investigation, Hale went before the prisoners to try to reassure them and level with them regarding the situation.

His plan was to speak to inmates through the bars separating him from the majority of Tucker prisoners with a public address system. His message that the abuse was over and that change was coming was met with deep cynicism on the part of the prisoners. Even word that the wardens had been fired was not reassuring to inmates. One inmate spoke, indicating "doubt and fear that the atrocious tortures of the past had in fact ended" (Hale, 1967).

Then things took a turn and opened the door for communication between the governor's aide and the men confined at Tucker. An inmate asked Hale to come near the cell entrance for a private conversation. After asking Hale if he really was an assistant to the governor, he invited Hale to come into the large cellblock to talk with them and listen to them. Gene Hale's own words best describe this rather remarkable meeting:

> The large barred door into the barracks cell was unlocked and opened. Inside the cell I walked, and faced the majority of the prisoners classified as rank prisoners. These were the ones who allegedly could not be trusted.
>
> Perspiration seeped from my brow, neck, shoulders, and back. My shirt was soaked, and perspiration seemed now to stream as I came face to face with the spokesman for the prisoners. The spokesman explained that I was to sit on a bunk bed to which he pointed. He explained that the prisoners would form a human ring around me in order that certain prison officials would not be able to see which prisoner talked to me as they feared reprisal and persecution if I left the prison.
>
> I sat on an old bunk bed where the smelly mattress was covered with a cotton sack, and watched the bugs crawl away as I sat down. The prisoners gathered around me, and all I could see were prisoners, prisoners, and more prisoners—convicted felons—and now I was a prisoner too.
>
> I tried to be firm, informative and honest, and I explained that they had been sentenced to this prison, and not invited; that I believed basically that there was good in every man. I did believe this of the majority as I sat there, surrounded by the prisoners knowing that I was subject to their will.
>
> Here I learned of the plan for the mass escape and the reasons therefor. I listened attentively, and I continued to wipe the perspiration from my face and neck.
>
> Either I was numb with fear or I believed and trusted these prisoners as they told their stories, as they asked only for fairness, human decency, and an end to the atrocities to which they had been subjected (Hale, 1967).

Perhaps the meeting that took place on that hot summer evening of 1966 symbolically represents the beginning of prison reform in Arkansas. In the past there had been periodic attention to problems, abuses, and reported atrocities, but the typical response was tentative, half-hearted, and most importantly temporary. Invariably, the attention died down and it was back to business as usual. Business as usual was to ignore the prison and its prisoners. The conventional wisdom was "Whatever happens there, happens; if it is harsh, then so be it; convicted felons deserve harsh treatment." For the first time an official of the state with the legitimacy and authority of the governor's office went before the inmates to say we are aware of what has been going on here, it is unacceptable, and it will not continue. For the first time the state was listening, albeit skeptically, to what the inmates were saying.

The fact that Hale received threats on his life and ultimately lost his job with the Attorney General's Office, due to his participation in and reporting of his experiences with this very early attempt at prison reform, indicated that this long-ignored issue could hit a nerve.

The Arkansas State Police, 1966

What had criminal investigators learned that prompted the governor to take such unprecedented steps? The complete report was 67 pages long, compiled largely from interviews with Tucker inmates. While it elaborated on the preliminary findings mentioned in earlier news conferences, it went well beyond those terse and guarded statements. The picture that emerges from the report was that Assistant Superintendent Bruton operated the Tucker farm as if it were an independent kingdom subject to little more than his personal whims and preferences. The Arkansas State Police 1966 report describes a Tucker of incredible corruption and cruelty. It catalogues in enormous detail commonplace occurrence of torture, misappropriation of state property and resources, bribery, loansharking, homicide, rape, blackmail, extortion, unsanitary and inhumane living conditions, and violation of existing correctional policy.

Several imaginative types of torture are described in the report, including forcing needles under the inmates' fingernails, using pliers on various parts of the body including genitals, beating inmates with chains and vehicle fan belts (Arkansas State Police, 1966), and knife-carving on the skin, to name a few (Hale, 1967). These were in addition to the use of the "hide," which was still legal at that time, although its administration often violated Board of Correction regulations. Common violations were exceeding the maximum of 10 lashes, using the hide on bare skin rather than on clothing, and allowing trusties to administer the whip. The strap used for whipping inmates was described as follows:

> The strap which is referred to throughout this opinion is made of leather and is between four and five feet long and four inches wide. This leather is bradded to a wooden handle approximately six inches in length. The strap is about one-fourth inch thick at the end attached to the wooden handle and is gradually tapered toward the end which comes in contact with the person being whipped. The evidence showed that there is more than one strap used at the Penitentiary but all are of approximately the same construction (*Jackson v. Bishop*, 1967, p. 809).

The federal court had not yet ruled that corporal punishment was a per se violation of the Eighth Amendment prohibition against cruel and unusual punishment. *Talley v. Stephens* (1965) had only required that the prison establish standards for the use and application of corporal punishment. This cautious decision was a nod to the weakening, but apparently not defunct hands-off doctrine of prison jurisprudence (Feeley & Rubin, 1998).

The inmates also described to the investigators, and thus announced to the world, a device called the Tucker telephone. The main part of this instrument of torture was an electric generator taken from an obsolete crank-type telephone. Appropriately, the device was maintained in a small building known as "the telephone booth" (Feeley & Rubin, 1998, p. 56). The generator was used to send jolts of electricity into the nude body of a prisoner strapped to a gurney. One electrode was attached to a person's toe, the other to his penis (Arkansas State Police, 1966). One inmate testified that several charges were introduced at a duration designed to stop just short of the inmates losing consciousness. Apparently, loss of consciousness would interfere with maximum effectiveness of torture. Assistant Superintendent Bruton reportedly "rang up" inmates on the Tucker telephone both to punish and to extract information from them (Arkansas State Police, 1966). Many inmates report having had the Tucker telephone used on them or having witnessed its use on others. It was reported that the device was a "standard punishment for all sorts of infractions" (Feeley & Rubin, 1998, p. 56).

FIGURE 2.3. Tucker unit telephone.

The Arkansas State Police report (1966) catalogues testimony from most inmates at Tucker. At first they were reluctant to talk to the state police, but when they were convinced that the investigation was legitimate and could bring change, the inmates offered a mountain of testimony. The following brief summary perhaps represents some of the major points raised in this lengthy report:

1. Trusty inmates used prison vehicles to drive into town to purchase whiskey and beer. Manufacture and sale of home brew was common. Drugs of various types were available for purchase.
2. Almost anything was available at a price. This included better food, better jobs, protection from violence, medical treatment, clothing, and even a place to sleep. Loans were made at 100% interest.
3. Food preparation and serving areas were filthy; the food served to rank men was unsanitary and severely inadequate nutritionally.
4. Those working on the long line (rank men) were described as 40 to 60 pounds under normal weight. Their clothing was dirty, torn or full of holes, and not the right size. Footwear was ill fitting or simply absent. Issuing underwear and socks was infrequent or just did not happen.

5. The living areas were described as filthy. Mattresses and sheets were dirty, discolored, and rotten. Showers were leaking, commodes and urinals were stopped up, and the entire living area had a "filthy smell."

6. Searches of the barracks turned up 61 knives, 5 fighting knuckles, 2 palm weights, 5 blackjacks or clubs, 3 straight razors, and 1 hatchet.

7. Wardens and others were given (or took) meat and other prison food items for their personal use and made use of prison laundry and auto repair service. Prison land and labor were used to raise livestock for private profit. Inmate labor was used to clear land for free-world people.

8. Inmates were beaten, kicked, shot, or whipped on numerous occasions by both trusties and wardens. Instruments for beating included such items as shovels, axe handles, chains, rubber hoses, tractor fan belts, blackjacks, hoe handles, and ropes with knots tied in them.

9. Money and other items sent to inmates by family or friends were routinely confiscated.

10. Inmates were forced to commit various sex acts for the amusement of trusties. Sex was voluntarily exchanged for goods such as food and services such as protection (Arkansas State Police, 1966).

There was considerable speculation that much of what the prisoners reported to investigators was fabricated. Nevertheless there was sufficient corroboration and physical evidence to convince even the most skeptical that Tucker had been the setting of extremes: extremes in the excessive use of physical force, extremes in deprived and squalid living circumstances, extremes in the economic and psychological exploits of prisoners, and extremes in gross and frequent violation of policy and, no doubt, law. Bill Skipper, one of the CID investigators in 1966, remarked in an interview in 1992, "I would not have believed what I was seeing, had I not seen it with my own eyes" (personal communication, November 10, 1992).

There was some mystery and intrigue regarding the release of the completed CID document. Although expected much earlier, the report was not released to Governor Faubus until just before he left office in January of 1967. Faubus and his staff speculated that state officials interested in developing ties with the new Republican administration followed the wishes of Governor-elect Rockefeller rather than Faubus with regard to this report. Everyone was aware that the report was a political "hot potato," unsure of how it would be interpreted and what it might precipitate. Gene Hale's release of his story on January 15 was a preemptory strike designed to reduce political uses of the document that could reflect negatively on the Faubus administration. Rockefeller released the full report just days after Hale's article appeared.

Jim Bruton

Superintendent Bruton's name was frequently mentioned by the Tucker inmates in their interviews with CID investigators. Bruton had given up his seat in the Arkansas House of Representatives to take the job at Tucker, where he remained for 12 years until his resignation just before the CID investigation began. Bruton enjoyed the confidence of prison board members who expressed doubts when Governor Faubus first insisted that Bruton was involved in wrongdoings.

Bruton was said to punish inmates for nothing more than simply wanting to whip someone. Inmates covertly tape-recorded whippings of inmates by Bruton. Not only did the recordings demonstrate violations of prison rules, they also provided a backstage look at the whippings in general as well as Bruton's approach to them. The criminal investigator (Atkinson) writing the Arkansas State Police report (1966) described Bruton's recorded voice during the whippings as "that of a very excited person bordering insanity." In hysterical profanity Bruton's excitement presented itself in cycles, increasing by degrees to a certain point, then diminishing and beginning again, while he whipped the inmates. A trusty stated that Bruton "acted like a man out of his mind" when he was whipping the inmates (Arkansas State Police, 1966, p. 58).

Bruton lead a very active life at Tucker. He was accused of kickback and extortion of inmates, of hay and livestock deals that were profitable to himself and his son, and of conversion of state resources to his own use. Inmates state that Bruton had a bed available that he would rent to inmates for visits from wives and girlfriends. Bruton reportedly approached wives and girlfriends stating that if they would have sex with him, he would make it easier on their loved ones. One inmate said that he was present when Bruton made an inmate with a bad heart run five miles, after which the man fell dead in the prison yard. Inmates report that it was common to see Bruton hit inmates "with anything he could get his hands on," including his cane or crutch (Arkansas State Police, 1966, p. 58).

A remarkable encounter occurred between Bruton and the principal state police investigator, Duke Atkinson, at Tucker prison in the summer of 1966. Bruton had submitted his resignation, but it was not yet effective as the investigation commenced. He was away from the prison the day the investigation began but burst on the scene on the second day of the investigation, expressing anger and dismay to Atkinson that the investigation was taking place without his prior knowledge. Atkinson told him that the investigation targeted only liquor traffic by inmates and was not intended to bring discredit on Bruton.

Satisfied and relieved by this response, Bruton relaxed and opened up to investigator Atkinson. He told him that liquor violations were as old as the penitentiary and the chances of changing that now were slim. Bruton explained that he was retiring under current retirement policy that was a better deal for him than a new plan to be implemented. He then asked if Atkinson would be interested in the job of assistant superintendent at Tucker. Further he told Atkinson that he thought he could arrange it and would be happy to see Atkinson have the job.

Bruton elaborated on the position of assistant superintendent at Tucker Farm. The job paid $8,000 per year, provided a new car each year, a 14-room house, a complete expense account, and all food furnished. He mentioned not to be concerned with the $8,000 salary as that would be the smallest benefit of the job. A lot of "gifts," he said, would be offered from various businesses and other "interested persons" and that it was "smart" to accept such gifts (Arkansas State Police, 1966, p. 12). Bruton also described to Atkinson how he had made "a

FIGURE 2.4. Tucker unit electric chairs.

 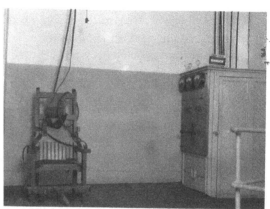

pile of money" with horses while at the prison. Bruton would buy horses, keep them on the prison grounds, have inmates care for them and break them, and he would sell them at a profit.

Bruton offered advice for operating the prison should investigator Atkinson get the job: "Run the goddamned place" and make sure that the inmates and the wardens know you are boss. "If an inmate gets out of hand," he counseled, "hit him with anything you can get your hands on," since that's the only thing that prisoners respect. It is wise in this job to "keep your mouth shut" and not let anyone know your business. If anything unexpected comes up, act as if "you knew all about it. ... Make everybody think you are the smartest son-of-a-bitch in the world, and you'll get by" (Arkansas State Police, 1966, p. 12).

Jim Beach, another state police investigator who assisted with the 1966 Tucker investigation, recalls an encounter with Bruton that involved administering the death penalty. Both death row and the electric chair were then located at Tucker. Reporters, law enforcement officers, and other witnesses were invited to view executions. On one occasion, as a public relations gesture, Bruton invited all witnesses down to Tucker for a large country breakfast feast prior to an electrocution. At the conclusion of the breakfast, Bruton stood and announced, "Let's go burn the bastard" (J. Beach, personal communication, November 12, 1992).

An Inmate's Version

An inmate who had escaped from Tucker told stories similar to those reported in the CID investigation. Billy Wayne Poe had been given a 7-year sentence to Tucker on an overdraft charge for checks totaling $60.70. Having escaped from Tucker in 1966, he surrendered to authorities in Detroit. When Michigan courts did not hear from Arkansas during the 60-day period given to initiate extradition proceedings, they released Poe. While at least temporarily free from prison, Poe also felt free to describe his experiences at Tucker (Steinmetz, 1967).

Poe admitted, "I was guilty, and I don't deny that, but I don't think I had to be treated like that for what I did." As an assistant to the inmate "doctor," who was not a physician but was a trusty in charge of the infirmary, Poe had witnessed the use of the Tucker telephone and the insertion of hypodermic needles under fingernails. "I've seen guys go crazy from the pain," Poe said. Other "treatments" in the infirmary included extraction of teeth by the inmate doctor without painkillers and forcing unruly prisoners to drink a concoction of turpentine and castor oil. Poe witnessed a young prisoner being beaten so severely in the infirmary that he broke a Coke® bottle to use on his throat to attempt suicide (Steinmetz, 1967).

Life in the barracks for rank inmates like himself was described by Poe as perilous and terrifying. He explained, "You did not have anything you could call your own." On his first Christmas in Tucker he received a gift from home that included a money order and house shoes. "They had already cashed my money order. He [a trusty] just showed the money to me and put it in his pocket." When the trusty picked up the house shoes, Poe grabbed them from him. "I was swarmed by trusties, and I was held down by two of them and beaten. One kicked me in the mouth, more than once, and knocked four teeth out" (Steinmetz, 1967).

It was necessary for Poe's mother to pay the inmate doctor $50 to make arrangements for the false teeth. Poe's mother said she paid out a total of $2,000 during the time her son was in prison to protect him. Poe explained that all the trusties knew that he was receiving money from the outside and all of them tried to get it. If one trusty got his money others would beat him or otherwise mistreat him. When visitors were at Tucker, trusties would "drop hints about how you might get beat up or something if your folks don't pay off" (Steinmetz, 1967).

In the fields, said Poe, the rank men were subject to wanton beatings by the trusty guards. "You get out of line, and they'll shoot you or beat you with a blackjack." At times the trusty riders would mistreat rank prisoners simply for their own entertainment. For example, two trusties on horseback would ride up to an inmate, lift him up, and drag him swiftly through the cotton to the end of the row to see how far they could throw the inmate through the air. Or they might just whip everyone just to "tighten them up," laughing as they did so.

On the other hand, an inmate interviewed for the *Arkansas Democrat* in November of 1966 pointed out that impressive improvements had occurred in Tucker since the changes were made the previous summer. He mentioned that educational, religious, and vocational programs had been instituted along with recreational programs that included baseball, boxing, library, movies, and so on. He also stated that food services had improved enormously, as had the working conditions in the field. "Now," he said, "we are treated like human beings."

The Strike at Cummins

When the trouble flared up at Tucker, Governor Faubus had acted quickly to remove offending staff members, initiate a thorough investigation, and make some improvements in facilities and routines. However, Faubus was insistent that the problems at Tucker were unusual incidents and that the basic organization and operation of Arkansas prisons were sound. Although a crisis had occurred, it had been addressed, and now the prisons could continue as they had for many years. According to Faubus there was nothing basically deficient about the system. It was an honorable and just prison system that served the state well and at minimal expense. Of the Tucker situation Faubus (1967) said, "Discoveries in the investigation and facts gained by me cast no bad reflection on the trusty system."

In another statement offered to support the point that the Tucker situation was atypical, Faubus announced that there were no comparable problems, "no wrongdoings" at Cummins, the main prison that held the vast majority of Arkansas inmates (Donald, 1966). However, on the very day that he made that statement a group of Cummins inmates staged a strike. Faubus, who had just held a news conference at Tucker regarding situation there, quickly traveled to Cummins to consult with Superintendent Bishop about this new development. As Faubus (1967) later described it, "One pot had settled, the other was starting to boil over."

The strike involved 144 inmates, some of whom refused to leave their barracks to work in the fields and others who went to the fields but refused to work. The latter were returned to the barracks and left confined with other strikers while Superintendent Bishop and Faubus met to develop their plans. The other approximately 1,000 inmates at Cummins did not participate in the strike (Douthit, 1966b; Trimble & Valachovic, 1966).

The initial interpretation of the strike was that it resulted from what Faubus called a mistaken impression that the strap had been abolished in Arkansas prisons. A lawsuit was pending in U.S. District Court regarding the strap, and its abolishment had been discussed on numerous occasions, but it remained a mainstay of Arkansas penitentiary discipline. News reports had just been released reporting that the strap would no longer be used; however, Faubus claimed that what should have been reported was that repeal of the strap was under consideration. Reportedly striking inmates taunted trusty guards stating that since the strap had been abolished that there was no way they could be punished.

Governor Faubus (1967) recalls that the following points emerged from his meeting with Bishop about the Cummins strike:

1. Most inmates at Cummins were not participating in the strike.
2. The rebels must not, under any conditions, be permitted to gain the upper hand.
3. Ring leaders must be identified and punished.
4. Strike participants must suffer loss of privileges.
5. Faubus would release news of the strike at a press conference.
6. Sufficient force would be on hand to ensure success, using as little force as possible, but maximum force if necessary.

In his news conference Faubus described the strike at Cummins and shared some of his thinking about it: "This entire incident was caused by a troublemaking group encouraged by recent court decisions, and the mistaken assumption that the use of the strap had been abolished" (Trimble & Valachovic, 1966). Faubus also indicated that no abuses of authority had been found at Cummins, as had recently been revealed at Tucker.

To ensure that sufficient force was available Faubus ordered about 30 state police officers to Cummins when he first learned of the strike (Trimble, 1966). The situation at Cummins remained relatively quiet, interrupted by a single incident of striking inmates attacking some of the non-striking inmates when they returned from work (Trimble & Valachovic, 1966). Subsequently, the state police separated the strikers from the rest of the inmates at Cummins, placing 104 striking Black inmates in one barracks and the 42 White strike participants in another ("Strap Ends Strike by 146 Prisoners; Tear Gas is Used," 1966). The strike began on a Friday and the situation remained calm throughout the rest of the weekend (Trimble & Valachovic, 1966).

Following meetings with Governor Faubus and the prison board, Bishop established Monday as the deadline for the strikers to abandon their efforts and to return to work. The board authorized Bishop to use any legal means needed to restore order to Cummins. Bishop also reported that rumors had begun to surface that some of the strikers were unhappy with the strike and wanted to return to work ("Striking Prisoners Remain in Isolation; Bishop Says Return to Work 'Rumored,'" 1966). Officials had made it clear that those who had participated in the strike would be losing "good time" accumulation. Good time gives an inmate additional or bonus credit for time served, thus shortening the total length of time to be served in prison ("Striking Prisoners Remain in Isolation; Bishop Says Return to Work 'Rumored,'" 1966).

When the deadline of 7:00 a.m. Monday came, Bishop, along with wardens and trusties, approached the barracks that housed the strikers, calling them out to work. When the inmates refused to leave the barracks, wardens sent trusties into the barracks to try to persuade inmates to end the strike and return to work. The striking inmates attacked the trusties, who withdrew from the barracks having sustained only minor injuries. The strikers were standing firm ("Strap Ends Strike by 146 Prisoners; Tear Gas is Used," 1966).

Bishop, when asked earlier how would he respond if the strike continued beyond the deadline, commented, "We'll cross that bridge when we come to it" ("Striking Prisoners Remain in Isolation; Bishop Says Return to Work 'Rumored,'" 1966). The bridge was crossed with a show of force. The state police fired tear gas shells into the barracks housing the Black strikers and fired gunshots over their heads. This was described as having a "quieting effect" on the men ("Strap Ends Strike by 146 Prisoners; Tear Gas is Used," 1966). Bishop then called 10 of the Blacks out of the barracks. As these 10 came out one by one, each received the maximum punishment of 10 lashes with the strap. After the lashes were administered, remaining inmates' acquiesced to authorities, saying they were ready to go back to work ("Strap Ends Strike by 146 Prisoners; Tear Gas is Used," 1966; "Striking Prisoners Remain in Isolation; Bishop Says Return to Work 'Rumored,'" 1966). Intending to follow the same procedure with White inmates, Bishop and the wardens found that White inmates were ready to give up the strike. One White inmate who was strapped still refused to return to work and was placed in isolation on a diet of bread and water ("Striking Prisoners Remain in Isolation; Bishop Says Return to Work 'Rumored,'" 1966). By 8:00 a.m. the strike had been broken.

After calm was restored and Cummins was back to its normal operation, Superintendent Bishop elaborated his understanding of what precipitated the incident. Bishop maintained that no one could be certain what brought it on due to conflicting inmate accounts. However, it appeared to be more complex than the early speculation that inmates saw no reason to comply based on the report that the strap had been abolished. Obviously, those at the bottom of the prison structure—the rank inmates—initiated the strike. In the first moments of the strike prisoners complained of abuses by trusties, specifically those who supervised them in the fields, the "line riders" (Valachovic, 1966). Eventually, a list of written grievances was given to Bishop as the strike continued. This grievance list raised the following objectives: (a) improved food, (b) reduction of working hours, (c) arbitration committees to raise complaints directly with the superintendent, (d) clothing that would fit, and (e) better treatment from riders (trusties) in the fields (Valachovic, 1966). Informal discussions with other inmates produced the following demands: an 8-hour, 5-day work week; state provided toothbrushes and materials with which they could write letters; open visits; and working in the fields only when they were dry. Although officials were not confronted by strikers about the use of the strap, as might be expected, it was on their minds. Bishop overheard one inmate remark to another who was a spokesperson, "Why don't you tell the man the truth? Why don't you tell him about the strap?" (Valachovic, 1966).

Officials made minimal response to the demands, requests, and complaints of the strikers. In talking with inmates during the strike, Bishop promised to improve their food, but referred to the other complaints as "general bitching." Cummins inmates who had been involved in the strike were able to smuggle a letter to the *Arkansas Gazette*. In their opinion, there was more to the Cummins strike story than had been told. "There are a lot of things our superintendent can't divulge. Why? For the simple reason that he don't know." The letter contended that brutality by wardens and trusties, along with bad food and working conditions, prompted their strike: "We could take no more. So we felt something had to be done. So we call a sit-down." The conditions described in their letter sound similar to the conditions just addressed at Tucker: beatings, harsh and unsanitary living conditions, forced homosexuality, living in a barracks "with 200 to 250 other men with rats, roaches, mattresses and beds which ha[d] been [t]here since the place was buil[t]." The letter states that the strike and its consequences were "all because we ask to be treated like human beings and men and not like animals" ("Smuggled Letter Reports Reasons For Prison Strike," 1966).

Prison Reform in the Faubus Administration

So, what can be made of prison reform in the Faubus years? First, one must not forget the context. Prisons through the mid-1960s were not considered much of an issue. They were isolated geographically, socially, and psychologically. There was not a great deal of awareness or concern about prisons, prisoners, or correctional issues. An unspoken, unwritten, but nevertheless operative principle in correctional administration at that time was to keep prisons out of sight and out of mind. The hands-off view of courts to prison operations also served to depress public awareness and legal intervention.

Arkansas had for decades fully complied with that operating principle. Prisons were seen as a necessity; they were seen as a place where the most deviant, irresponsible, and "evil" were separated from the conventional, responsible, and "good." The goals of the prison experience and the means of achieving those goals were given little if any thought.

There were, however, two widely accepted guidelines for the operation of Arkansas prisons. Decision makers such as legislators and governors, the press, and the citizens generally shared these guidelines; they were not widely discussed, and rarely written about. They were simply accepted. The first guideline was that the prison experience ought to be punishing. Arkansas law sentenced persons convicted of crime to "hard labor." It has been settled law from early statehood even to the present day that a sentence to a term in the penitentiary is a sentence at "hard labor" (*Ward v. Little Rock,* 1883, p. 531; *McArty v. Hobbs,* 2012, p. 3). The commonly accepted arguments for punishment as a wise and useful response to crime resonated with the Arkansas consciousness and the Arkansas experience. Persons who have violated the criminal laws have upset the moral balance, thus they ought to pay a debt to society. Also, if we make the consequence of crime a painful punishing experience, it will serve as an example to others contemplating crime and thus will deter future acts of crime.

The second guideline of correctional administration in Arkansas was to operate prisons at maximum economic efficiency. This meant spending as little as possible of the state's money on operating prisons. It also meant that if the prisons could be run at a profit to state revenues, so much the better. Arkansas was no doubt a poor state. While there was consensus that Arkansas needed a prison, the idea of spending precious state resources on prisons was not viewed favorably (Feeley & Rubin, 1998). Examined on this criterion, Arkansas had established an enviable record.

The prison system that the Faubus administration inherited and administered received little attention in its early years and for many years prior to that. It was assumed that the prison could operate on its own with little outside interference, and it did. It was assumed that it would be a harsh and punishing experience for prisoners, and it was. It was assumed that the system would not place financial demands on the state, and it did not.

The equilibrium in correctional administration that had been established and operated for many years was upset in 1965 and 1966. Most of this change was probably due to currents that were flowing in the larger American socio-cultural system. Realities previously taken for granted were suddenly becoming closely scrutinized. Authority was no longer being accepted simply because it was authority. The rights of individuals for categories of persons not among the privileged were undergoing a vast national reconsideration. Also, the hands-off view of courts to questions of prison administration were beginning to fade (Feeley & Rubin, 1998).

Governor Faubus had radar that was highly sensitive to social and political shifts. He sensed, correctly, that prisons were about to become a political issue. At first he seemed to dismiss strains toward change in the prisons as crass dirty politics. Such tendencies, he felt, were based on a distortion of facts used to discredit the responsible operation of what could be defended as a model penitentiary system.

Largely through what was revealed in both the Tucker incident and the Cummins strike, Faubus found it necessary to admit that perhaps the system was not as faultless, and its operation was not as responsible, as he had thought. This was occurring precisely at a time when the notion of what was considered responsible organization and practice for prisons and prisoners was shifting. Prison reform was even beginning to find its voice in such persons as the members of the Arkansas Prison Board, in the superintendent of Arkansas prisons, his trusted aid Gene Hale, and in editorials in both the "liberal" *Arkansas Gazette* and the "conservative" *Arkansas Democrat*.

While evolving societal and political attitudes were important, reforms were largely promoted by the not insignificant power of the federal courts to require adherence to minimal constitutional standards. The first federal court case to question the conditions in the Arkansas prisons was *Talley v. Stephens* (1965), where Judge J. Smith Henley first considered issues regarding the use of whipping inmates as a form of punishment. As stated, this case did not prohibit corporal punishment but did take the first step of requiring the state to develop standards and safeguards for the practice and enjoined use of corporal punishment until such standards were established. Subsequent to the *Talley* decision the Arkansas Prison Board did implement the following standards and procedures for the use of the strap as the method of corporal punishment:

Offenses and Punishment

A great part of your time here will be spent in the barracks you are assigned to. Barracks rules and procedure will be posted in the barracks. Your conduct, personal cleanliness and attitude while in the barracks is an important part of your prison record. "These major offenses will warrant corporal punishment:"

1. Homosexuality.
2. Agitation (defined as one who creates turmoil and disturbances).
3. Insubordination (resisting authority or refusing to obey orders).
4. Making or concealing of weapons.
5. Refusal to work when medically certified able to work.
6. Participating in or inciting a riot.
7. No inmate shall ever be authorized to inflict any corporal punishment under color of prison authority on another inmate.

> Punishment shall not, in any case, exceed Ten lashes with the strap, the number of lashes to be administered shall be determined by a Board of inquiry, consisting of at least two officials of the Arkansas State Penitentiary, The Superintendent or Assistant Superintendent, and the head Warden or an associate Warden. The Board of Inquiry will request that the accused inmate appear before the Board and speak in his own behalf. No Punishment will be administered in the field (*Jackson v. Bishop*, 1967, p. 808).

These procedures were not reviewed and approved by any court before their implementation. The subsequent federal court review and decisions regarding corporal punishment and other important issues regarding conditions of confinement will be an ongoing influence of Arkansas prison reform for the next decade and a half. Corporal punishment as a means of discipline for prisoners has a long history. State law never included corporal punishment as a sanctioned form of punishment or discipline, but the Arkansas Supreme Court, as early as the late 19th century, expressed misgivings about the propriety of corporal punishment but held that it was permissible to whip prisoners in state custody (*Werner v. State*, 1884).

While the *Talley v. Stephens* case (1965) did not abolish corporal punishment, it was at least a partial victory for inmates in that the Court did enjoin the use of the strap until administrative procedures were established by the prison, and the prison authorities were enjoined from interfering with the prisoners' right of access to the courts. The guaranteed right of access to the courts on the part of prisoners by *Talley v. Stephens* (1965) provided the path to reform that was paved by the subsequent cases and federal court intervention that will be discussed in the following chapters.

If one wishes to find fault with the Faubus administration in regard to prisons, a key point would be neglect. The surprise and dismay that Faubus and his staff expressed at the revelations that surfaced at Tucker and Cummins in 1966 indicate that they did not know what was taking place at the state prisons. A question that is easy to raise in hindsight is "Should they have known what was going on?" When he resigned in the summer of 1966, Jim Bruton had been at Tucker for 12 years. It is unlikely that what the CID investigators found had existed there only a few weeks. It is difficult to know with certainty because the data did not and do not exist to confirm what was happening. However, the fact that the data did not exist indicates that the supervision of persons like Bruton, and therefore of the prisons themselves, was extraordinarily loose and distant. Monitoring mechanisms and routine evaluation and feedback were virtually nonexistent.

Also nonexistent or virtually nonexistent was policy to guide prison operations. If the revelations at Tucker showed anything, they clearly demonstrated that the prison operated according to the whims and preferences of persons like Bruton, or perhaps even worse, the whims of inmate trusty guards and supervisors, who bore the responsibility for the majority of the day-to-day prison operations. For example, whipping prisoners with the bull hide had for many years been the primary social control mechanism to maintain order and discipline.

However, rather than establish its own policy (or even recognize the need for one) for using the whip, the Arkansas prison system had to be forced into such policy by the federal court.

The 1966 Tucker and Cummins incidents also demonstrate that lines of authority were not at all clear. Although Superintendent Bishop saw himself as over Assistant Superintendent Bruton, Bruton seems to have seen himself as answering to no one. Similarly, the Tucker incident demonstrated that the responsibility for running the prison system was clearly not for the prison board, the governor, and the superintendent. The clearest example of that was the firing of the Tucker wardens by Faubus in consultation with Bishop, but with no consultation with the prison board. When some members of the board took exception to this, Faubus (1967) replied, "I did not have time to contact every Tom, Dick and Harry."

It is also easy to fault Faubus for his uncompromising defense of the trusty system. While indeed this system was advantageous economically, it also was an organizational form that provided fertile soil for the growth of amazingly corrupt, cruel, and abusive practices.

On the other hand, one has to give the Faubus administration credit in regard to prison reform. When he became aware that there were problems at Tucker, Faubus immediately looked into it, found that there was a much larger problem involving possible criminal violations, ordered an investigation, and took immediate steps to correct the situation. Faubus did not attempt to cover up what was taking place at Tucker or Cummins. He announced the facts as they became available to him, along with his proposed actions. Faubus deserves credit for trying to learn all sides of the story. He sent his aide, Gene Hale, to Tucker in order to assist with the situation, but also to hear out the inmates as they gave their complaints. Faubus himself went to both Tucker and Cummins as the crises unfolded and talked directly with inmates.

Also, the Faubus administration must be given credit for actual changes that took place in Arkansas prisons. While some of these improvements may seem modest by current standards, at the time of their implementation they represented revolutionary changes in the Arkansas system. Examples of improvements were construction of a new hospital, new housing for inmates that replaced wooden barracks with fireproof structures, new kitchen and dining hall facilities, along with modernization of farming equipment and facilities. An education program was implemented, which for the first time was accredited by the state's education department (Faubus, 1991).

But, it was the attention to these issues by the federal courts that provided the real impetus for reform. *Talley v. Stephens* (1965) did not abolish the strap and corporal punishment but did require procedural safeguards and enjoined prison administrators from interfering with prisoners' access to the courts for redress of grievances. *Jackson v. Bishop* (1967) forbade the use of the infamous Tucker telephone or the use of the strap on bare skin. *Jackson* went on to require that additional procedures for use of corporal punishment be filed with the Court. As will be discussed in a subsequent chapter, the use of the strap was further reviewed by the 8th Circuit Court of Appeals (*Jackson v. Bishop*, 1968).

Conclusion

In summary, the issue of prisons and prison reform had in this time become an issue that would not go away. Inconceivable conditions had been exposed and at least temporarily addressed. The picture of Arkansas prisons that emerged at this time was nothing to brag about. For anyone who wanted to examine the question of blame there seemed to be plenty to spread around. Perhaps Gene Hale (1967) at the end of his report said it best: "As fact, we are all guilty FOR the prisons OF the guilty, or perhaps it should be written we are all guilty OF the prisons FOR the guilty." Regardless of what happened or did not happen and who was responsible for it, it was clear that prison reform was now in the spotlight and it was a safe bet that it would remain on the stage for several years.

REFERENCES

Arkansas State Police (1966). Case Report, Criminal Investigations Division, File Number 916-166-66. Report re Tucker State Prison Farm.

Cummins trusty shot to death. (1966, January 15). *Pine Bluff Commercial.*

Donald, L. (1966, September 2). 3 Wardens fired as CID uncovers Tucker scandal. *Arkansas Gazette.*

Douthit, G. (1966a, September 1). Firings, demotions shake penal farm. *Arkansas Democrat.*

Douthit, G. (1966b, September 3). Prison board meets on firings, strike. *Arkansas Democrat.*

Faubus, O. (1967, February 2). Faubus tells of prison probe. *Jonesboro Sun.*

Faubus, O. (1991). *The Faubus Years: January 11, 1955 to January 10, 1957.* Orval Faubus.

Feeley, M. M., & Rubin, E. L. (1998). *Judicial policy making and the modern state: How the courts reformed America's prisons.* Cambridge University Press.

Fugate, L. (1966, September 2). Ex-warden: Firing is "All a mistake." *Pine Bluff Commercial.*

Hale, E. (1967, January 15). A Faubus aide reports on Tucker Prison: Plot to seize weapons, unsanitary conditions, tortures are described. *Pine Bluff Commercial.*

Holt v. Sarver, 309 F. Supp. 362 (E.D. Ark. 1970)

Murton, T., & Hymas, J. (1969). *Accomplices to the crime: The Arkansas prison scandal.* Grove Press.

Prison chief resigns. (1965, October 11). *Arkansas Democrat.*

Strap ends strike by 146 prisoners; tear gas is used. (1966, September 6). *Arkansas Gazette.*

Smuggled letter reports reasons for prison strike. (1966, September 17). *Arkansas Gazette.*

Steinmetz, T. (1967, January 15). A convict's story-IV: "I used to lie awake … thinking about killing those guys." *Pine Bluff Commercial.*

Striking prisoners remain in isolation; Bishop says return to work "rumored." (1966, September 5). *Arkansas Gazette.*

Trimble, M. (1966, September 4). Board to request more buildings, prison employees. *Arkansas Gazette.*

Trimble, M., & Valachovic, E. (1966, September 3). 144 Cummins inmates hold sit-down strike. *Arkansas Gazette.*

Valachovic, E. (1966, September 7). Bishop reports calm at prison. *Arkansas Gazette.*

CASES CITED

Cooper v. Pate, 378 U.S. 546 (1964)

Jackson v. Bishop, 404 F.2d 571 (8th Cir. 1968)

Talley v. Stephens, 247 F. Supp. 683 (E.D. Ark. 1965)

Holt v. Sarver, 309 F. Supp. 362 (1970)

Ward v. Little Rock, 41 Ark. 526 (1883)

McArty v. Hobbs, 2012 Ark. 257 (2012)

Werner v. State, 44 Ark. 122 (1884)

Jackson v. Bishop, 268 F. Supp. 362 (1967)

KEY TERMS

Arkansas State Police CID Investigation

Court participation in prison issues

Gene Hale

Inmate perspective

Jim Bruton

Rehabilitation

Torture

Violations

QUESTIONS

1. Describe the hands-on versus hands-off approach. Which approach was instrumental in the U.S. Supreme Court case of *Cooper v. Pate* (1964) and why?

2. What were some of the findings associated with the CID investigation at Tucker? Which do you believe was the most significant finding? Why?

3. The CID investigation prompted the reporting and public exposure of the conditions at the Tucker farm. In your opinion, if the investigation and report on Tucker Farm was never written, do you think reform in the prison system would have happened? Why or why not?

4. What court case required that prisons establish standards for the use and application of corporal punishment? What is the significance of the ruling?

FIGURE CREDITS

3 | Prison Reform in the Early Months of the Rockefeller Administration

Introduction

Media attention, a new governor, and the slow but sure end of the old "hands-off" approach of prison organization, practices, and treatment of prisoners set the stage for the beginnings of prison reform in Arkansas.

The Arkansas prisons were not much of an issue with Arkansans or with their state officials until the scandals were publicized in the transition between the Faubus and the Rockefeller administrations. Previously, when news of the prisons, particularly criticism of the system, reached public awareness, that awareness was short-lived and without fervor. Those who expected this pattern to repeat itself in the late 1960s were in for a big surprise.

Rockefeller Administration and Reform

Governor Rockefeller was appalled by the Arkansas prison system, calling it "probably the most barbaric prison system in the United States" (Ward, 1978, p. 103). When Winthrop Rockefeller took office in January of 1967 the scandal and problems surrounding the Tucker prison were far from over. Rockefeller was the first Republican to be elected governor of the State of Arkansas since the Reconstruction Era following the Civil War. In the first month in office the new administration was deliberating what to do with the potentially explosive state police Criminal Investigation Division (CID) investigation report and its accounts of atrocity, corruption, violence, and inhumanity at Tucker. Before the decision was made, Eugene Hale's release of the essential elements of the report ended the indecisiveness and mystery. Rockefeller then released the document in its entirety to the press but asked the press to exercise discretion given the inflammatory nature of the report (Arkansas State Police, 1966; Ward, 1978).

The situation at Tucker in the early days of the new governor's administration was far from stable. In February of 1967, Rockefeller fired Pink Booher, the assistant superintendent in charge of Tucker, along with three other free-world officials. Information gathered from inmates reached Rockefeller that "goon squads were operating the prison," beating up prisoners at will (Douthit, 1967a). Tension and conflict between the trusties and Booher had escalated into crisis proportions. At one point Booher was found by state police to be holed up in his Tucker office with a Thompson submachine gun in a standoff with Tucker trusties (Murton & Hyams, 1969). The armed trusties threatened to shoot him if he entered parts of the prison occupied by the inmates (Murton, 1970, p. 13). As stated earlier, nearly all of the de facto guards were armed "trusty" prisoners (Murton & Hyams, 1969). Rockefeller at that point found it necessary to call in the Arkansas State Police to maintain order.

Rockefeller not only expressed interest in prison reform, but also used it as a campaign issue. Prison reform was explicitly mentioned in the Republican Party's platform. In an address shortly after the CID report was released, Rockefeller reiterated the need for prison reform to the people of Arkansas and asked for the assistance of the legislature. He pointed out that there was no easy solution to the prison problem. He suggested the need for commitment of resources combined with sound planning: "At this time I think it is necessary that we commit ourselves irrevocably to the program of [prison] reform" (Ward, 1978, p. 103).

Thomas Murton: The Real Brubaker

Rockefeller was not hesitant, as his predecessors had been, to draw on the experience and expertise of correctional experts outside Arkansas. One such expert whom Rockefeller consulted was Thomas Murton, a professor of criminal justice at Southern Illinois University. Murton offered his services to make an assessment of the situation at Tucker. It was in part on Murton's advice that Rockefeller acted to fire four of the top staff at Tucker.

Murton had both academic and administrative experience in corrections. He was a doctoral candidate in the criminology program at University of California

FIGURE 3.1. Arkansas Department of Corrections warden, Thomas Murton.

at Berkeley and had administered prisons in Alaska both for the military and for the state. Rockefeller had expressed interest in finding a reformer who could begin changing Arkansas's archaic prison system. Murton made an initial visit to the Tucker prison farm and stated the "eighteenth century (penological) methods used there ... w[ere] like going through a time tunnel" (Murton & Hyams, 1969, pp. 17–18). It was a tough assignment in this environment that offered little in resources and perhaps even less in popular support for change. The governor and his staff saw Murton as bright, informed, courageous, and tough. When Murton mentioned to Rockefeller that he would like to have a chance to bring about change in the Arkansas system, Rockefeller had found his reformer. Murton told the governor and his staff, "I'd like to go to Tucker and demonstrate to the people of Arkansas that you can run a prison without torture and brutality" (Murton & Hyams, 1969, p. 18).

The prison scandals captured the imagination of the Arkansas legislature and its members were not hesitant to become involved, particularly since the new administration was Republican and the legislature was almost wholly Democrat. A five-member legislative investigative committee indicated that deficiencies in the system were due in part to the small number of state-employed personnel, as well as inadequate physical facilities. They also expressed an interest in having the prisons run by the prison board rather than through the governor's office. For years the few free-world employees of the prison system had been subject to political appointment and control of the governor's office (Douthit, 1967b). Two members of the legislative investigative committee, Ivan Rose of Rogers and Van Taylor of Waldron, went to Tucker and questioned prisoners regarding conditions there. Their responses confirmed that the living conditions were still bleak and dangerous. Many inmates, with good reason, feared for their safety.

Regime Change at the Tucker Farm

Murton, in one of his earliest interviews as assistant superintendent at Tucker, made it clear that the trusty system must end, although he felt that it would have to be phased out over a period of time. Guards, according to Murton, "should be part of the paid staff and prisoners should not be allowed to carry guns" ("Penologist Named as Chief at Tucker," 1967).

The Tucker that Murton entered was extremely unstable. In his consultations with Rockefeller prior to being hired, Murton predicted that a major disturbance or riot could happen in a matter of hours (Murton & Hyams, 1969). Murton's comments regarding uprooting the old prison system had not gone unnoticed by the Tucker inmates.

Murton's plans for change in the prison were dramatic and ambitious. He believed that the Arkansas system could be changed from one of the worst to one of the best in the nation. "My long range goal was to eliminate the exploitation of inmates by other inmates or by non-prisoners for personal gain. I wanted to change the purpose and effect of the institution and I wanted to change the inmates' life [sic] at the institution (Murton & Hyams, 1969, pp. 18–19). He furthermore observed that change might be easier in Arkansas than elsewhere, in that Arkansas might be able to skip the slow evolutionary steps necessary in other states.

Perhaps it also should be mentioned that Murton's ideas for reform were being expressed in very general terms at this point. It is not clear if he had yet formulated his specific objectives for Tucker or if he purposely wanted to remain somewhat vague to keep his options open. Perhaps both.

Murton sensed that Arkansans had developed a rather high tolerance for abuse and perhaps atrocity in the prisons. His solution was to demonstrate publicly how bad the system was in order to convince the citizens of Arkansas of the inevitability of change. He reasoned that once the public saw the system for what it had become through the years they would be eager to reform it and ensure that it would not fall back to the previous horrors

O.E. Bishop, who had been hired by Faubus, was still in the position of super-intendent of Arkansas prisons. There was some discussion that Rockefeller might fire Bishop in order to replace him with Murton. The decision was made that Bishop be left in charge of Cummins, while placing Murton in charge of Tucker. Although technically Bishop was to be over Murton, it was agreed that Murton would have full control of Tucker (Murton & Hyams, 1969). Murton wanted to have an opportunity to reform Tucker before moving on to Cummins or being over the entire system. Murton also agreed to continue as correctional consultant to the governor and to work with the prison study commission that was being formed.

Murton's initial impression of Tucker was summed up in what he called "an atmosphere of total despair." He continued, "Their eyes, their expressions, and their demeanor were a vivid portrayal of hopelessness" (Murton, 1970, p. 13). He was also struck by the firmly entrenched oligarchy whereby all matters affecting the life and work of inmates were firmly in the control of a few powerful inmates who actually operated the prison. According to Murton, this trusty method of running a prison had become solidly entrenched due to apathy and indifference on the part of both the general population and state officials, and to the vested interests, economic and otherwise, which had become associated with that method of running the prisons. It became immediately apparent to Murton that the system was maintained by rewards and privileges granted to trusties, such as drugs, liquor, gambling, sex, and profits from various forms of illegal trafficking (Murton, 1970).

In late February 1967, Murton entered Tucker as its new assistant super-intendent without the assistance of civilian staff members other than himself. What he did have was a detachment of 15 Arkansas State Police officers and a tense inmate population. Murton immediately addressed the inmates' exclusive control of weapons. Although there were 15 Arkansas State Police officers on site at Tucker, they had to give up their weapons to inmates as a condition of coming onto the Tucker compound. This had been a longstanding rule in Arkansas pris-ons. Governor Rockefeller discovered when he first visited Tucker that he would not be allowed on the grounds at the prison until his bodyguard surrendered his gun to an inmate at the front gate (Ward, 1978).

On his first morning at Tucker, Murton, accompanied by the ranking state police officers, approached trusties in towers and gate houses to ask for permis-sion to arm the police. The argument that Murton offered was that the police and the inmate guards could be of assistance to each other if both were armed. This seemed reasonable to the inmate guards and thus, for the first time, police officers, who had been given the assignment of keeping order in the prison, were allowed to be armed (Murton & Hyams, 1969).

Murton's first policy change was to abolish corporal punishment. He was firmly convinced that the prison could not be properly run by depending on the bull hide to maintain control. Use of the strap had been debated for years, and there had been brief experimental suspensions of its use, but this was the first time policy prohibited its use.

Superintendent Bishop continued to use the strap at Cummins and believed that it would be impossible to run Cummins without it. Realizing that having the strap abolished at Tucker while still using it at Cummins was going to create problems for him at Cummins, Bishop asked Murton to moderate his stand on corporal punishment to at least "allow for the possibility" that the strap could be used at Tucker. Murton would not compromise the substance or intent of his policy (Murton & Hyams, 1969).

The Tucker trusties were suspicious of Murton's reforms and knew that such reforms would bring an end to their privileged positions. Murton had made no secret of his goal of replacing the trusties with free-world guards. However, at that time it was impossible for Murton to do so. Resources were simply not available for such a drastic move. This may have been advantageous in that it bought time both for Murton and the trusties, thus diffusing an immediate confrontation that could have placed Murton's reform in jeopardy.

Nevertheless, given the prospect of such ominous changes, the trusties threatened to strike (Murton & Hyams, 1969). Murton knew that a strike would be disastrous because of the reality that the prisoners were responsible for the basic operations of the prison. Murton assembled the trusties to try to calm their fears, to establish rapport with them, and most importantly to enlist their assistance. He reiterated to them his long-range goals but pointed out that he would have to move in stages. He told them that he wanted to have an open press policy. He explained that this would keep the administration of the prison honest in that the outside people would no longer be kept in the dark about what was happening in the prison. He promised trusties that they would not be returned to the ranks that could place them in a life-threatening situation. He explained that he wanted to develop a school program and a vocational program and to proceed with improving food and dining facilities.

Much to the relief of the trusties, Murton said that for the time being he would allow alcohol and gambling to remain. These would be removed in the future, but only after advanced notice to the inmates. Murton also told the assembled trusties that they would no longer receive a parole for killing escaping inmates. Perhaps Murton's strongest card was played when he asked the inmates to assist him in running the prison. At one point he said, "We'll run the prison together" (Murton & Hyams, 1969, p. 29).

Murton also spoke with the rank men, announcing to them that the trusties would no longer abuse them, nor would corporal punishment be used. However, he did remind the inmates that trusty guards would still be armed and were still under order to shoot a man who was attempting escape. He promised them improved food, clothing, shelter, and working conditions and that he would make other improvements. Not wanting to bring too much threatening change at once, he told the rank inmates that for the time being they could keep their homemade weapons. He announced the end of promotion through the purchase of new jobs. Promotion thereafter would be based on merit. He appealed to the rank inmates to work with him and promised that if they did so it would lead to a general improvement of conditions (Murton & Hyams, 1969). In response to an inmate's question, Murton said he would look into establishing a program, similar to the one at Cummins, where inmates could earn money by donating blood. He also assured the inmates that he would be looking into ways to improve good time and parole policy, as well as liberalizing visitation and mail procedures (Murton & Hyams, 1969).

It appeared that Murton was off to a good start with the inmates. Anyone who could make the kind of improvements he was talking about was worth listening to. He had displaced any threat of disturbance and had the attention of the inmates. He did not fit the image of the kind of prison official that inmates had become used to. Many of the inmates were suspicious but willing to wait and see what developed. The inmates who had the most to lose were the very ones who had profited most at the expense of the other inmates.

Murton was allotted a few new staff positions with which he could hire free-world employees. He carefully chose persons whom he felt could assist him with his Tucker revolution. For example, he hired Bea and Frank Crawford, a married couple with whom he had worked in Alaska prisons. Bea was placed in charge of the kitchen, where she immediately dealt with the filthy and dangerous conditions she found. With the assistance of Murton, she abolished the free market competition in food that allowed those with money to get better food and left intolerable food for others. She also discontinued separate meal services for staff, trusties, and rank. Three meals a day were served in which everyone ate the same food. Both the quality and quantity of food improved (Murton & Hyams, 1969). The resources for good nutritious food had always been there; Tucker was a productive farm. What was needed was management of those resources. Bringing immediate change in food services made a statement regarding Murton's intentions and his ability to get things done.

An auxiliary operation of the kitchen at Tucker for many years had been production of homemade booze. Murton found it fairly easy to cut off the supplies of free-world alcohol but found it very difficult to stop home brew. In the past drinking was often tolerated and ignored. At times it was even encouraged by the staff, in part because the staff found alcohol profitable for themselves. Alcohol consumption had even been justified as a means of cutting down on escapes (Murton & Hyams, 1969). To interfere with home-brew production, yeast was locked up, the availability of fruit was reduced, and frequent shakedowns were instituted (Murton & Hyams, 1969).

Frank Crawford, Bea's husband, was placed in charge of Tucker farming operations. Whatever else Tucker was, it was a farm that produced funds to run the prison and to make a profit for the state. Crops grown at Tucker included strawberries, cucumbers, cane, potatoes, corn, rice, oats, and cotton. It was a challenging agricultural operation. Although there were 300 inmates on the farm, a substantial number of these were allocated to security, food service, record keeping, and similar functions. It was an understatement to say that modern farming technologies were not employed at Tucker. Thus, there was more farm work to be done than there was labor to do it. In order to get the work done, the long lines worked 14 to 16 hours a day. Traditionally, they had worked under threat of violence, poorly clothed and fed, in conditions similar to, but perhaps worse than, slavery.

In touring the farm, Murton found that the farm, much like the prison, had been severely neglected. Buildings were in poor repair, farm work was behind schedule, livestock had been mistreated, and what little farm equipment they had was obsolete and in disrepair (Murton & Hyams, 1969).

Early into his Tucker employment, Murton summed up his impressions as follows:

> It seems like we can't get hold of this institution. It's just one big can of worms. Where you grab one piece, you shake up the whole enterprise. There are people cooking all over the farm. They've got their own houses, their own refrigerators, their own stoves, their own cooking equipment and food. There are still payoffs, purchases of goods and services. We've got dope inside. Its [sic] just one big funny farm. When you want to make one minor change you have to revamp the entire system. The complexity of the operation is beyond belief. I've dubbed the place the "Tucker Time Tunnel." Enter this institution and you go back one hundred years in penology (Murton & Hyams, 1969, p. 48).

Murton once joked with inmates that normally when he took over an institution he would immediately begin telling people what to do. That was not so smart, he said, at Tucker, because it was the inmates who ran the place. While the inmates got a good laugh at hearing that, it was no joke. The inmates not only had the guns and the keys to the prison, they also controlled information flow as well as all processes that made up the prison operation. The prisoners had an enormous amount of power. The power could be exercised legitimately from the viewpoint of the state by preventing escapes and producing crops, but it could also, as we have seen, be exercised to sordid purposes.

Murton saw immediately that the inmate power structure was capable of undercutting any effort to reform the system. He knew also that he was going to have to accommodate himself and his plans to inmate power arrangements if he had any chance of bringing about change. His general tactic was to improve horrible conditions, thereby indicating a commitment on his part to inmate welfare, while slowly displacing the extent to which trusties controlled the destiny of the prison and its inmates. To do so it was necessary to have more state employees as prison staff. Although Murton claimed that he received no assistance from outside sources, the legislature in the spring of 1967 authorized an increase in staff from 6 to 38 (Murton, 1970).

In one sense a person might view the primary task of reform at Tucker as being the job of "breaking the power structure" (Murton, 1970, p. 13). Although he used those very words, Murton's approach was somewhat different. Most institutions must depend on inmates to some greater or lesser extent to keep the institution operating and to maintain order. Thus, the inmates have a source of power. This power source was, of course, highly exaggerated at Tucker. In this case the state had given so much responsibility to the inmates that it found it extraordinarily dependent on the inmates.

Self-Government

Murton decided to accept the existence of inmate power but at the same time sought to convert it to a legitimate form of self-government that could benefit inmates rather than support the exploitation of some by others. Murton believed that such self-government could also serve the interests and goals of the state. In an early account of his experiences at Tucker, Murton stated, "In those [first] three months we had broken the inmate power structure" (Murton & Hyams, 1969, p. 76). But upon later reflection, he described the process in more realistic terms of accommodating the existing power structure or co-opting it to his own purposes of enhancing inmate welfare. This objective was not difficult to sell to the deprived inmates, and, therefore, was rather easily legitimated.

Murton's approach to inmate self-government became formalized in the Farm Council and the Disciplinary Committee. The Farm Council was an inmate body elected by the inmates themselves. They were given some considerable authority in decision making at Tucker Farm. Murton had experimented with such a council previously in his Alaska experience and had planted the idea with Tucker inmates. In the election held in March 1967, inmates elected two Farm Council members from each barracks. The election was set up and monitored by the inmates themselves. While they were free to elect anyone they wished, Murton had urged the inmates to avoid electing persons who had enjoyed power through the various rackets (i.e., the "wheels"). Thus a new power structure came into being to replace the previous power arrangements, which for decades had rested on buying, selling, exploitation, and brute force (Murton & Hyams, 1969).

A set of inmate placement decisions must be made in all correctional facilities. These decisions are commonly called classification, and in other modern prisons were performed by civilian staff. Typical classification decisions involve job placement, barracks or cell placement, level of custody, privileges, and related matters. A major responsibility of the Farm Council was to classify inmates. Each Saturday afternoon the Farm Council met in the superintendent's office as the classification committee. Murton reported that none of the men classified for minimum custody by the council ever attempted to escape (Murton & Hyams, 1969).

Additionally, half of the council made up a disciplinary committee who made decisions regarding consequences for violation of institutional rules. Much like a disciplinary committee composed of prison staff, this committee heard complaints against inmates, determined guilt or innocence, and determined the disposition of the matter. Murton reserved the right to veto decisions by inmate representative bodies but never found it necessary to do so. In disciplinary matters, inmates could choose to have their case heard before the disciplinary committee or could have it heard and decided by Murton. In all cases except two, inmates went to the committee.

The punishments imposed were not nearly so harsh as they were in the past, when the strap was the most common punishment. Nevertheless, the punishments given were, according to Murton, just as effective in maintaining order. Common punishments or consequences were loss of visiting privileges, loss of commissary or mail privileges, and, for serious matters, confinement in isolation for a period between 30 and 60 days (Murton & Hyams, 1969).

Homosexuality

Homosexuality was a problem that required attention. Homosexual behavior is not uncommon in sexually segregated institutional living arrangements, particularly in prisons. Murton estimated that 80% of Tucker Farm inmates had homosexual experiences while incarcerated. While some of the homosexual encounters were no doubt consensual and would have taken place elsewhere, sex had been institutionalized as part of the Tucker exchange system (Murton & Hyams, 1969). For example, it was not uncommon for young inmates to trade sexual favors in return for desirable jobs or protection from other inmates. Murton's explanation of the high incidence of homosexuality at Tucker was simple: "The inmate power structure was based on exploitation, and one method of exploitation was sex" (Murton & Hyams, 1969, p. 90). One 14-year-old inmate who was placed in an isolation cell with other inmates was almost beaten to death in a rape before submitting (Murton & Hyams, 1969).

One particularly troublesome inmate in regard to homosexual behavior was a 62-year-old who was known as Hazel. Hazel made no secret of his sexual appetite and inclinations. By forcing himself on others, he was disruptive in almost every setting. There were a number of older predatory males like Hazel who pursued younger inmates. Some Tucker inmates were as young as 14. Given the architecture of the living arrangements, a large barracks that housed from 100 to 150 inmates, it was very difficult to provide protection from unwanted advances and homosexual assaults. Murton found a partial solution by removing the sexual predators from trusty positions, where abuse of power had been a way of life. Additionally, Murton sought to interrupt or replace exchanges of goods and services for which inmates had found it necessary or desirable to trade their bodies (Murton & Hyams, 1969). Murton also tried to isolate the inmates who were causing continuous problems. For example, he had them placed in work settings where they worked alone.

Nevertheless, problems associated with homosexuality continued, particularly in certain barracks. Murton's ultimate weapon to solve the problem was an inmate called Chainsaw Jack. Jack was in prison because he had used a chainsaw to murder a man who had made a homosexual advance toward him. Chainsaw Jack was placed in charge of preventing homosexual conduct in selected barracks. He announced, "If I catch two of you in the same bed, I am going to get the chainsaw up front and come back there and straighten you out" (Murton & Hyams, 1969, p. 92). While this was no doubt a bluff, apparently Jack had a convincing manner of presentation. Problems with homosexuality were dramatically curtailed.

Some of the problems at Tucker were a consequence of physical facilities. For example, the problems of homosexuality were exacerbated because of barracks living arrangements where men could move about at will. Also, the isolation cells were so few in number that it was impossible to place persons in true solitary confinement. They were in fact confined with several others in a space short on square feet but long on time. These isolation cells were so antiquated that they did not have adequate locks or other common security provisions. The inmates found, much to their delight, that it was quite easy to break out of isolation cells. Murton, irritated by this, ordered large padlocks and chains to improve security. These new locks were not much of a challenge to lock-picking experts, and Murton found ostensibly confined inmates roaming around prison grounds. Murton ultimately threatened to weld the doors of the cells shut in order to keep the men secure. The inmates tested him on this, whereupon he did in fact weld some inmates in an isolation cell for a period of 10 days. This proved to be a period of considerable inconvenience to the inmates. When the welded doors were opened, there were no further attempts to break out of isolation (Murton & Hyams, 1969).

Another example of Murton's work at Tucker was his dealing with death row inmates. Traditionally, inmates with a death sentence are isolated from the rest of the prison population and live in very secure quarters. The electric chair and all death row inmates, eight Blacks and one White, were housed at Tucker. In an early visit to death row, Murton found that some of the men had been there for as long as 8 years without having gone out of the cellblock. Under one of the former superintendents, these inmates stayed in their cells at all times with the exception of 3 or 4 minutes each New Year's Eve when they could go into the corridor of the cellblock just in front of their cells. He also learned that in the past one inmate had spent 14 years in his cell except for two releases to briefly confer with his attorney.

The cells in which the death row inmates were held measured six by nine feet, and most cells contained two men. The cells were ill equipped, extremely dirty and smelly, and had little heat in the winter. Floodlights were aimed into each cell, both day and night. The condemned prisoners had no contact with the prison that surrounded them, much less with the outside world.

Murton first allowed death row inmates to clean up and even paint their cells; gave them books, papers, and magazines; bought a TV set for them; and began giving them access to the corridor in front of their cells several times a day. Thus, they could move about and play cards or other games. Murton also was able to provide some funding for legal assistance for the condemned prisoners. One death row inmate had to be taken to the state hospital, having undergone steady mental deterioration during the time he had been confined.

Eventually, Murton found it possible to give more and more freedom to the death row inmates. In the summer of 1967 they were, for the first time, allowed to leave the death row building, moving for the first time in a long, long time into the outside world. Murton describes what must have been a very dramatic scene in the following words: "They walked out into the yard, they kissed the ground and lifted their faces to look at the sky in wonderment. They ran wildly, kicking dirt like a bunch of skittish colts that had been locked up in a barn" (Murton & Hyams, 1969, pp. 80–81). The work task assigned to them was to build a baseball diamond, which they completed. They formed a baseball team that played other Tucker teams.

As time passed Murton integrated the death row inmates more and more into the regular prison population, including having them eat with the regular inmates. This was an unheard-of practice, even in the most progressive of U.S. prisons. In addition to being an integration of death row and non-death row inmates, it also provided an occasion for racial integration. Previously, Black and White inmates were segregated for dining and almost all activities. State law required that the Black and White prisoners be segregated. The Blacks on death row were the only Black inmates at Tucker. Although there was initial resistance to this on the part of some White inmates, it was accepted and continued without incident (Murton & Hyams, 1969). Cummins appears to have been integrated only to the extent that the Cummins trusties included both White and Black prisoners who were housed in segregated barracks (Feeley & Rubin, 1998).

By late summer of 1967, death row inmates were virtually indistinguishable from regular inmates. They were given regular job assignments such as working in the laundry or commissary, doing painting or carpentry, and so on. They proved to be good employees. Murton's explanation of his approach to dealing with death row inmates was straightforward: "If a man is treated like a human being, he will respond like one" (Murton & Hyams, 1969, p. 82).

Perhaps Murton's strongest attack on the old system came in the form of disrupting its economic base. The primary medium of exchange in the prison was called "Brozine," a type of prison money. Brozine could be used to exchange for anything, including food, jobs, sex, clothes, and of course gambling. Murton planned to eliminate Brozine in order to curtail illegitimate and disruptive exchange. Brozine was to be replaced by a ledger system that would disallow the transfer of funds from one inmate to another. This was to be a major change for Tucker since Brozine had been the medium of exchange for the past 50 years.

Murton gave the inmates a few weeks' warning regarding the removal of Brozine to give them an opportunity to settle gambling debts, loans, and so on. The removal of Brozine prompted a series of escapes from Tucker. The escapes were almost exclusively limited to trusties whose world had been turned upside down by the Murton changes. Trusties up to that time enjoyed quite a good life, often better than they could have expected on the outside world. Having one's own shack, opportunities for income, access to women, booze, currency, and food was all coming to an end. The end of gambling as it had existed for years seemed to be the last straw. Some of these inmates requested transfers to Cummins Farm, still running on the old system. Others had to accommodate to the new system or escape. Of course, for trusties escape was a simple matter; the inmate just left. Murton points out that the freedom of movement was so great for trusties that often it was difficult to tell who had escaped (Murton & Hyams, 1969).

Arkansas prisons were beginning to receive some notoriety outside of the state in regard to prison conditions. The state of Oregon went so far as to resist extradition to Arkansas. On one occasion, an Oregon judge refused to return four Arkansas inmates who had escaped on the basis that to return the inmates would give encouragement to Arkansas by

> aiding and abetting her in the management of her institutes of terror, horror, and despicable evil. The judge continued his analysis of the Arkansas system stating that Cummins and Tucker gave evidence of barbarity, cruelty, torture, bestiality, corruption, terror, and animal viciousness that reeks of Dachau and Auschwitz (Murton & Hyams, 1969, p. 71).

All in all, Murton was able, in a time of less than 1 year, to make some impressive if not remarkable changes in Tucker Prison Farm. In one of his writings Murton gave the following summary of his Tucker accomplishments:

> We were able in a few months to feed and clothe the inmates, hire competent staff, upgrade the agricultural programs, establish educational and vocational programs, provide a rational religious counseling service (to replace forced church attendance under the gun), eliminate corruption, move trusties into the barracks, and practically eliminate the rapes and other homosexual assaults. Inmates were no longer required to act as servants for the staff; they no longer worked outside tilling the soil for private citizens. Prison food no longer went "out the gate" into private hands; livestock management was upgraded by acquisition of new breeding stock and the institution of sound animal husbandry practices. We ultimately broke the convict power structure by eliminating the monetary exchange that had maintained the inmate economy, with the attendant gambling loan rackets and assaults (Murton, 1970, p. 13).

By Murton's account Tucker, by the fall of 1967, was a very different place from what it had been. Journalists who had open access to Tucker at this time also confirm this. Murton's vision of creating a community at Tucker was taking shape. A prison band had been formed, dances were held (not without controversial reviews outside the prison), and the situation appeared to be calm, orderly, and humane.

Problems With the System

A few years after Murton was no longer employed in Arkansas, he wrote that his reforms at Tucker took place with virtually no assistance from other criminal justice agencies, the state legislature, the Arkansas Prison Board, other state agencies, or the public (Murton, 1970). Murton was able to enlist the assistance of several inmates along with the staff he had hired at Tucker. However, he seemed to have considerable difficulty securing the support and assistance of persons and agencies outside the prison. He felt harassed by agencies such as the State Purchasing Agency, where he found it difficult to negotiate the policies and procedures and to deal with the persons who administered them. It was very difficult to get action on purchase requests for many items such as farming equipment, building materials, a boiler, and so on.

Murton became so infuriated by the problems with purchasing that he prepared a 19-page status report that he distributed to members of the prison board and to the press. The document charged Cummins officials who administered prison budgets, and state purchasing personnel, with "specific instances of harassment and interference" (Murton & Hyams, 1969, p. 123). This had the effect of escalating a conflict with Superintendent Bishop. Murton and Bishop were questioned before the prison board regarding their differences (Murton &

Hyams, 1969). Following this dispute, the business manager of Cummins was fired and the head of the department resigned (Murton & Hyams, 1969). While Murton had his problems working with the system, members of the system also had trouble working with Murton.

Conclusion

A reform-minded governor who was appalled by the atrocity that was the Arkansas prison system hired Thomas Murton to take control of the Tucker Prison Farm. In a relatively short period of time, Murton successfully ended the corruption of the few free-world administrators and wardens. The fact that the bulk of the prison operations were under the control of trusty prisoners made reform of the inmate culture more problematic. But Murton was persistent, pragmatic and ultimately successful in this level as well. Entrenched state bureaucracies also proved to be difficult to deal with. Murton's successes at Tucker would pave the way for even greater challenges in the largest and most notorious Arkansas prison: Cummins Farm.

REFERENCES

Douthit, G. (1967a, February 7, p. 1). Prison board to be called. *Arkansas Democrat.*

Douthit, G. (1967b, February 16, p. 1). Prison team urges sweeping changes. *Arkansas Democrat.*

Feeley, M. M., & Rubin, E. L. (1998). *Judicial policy making and the modern state: How the courts reformed America's prisons.* Cambridge University Press.

Murton, T. (1970). Too good for Arkansas: One year of prison reform. *The Nation, 210*(1), 12–14.

Murton, T., & Hyams, J. (1969). *Accomplices to the crime: The Arkansas prison scandal.* Grove Press.

Penologist named as chief at Tucker. (1967, February 14). *Arkansas Democrat.*

Ward, J. L. (1978). *The Arkansas Rockefeller.* Louisiana State University Press.

KEY TERMS

Death row inmates	Reformation
Farm Council	Rockefeller Administration
Homosexuality	Self-government
Inmate power	Thomas Murton

QUESTIONS

1. Who assisted in prohibiting corporal punishment at Tucker Farm? What was the issue associated with corporal punishment at both Cummins and Tucker Farm? If you were superintendent of a prison, which kinds of punishments would you administer and why?

2. Murton believed in an "open press" policy. After a person is incarcerated and removed from society, do you think the public should be aware of what occurs in prison? Why or why not?

3. The inmates were apprehensive about Murton's ability to change the organizational structures within the prison. However, what event(s) demonstrated his intentions and his ability to get things done? What changed in the prison as a result?

4. What were the Farm Council and the Disciplinary Committee? What was their role and responsibility within the prison, and how did this new power structure differ from the old one?

5. Compare the common punishment and consequences in the past to the methods under Murton.

FIGURE CREDITS

Fig. 3.1: Copyright © by Arkansas Department of Corrections. Reprinted with permission.

4 | Reform at Cummins Under Murton

Introduction

Probably the most notorious period in the history of Arkansas prisons came in the weeks that Tom Murton, the controversial reformer hired by Governor Rockefeller, served as superintendent of the Arkansas prisons. The prisons received statewide front-page coverage and national media attention, and in time a full-length movie, *Brubaker* (Silverman & Rosenberg, 1980), starring Robert Redford, was made based on Murton's version of the story. Murton first achieved some success in making reforms at the Tucker Farm and then was brought in to address much of the same corruption and deplorable conditions at the Cummins Farm.

Murton Comes to Cummins

Having served as assistant superintendent of Tucker Farm for about 1 year, Murton accomplished impressive reforms in the smaller of the two Arkansas prison farms. Although courageous and assertive in accomplishing his tasks, support for Murton began to wear thin at times among legislators, prison board members, and the governor and his staff. Murton frequently became frustrated in his efforts to bring about change and was not hesitant to express his frustrations through sarcastic criticism. He often found himself in conflict with various persons and agencies whose cooperation and assistance he needed. Some Arkansans were offended by his reform tactic of publicly criticizing and ridiculing Arkansas and its prison system as a means of soliciting support for his prison reform efforts. Governor Rockefeller observed, "Murton's ego equals only his ability as a penologist" (Ward, 1978, p. 104). Although his support of Murton at times vacillated, Governor Rockefeller decided that he generally agreed with Murton's approach and wanted him to remain on the job.

Since the summer of 1966 when the prison "scandals" began receiving so much attention, most of the focus was on events and conditions at Tucker Farm. However in late October 1967, observations by Dr. Edward Barron, the prison physician, raised serious doubts about conditions at Cummins Farm. Having

FIGURE 4.1. Cummins unit administration building, 1949.

served as penitentiary physician for less than 2 months, Dr. Barron indicated not only that medical treatment was seriously deficient and unmonitored, but also sanitation and health conditions were in need of immediate correction and were "incredible." A health inspection by state health inspectors found "about 100 unacceptable health standards in the [Cummins] complex" (Forster, 1967a). Conditions were particularly filthy in solitary confinement cells. An example was the women's solitary confinement cell that had no toilet facility other than a large tin can. He found large amounts of prescription drugs and injections were being administered "like water" by inmates with no record keeping. Even more surprising to him, Barron discovered and broke up a "drug ring" in the penitentiary that was selling "any type of drug that anyone could conceivably get high on" (Forster, 1967a). Barron assigned responsibility for such prison conditions to "the indifference of the people of the state to the prison system" (Forster, 1967a).

The day after Dr. Barron's comments were made public, prison superintendent O.E. Bishop resigned, stating "It got to the point that I couldn't run the penitentiary like I th[ought] it ought to be run" (Douthit, 1967a). John Haley, chair of the penitentiary board said that Bishop was caught between two factions, one of which was pressing for reform and the other of which was interested in keeping the prisons as they had operated in the past, particularly in regard to making a profit (Douthit, 1967b).

Bishop's resignation, which was to become effective December 31, 1967, opened up the position of superintendent, which had responsibility for the operation of Cummins Farm as well as overall responsibility for the system. Murton, then assistant superintendent in charge of Tucker Farm, had expressed interest in the position of superintendent for some time and had recently met with the governor to resolve differences shortly before Bishop resigned. However, Rockefeller's cooling enthusiasm for Murton seemed evident in his comment that he wanted a trained penologist in the position of superintendent and that Murton "was not being ruled out as a possibility" (Douthit, 1967d).

Shortly after it was revealed to the public that Murton had been gradually integrating death row inmates into the regular inmate population and routines (Douthit, 1967c), Murton formally applied for the position of superintendent of Arkansas penitentiaries. At the same time he suggested that Robert Van Winkle, who was hired by Murton, be placed in charge of Tucker ("Murton Applies for top Prison Office," 1967d).

The only other serious applicant for the job was John Price, who had been with the system for several years and had served as assistant to Superintendent Bishop (Douthit, 1967d). Rockefeller let it be known that his choice for the job was Murton, indicating that to hire Murton would be to recognize the need for a professional penologist and for reform, while to hire Price would be staying with the "old school" (Douthit, 1967; "Selection of Murton Not Assured," 1967d).

The prison board, still dominated by Faubus appointees, was much concerned with the cost of reforms. They also were ambivalent about Murton and gave no public assurance about going along with Rockefeller's recommendation. The chairman of the board was concerned about the ability of the state to fund prison reform, and of the loss of revenue from a de-emphasis on farm production ("Selection of Murton Not Assured," 1967e). He elaborated, "If we are going to institute the kind of system Mr. Murton would like to have, it's going to take about $2 million extra money. … Unless the legislature wants to appropriate the money to put this system on the footing Mr. Murton would like it to be on, we can't operate very long" ("Selection of Murton Not Assured," 1967e).

Murton also faced opposition from persons in Lincoln County, the county in which Cummins Farm is located. Residents circulated a petition requesting that Murton's appointment be blocked. The only issue mentioned in the petition was fear of security if Murton were placed in charge of Cummins (Douthit, 1967b). Murton did not comment on the petitions other than to say that more persons had escaped from Cummins under previous administration than had done so under his administration of Tucker (Douthit, 1967b).

The specific objections to Murton's being appointed superintendent mentioned by the three board members who opposed him were his general lack of administrative experience and his lack of experience running a large penal institution, his expenditure of funds, and his tendency to take action without consulting with the board (Douthit, 1967c; "Rockefeller Mellows on Murton Position," 1967). An example of the latter was Murton's independent approval for several inmates from Tucker to travel to Little Rock to participate in the production of a drama that depicted prison brutality (Forster, 1967b).

During deliberation of his appointment as superintendent, Murton attracted attention and controversy on another front. He was quoted as making comments about a panel of inmates from Cummins who traveled outside the prison to explain prison life in public appearances. Murton accused the panel and an inmate band of "drinking and sexual exploits" on their trips away from Cummins Farm (Associated Press, 1967). Members of the inmate panel accused Murton of "character assassination" and filed a slander lawsuit against him ("Slander Suit Names Murton," 1967).

The controversy over the appointment of a superintendent continued for several weeks. The board determined that Murton would become the acting superintendent upon Bishop's resignation by merit of his title of assistant superintendent. This, however, left unresolved the issue of permanent superintendent. Rockefeller remained steadfast in his support of Murton and the need for a professional penologist to head the system. While the board had the authority to hire a superintendent, they could not effectively do so without the approval of the governor who had the authority to fire the superintendent ("Board, Governor Impasse Continues," 1967). The board voted, perhaps unnecessarily, to appoint Murton as the acting superintendent, pending a permanent appointment (Douthit, 1967f). Thus, the deadlock continued as Murton prepared, at least temporarily, to begin his work at Cummins.

Murton's impressions were that Cummins was a hostile and dangerous environment for him. The trusties at Cummins were aware of changes Murton had made at Tucker and were not pleased with the prospect of such programs being implemented at Cummins (Murton & Hyams, 1969). Rumors circulated that trusties would create disturbances and not cooperate with Murton. The general atmosphere was tense and unsettled (Murton & Hyams, 1969). It was also rumored that Murton would be shot upon entering Cummins. This would be a relatively easy task for armed trusties (Murton & Hyams, 1969).

Reforms at Cummins

Murton announced that his entrance to Cummins would be January 4, 1968, but he actually arrived without incident as Cummins' new superintendent on the morning of January 1. In his first few days as superintendent, Murton split his time between Cummins and Tucker.

Among his first actions, Acting Superintendent Murton fired an executioner who had been on the penitentiary payroll for $1,500 a year. This was a questionable position and salary considering the fact that between 1961 and the time of Murton's arrival in Arkansas only one person, Charles Fields in 1964, had been put to death in the state (Espy & Smyka, 1994). He transferred trusties and staff whom he trusted from Tucker to Cummins. He changed kitchen operations and feeding schedules so that all persons using the prison mess facilities ate the same food on the same line. He destroyed numerous "squatter shacks," which had been built and occupied by trusties around the 16,000-acre Cummins farm. All prisoners were returned to the barracks. He discontinued the provision of goods and services for free-world persons. He had started his assault on the old system, as it existed at Cummins.

Before leaving, Bishop had set up an inmate council at Cummins, somewhat patterned after that implemented by Murton at Tucker. According to Murton, the recommendations of the Cummins council had been ignored, which infuriated the inmates. Members of the council, along with other powerful inmates, conspired to "burn the prison down" and undermine Murton's efforts to reform the prison. Murton met with the council and began to sort through their requests, some of which he granted, others of which he denied. Apparently, it was a very confrontational meeting. Murton informed them that he intended to run the prison and told them never to threaten to start trouble again or he would "wipe them out" (Murton & Hyams, 1969, p. 165).

As had been the case at Tucker, Murton found it necessary to make concessions to inmates and staff on at least a temporary basis. For example, he announced that Brozine, the prison currency, would be continued for some time, although it would at some point be phased out. Murton promised to give a reasonable period of advance notice of the abolition of Brozine to allow inmates who had extended loans to make collection. Trusties would continue as guards for at least 2 years. Murton gave Clay Smith authority to act as superintendent in his absence and even gave him permission to continue using the strap. Smith was one of the "old guard" wardens at Cummins who fully expected to be fired by Murton rather than promoted (Murton & Hyams, 1969). Murton later admitted that his intentions in appointing Smith were to give responsibility for keeping order to the very man who had planned disruption in Cummins for Murton's arrival (Murton & Hyams, 1969).

By January 19, 1968, Murton reported that in spite of suspicion and mistrust of him by inmates, things were going well in his takeover of Cummins. "So far I have been able to stay on top. I don't anticipate any major problems" (Donald, 1968a).

Murton used a series of memos to communicate with inmates and staff at Cummins. In one of the memos Murton sarcastically highlighted the absurdity of not having an accurate count of Cummins inmates. He announced a contest to determine both how many inmates there were at Cummins and how many inmates there should be: "There are no restrictions on methods to get the answer … dart board, Ouija board, roulette wheel. Your cooperation in determining the correct population count is most appreciated and necessary" (Donald, 1968b). Murton ultimately determined that there were 1,287 prisoners who were at Cummins, but never did ascertain how many should have been at the prison (Murton & Hyams, 1969). Even this number may have been inaccurate. The archives of the Arkansas Department of Correction indicate that the total inmate population of the agency on December 31, 1967, was 1,352 (S. Graves, personal communication, April 3, 2019). That number would include both the Tucker and Cummins farms.

Shortly after Murton took over at Cummins, the conflict between the governor and the prison board was settled. Three of the five members of the penitentiary board resigned their positions, opening the opportunity for Rockefeller to make his own appointments to the board. Thus, his administration would have full control of prisons, including appointment of the permanent superintendent (Murton & Hyams, 1969). Murton was appointed superintendent by the new board on January 15, 1968 ("Lack of Finances One Problem of Penal Board," 1968).

Dances and Babies

A controversy surfaced during Murton's first month at Cummins. Prior to leaving Tucker, Murton had instituted Saturday night dances held at Tucker for selected inmates, their wives or girlfriends, and staff. When he moved to Cummins, the dances at Tucker continued, with female inmates being transported from the women's unit at Cummins to participate. Murton defended the dances as providing an incentive for inmates and providing balance in the prison community (Douthit, 1968i). "It was really a good thing from the idea of making them realize they were still human" (1968). Although Murton described the dances as good, clean fun that presented no problems of control, rumors circulated that the

FIGURE 4.2. Women at the Cummins Women's Prison, 1949.

dances were unruly, even drunken occasions. "Nobody got raped, there was no booze, there were no pills. There was some necking" (Douthit, 1968i).

Murton recognized that the idea of dances at a prison might be shocking to some people in Arkansas but maintained that such practices are generally accepted in modern prisons (Douthit, 1968i). Some members of the legislature made "caustic comments" about the dances at Tucker, in part because the dances were racially integrated. Members of the penitentiary board objected to Murton initiating dances without consulting with them (Douthit, 1968i). There was also some public reaction, most of which was negative. Murton received letters critical of the dances (Murton & Hyams, 1969). Additionally, the daughters of a murder victim took considerable exception to the fact that the man convicted of the murder and placed on death row was shown in a news photo playing in the band for the Tucker dances (Lemke, 1968).

To demonstrate that the dances were legitimate affairs and were conducted in an orderly manner, Murton and the current Tucker superintendent, Robert Van Winkle, invited the press and state officials, including penitentiary board members and a visiting prison consultant from California to evaluate the dances. The press gave extensive coverage, including photos, and the consultant said that such a dance "is a good influence in the regeneration of men" (Douthit, 1968i). While some were satisfied with this explanation, many remained skeptical of this correctional technique so highly approved by "experts."

Yet another set of decisions placed Murton in the public spotlight as Arkansas's new prison superintendent. A 38-year-old inmate at the women's reformatory, Ann Shappy, gave birth to a baby boy in a hospital in Little Rock. She had been convicted on a morals charge involving assisting in the rape of one of her daughters.

Although she was in the hospital for 2 weeks following the birth, she was returned to prison without ever having seen her baby (Murton & Hyams, 1969).

Murton inquired about the status of the baby and found that the state welfare department intended to place him for adoption. Ann Shappy had signed no release and there had been no hearing on the matter. Murton decided that she was entitled to have her baby. Murton, Shappy, and Bea Crawford drove to the hospital and took little Woody Dwayne to the women's reformatory where they set up a nursery. The other women in the reformatory were delighted (Murton & Hyams, 1969).

Members of the state welfare department were less enthusiastic with the placement of the baby, not only because Ann Shappy was an inmate in the state prison, having been convicted of a felony, but also because four of her seven children had been wards of the state welfare department. They determined that the baby should be placed in a foster home. After the story and picture appeared in the state press, pressure increased on the welfare department to remove the baby from the prison.

Thus began a tug of war between the welfare department and Murton over the fate of the baby. For Murton, keeping the mother and baby together was a matter of highest principle. Inmates, he reiterated, must be treated with dignity and as human beings. On the other hand, the welfare department felt it must act in what it regarded as the best interests of the child. In Murton's words, this four-and-a-half-pound infant seemed to have the entire officialdom of Arkansas in a turmoil (Murton & Hyams, 1969). The governor's office insisted that the baby be removed. Ultimately, Mrs. Shappy decided to give in to the wishes of the welfare department and give up her baby (Murton & Hyams, 1969).

"Bodiesburg"

It was in this atmosphere of seemingly endless publicity and controversy that the Waterloo for Thomas Murton emerged. Soon after Murton became superintendent of Cummins, Dr. Edwin Barron, the prison physician, reported to Murton that he had examined and become suspicious of patterns in prisoners' death certificates. There appeared to be an unusually high death rate and an uncommonly high number of deaths among young men attributed to heart disease ("Murton Indicates He Won't Quit Yet," 1968.) Soon after he came to Arkansas, Murton had heard both that many inmates had died as a result of foul play in the prison and that they were buried on prison grounds. He had searched for graves at Tucker with the idea that uncovering the graves would also be a means of revealing the prison's sordid past. He had found no such graves at Tucker.

Inmate Reuben Johnson, who had been an inmate in Arkansas prisons periodically for 31 years, told Dr. Barron that he had witnessed the killing of another inmate by a warden at Cummins in 1947, and that he personally had assisted with the burial of that inmate and several others who were killed during his years at Cummins. He said that he could point out the exact location of those graves and others that constituted an area known as "Bodiesburg" among the inmates. He also told of another location on the farm where other inmates had been buried (Murton & Hyams, 1969).

Frank Crawford, hired by Murton to be in charge of farming operations, first at Tucker and later at Cummins, noticed "sunken holes" by the levee. An inmate told Crawford that this was where over 100 inmates had been buried. It was the same location that Reuben Johnson claimed to have buried three inmates (Murton & Hyams, 1969).

At roughly the same time that Dr. Barron's and Reuben Johnson's revelations regarding the possibility of buried inmates reached Murton, a *New York Times* reporter, Walter Rugaber, was at Cummins to prepare a story on Murton's taking over supervision of Cummins. He asked Murton about rumors that inmates had been buried on the farm. Murton replied that not only had he heard the rumors, but also that it was his belief that "a number of inmates had been shot or beaten to death in the past and secretly buried on the grounds" (Murton & Hyams, 1969, p. 184). When the story ran in the *New York Times* with its reference to Murton's suspicions, reporters from all over the world became interested (Murton & Hyams, 1969). Although interested in digging, Murton was in no hurry to begin since there were other matters occupying his attention and requiring available labor.

Adding to the suspicion raised by inmate stories was a list dating back many years of over 200 inmates who were regarded as unapprehended escapees ("Prison Farm to be Combed for Graves," 1968.) It seemed unlikely to Murton and others that all of these persons had escaped and were never heard from again.

On January 29, 1968, a CBS Television crew came to Cummins to begin a feature story on the Arkansas prison farms. On the same day local TV newspersons came to Cummins to ask if digging was going to take place. Murton responded that if weather conditions were unfavorable for farming duties, which was likely on that very day, he would make inmate labor available for digging (Murton & Hyams, 1969).

About noon on January 29, fifteen Black inmates and Reuben Johnson, under the supervision of Warden Harold Porter, took a bus to the levee, followed by members of the press, to begin digging at the locations Johnson identified as unmarked gravesites. At 2:30 p.m. the men discovered what was left of plank coffins in all three locations identified by Reuben Johnson. As persons from the news media took pictures, the inmates carefully dug up and removed the skeletal remains of three adults.

Murton observed that one of the bodies had a crushed skull. The bones of the other bodies were whole, although it appeared that the skulls were not attached. The legs apparently had been severed from one of the bodies. Murton speculated that this had been done so the body would fit the coffin (Buckley, 1968). With news representatives on site when the bodies were dug up, both newspaper and TV gave the story top news priority that evening and for many days to follow. The story did not remain local and was immediately picked up by national media. Another, in what was becoming a long series of revelations about the Arkansas prisons, was being read about and discussed throughout the nation if not the world.

Governor Rockefeller was out of state when the excavations took place (Murton & Hyams, 1969). Unsurprisingly, the governor was not pleased to learn of the new developments in the Arkansas penitentiary by reading about them in the *New York Times*. Murton claims that Bob Scott of the governor's staff gave him approval to begin digging (Murton & Hyams, 1969). Tom Eisele, acting on behalf of the governor, ordered that the investigation be turned over to the Arkansas State Police and that Lynn Davis, former director of the state police, prepare a report on the matter for the governor (Murton & Hyams, 1969). Although Murton intended to continue digging the next day, the state police announced that there would be no more digging "at this time" ("Convict Says He Buried '10 or 12,'" 1968).

Just prior to the excavation of the graves, Murton wrote a letter to John Haley stating his intention to resign following an upcoming special session of the legislature "unless the board would give me authority to run the prison" (Murton & Hyams, 1969, p. 187). Murton was discouraged about the prospects of reforming Cummins. "I don't like to attempt a job where I don't have a chance" (Dumas, 1968). "I was bone tired just trying to keep my head above water" (Murton & Hyams, 1969, p. 187). However, soon after the bodies were discovered, Murton sought to make it clear that he was not resigning (Lewis, 1968). Board Chairman Haley praised Murton's accomplishments and even described him as capable and brilliant, but at the same time he and the board began considering possible replacements for Murton (Dumas, 1968).

The national media attention was embarrassing. Governor Rockefeller expressed concern over what he described as sensationalism. Nevertheless, Arkansas officials called for a complete investigation of the deaths and burials on the prison grounds. Rockefeller himself promised a complete report on the matter (Valachovic, 1968a). At a press conference the governor declared an investigation would be pushed fearlessly but in an orderly manner—and let the chips fall where they may" ("Exhume Bodies, WR Says," 1968). In the early days of the revelations regarding the bodies, Murton met with and quoted the governor as saying "we could be on the brink of uncovering a scandal of untold proportions" (Murton & Hyams, 1969). Nevertheless, the governor called for a straightforward investigation: "It is my intention to continue in an orderly fashion to identify existing graves, move the remains to a proper and dignified cemetery with either the CID of the State Police or a coroner in attendance. Any signs of foul play will be followed up" (Douthit, 1968a). Members of the legislature stated the need for a full investigation to determine whether these were routine, legal burials or if they were burials of prisoners who had been killed in prison with no investigation of their deaths (Douthit, 1968a).

United States Congressman (later governor and U.S. senator) David Pryor, in a powerful public speech, said that the state must face the truth of the prison situation and clear it up completely. It is tempting, he said, to try to avoid the painful truth about the prisons that he referred to as "Arkansas' greatest shame." The penitentiary, said Pryor, "is a subject so highly charged with controversy and confusion—so shrouded in mystery, intrigue and secrecy for generations, that we have comfortably refused to dirty our hands. ... We must discover and bring to light the causes of our troubles—the causes of unjust and inhuman practices and the final elimination of these cancerous conditions. No longer is it an issue of politics. It is an issue of conscience" ("Reform Prison, Pryor Warns," 1968). Pryor predicted that if the state of Arkansas did not solve the problems of the penitentiary, the federal government would become involved.

Murton reported that inmate reaction to the excavation was jubilant. The inmates "were cheering and slapping each other on the back. It was like New Year's Eve. Their story had finally hit the outside world" (Murton & Hyams, 1969, p. 186). Inmates and former inmates offered further information about brutality and death in Cummins and Tucker. Examples of what they reported are seen in the following excerpts from affidavits:

> I can show you where a superintendent killed a man and buried him at Tucker. He beat the man until he couldn't get up, then he told him to go to work. When the man couldn't do it, the superintendent shot him. I helped bury the man.
>
> In 1943 I was chopping cotton when I saw a twenty-one year old [sic] inmate beaten to death.
>
> I witnessed a murder at Cummins on May 13, 1957.
>
> Halfway between the old Seven Camp barn and the ditch is the grave where two colored men and a [W]hite man were buried after being killed (Murton & Hyams, 1969, pp. 188–189).

Some of those who were making allegations about past brutality received threats. Reuben Johnson was moved to Tucker for safekeeping after threats were made on his life (Murton & Hyams, 1969). Although the allegations were of matters in the past, nerves were being struck.

Murton Versus the Prison Board

As time progressed, interest in getting to the bottom of Arkansas's prison scandal waned and interest in simply getting it over with waxed. An indication of this shift was found in a resolution passed by the Arkansas Legislative Council, which asked for a thorough investigation of the graves and bodies at Cummins but directed investigators not only to look into the circumstances of the deaths, but also the opening of the graves for possible criminal violations. Thus, the search for blame began to shift from those who engaged in acts of brutality toward prisoners to those who further exposed the scandal. Members of the Council expressed anger and regret over the publicity stemming from excavation of bodies at Cummins and charged that the Republican Party was "getting considerable mileage" from the publicity over the matter. In ironic phrasing, the members of the council said that the people of Arkansas were "gravely" concerned over the national publicity resulting from the exhumation at Cummins (Valachovic, 1968a).

Decision makers at the highest levels vacillated over what to do as people throughout the nation pondered the question, as expressed by Congressman Pryor, "Where is the conscience of Arkansas?" ("Reform Prison, Pryor Warns," 1968). As Chairman Haley continued to seek a replacement for Murton, the entire prison board voted its approval for Murton to dig for more bodies in the unmarked gravesites with state police investigators on hand to seek evidence of foul play. All bodies found were to be given a proper burial in officially established cemeteries for indigents at Cummins and Tucker ("FBI asked to Talk to Former Inmate Who 'Saw Deaths,'" 1968).

Governor Rockefeller responded to the board's granting Murton permission to continue digging by ordering that no more digging would take place until he approved it. He reiterated that the state police would be in charge of any digging and would report directly to him. Before any further digging would take place, he added, a decision must be made regarding the legality of such exhumations. Rockefeller criticized the state police for not keeping him informed of developments and openly criticized Murton for his operating with such extreme independence and apparent disregard for "the total picture." He further commented that it placed him, as governor, in a difficult position to find out what was going on in the penitentiary through the press (Valachovic, 1968c). The governor's frustration with this most recent aspect of the prison scandal was becoming apparent.

Murton's impression was that the investigation being conducted by the state police at Cummins was superficial. He stated, "It was apparent from the start that they [state police] were not planning anything but to put a lid on the publicity with a whitewash investigation" (Murton & Hyams, 1969, p. 190). The Criminal Investigation Division (CID) officer in charge, Major Bill Streubing, made statements to the press prior to traveling to Cummins to begin the investigation that the bodies dug up were from an old paupers' graveyard. ("Murton Status Haunts Pen; Check of Skeletons Slated," 1968.)

Murton and Rockefeller continued to air their differences in the press, which seemed to focus more of the controversy surrounding Murton's handling of the situation and less on the death of prisoners. Murton argued, contrary to Rockefeller's complaints, that he not only kept the governor's office informed during the digging, but he had secured approval from Bob Scott, aid to the governor, to begin digging in the first place. Murton maintained that when the first body was discovered, he ordered an assistant to call Bob Scott immediately (Associated Press, 1968).

The controversy continued to simmer and often boiled over into various state arenas. State Senator Virgil Fletcher, in a speech to the Senate, charged that Murton "had damaged Arkansas and its prison system by digging up graves at Cummins Farm before the national press" ("Fletcher Says Murton's Act Harmed State," 1968). A few days earlier Fletcher had invited Charles Clark of Little Rock, a former Arkansas penitentiary inmate, who defended the prisons against the "vicious rumors" being circulated. He testified that Cummins was unequalled as an institution for the regeneration of men and claimed "there is no justifiable criticism of the existing system" (Smith, 1968). After his prison release Clark had helped to found the Patriotic Party in Arkansas, an anti-tax, anti-communist, anti-labor union, pro-military political party. The Senate enthusiastically received Mr. Clark's testimony and gave him a standing ovation (Smith, 1968).

The first reports based on examination of the skeletons by a pathologist differed sharply from Murton's account. Dr. Rodney Carlton, deputy state medical examiner, said that two of the skeletal remains showed no evidence of trauma or violent death (Valachovic, 1968d). The third showed multiple fractures, some of which were fresh. The older fractures are consistent with fractures due to blunt trauma, but Carlton indicated that his inclination was that the fractures were sustained after death. None of the skeletons showed evidence of decapitation, amputation, or other mutilation (Valachovic, 1968d). Carlton suggested that pathologists be present at any future exhumation.

State Police Director Carl Miller was directed by Governor Rockefeller to ask state Attorney General Joe Purcell for an opinion on the legality of opening more graves at Cummins (Douthit, 1968g) The attorney general's staff advised Miller that a court order would be required to continue digging the graves. Existing Arkansas law directed officials to seek such a court order, and for judges to grant it in instances where an individual dies in prison and is subsequently buried without an autopsy ("Fletcher says Murton's Acts Harmed State," 1968).

Circuit Judge Henry Smith of Pine Bluff was interested in having this matter investigated but seemed only mildly inclined to continue probing the causes of inmates' deaths. Smith, whose nephew had served as farm manager under O.E. Bishop at Cummins, ordered a grand jury to investigate the operation of Cummins, the reports that inmates were murdered and buried on prison grounds, and whether state officials violated the law when they dug up the skeletons ("Delay Opening Prison Graves, WR is Advised," 1968; Hines, 1968). As part of their investigation the grand jury traveled to Cummins in part to see the three opened graves and the 20 other depressions in the ground identified by inmates as graves ("Delay Opening Prison Graves, WR is Advised," 1968).

The grand jury was in session for 3 weeks and heard testimony from 82 persons ("Grand Jury Hears Last Testimony," 1968). The grand jury issued no indictments but issued a number of opinions and recommendations ("Jury Says Murton Publicity Seeker," 1968). The final report indicated that the digging of the graves "was designed as a publicity stunt for the personal benefit of Thomas O. Murton ... at the expense of the state of Arkansas. ... We recommend that there be no more digging in the Prison cemetery" (1968). The jurors also called for the return of the strap and the electric chair. The report indicated that solitary confinement was more brutal than corporal punishment, and that they found no credible evidence to substantiate charges of brutality by the use of corporal punishment at Cummins. Such allegations come from "known troublemakers." They asked that the area where the bodies were dug up be officially designated as the Cummins Cemetery, declaring that it was used as a cemetery as long ago as 1923. They called for the immediate dismissal of Murton and generally defended the organization and practices of Cummins as it was prior to Murton being placed in charge of the prison farm ("Jury Says Murton Publicity Seeker," 1968).

Although the investigation continued, no more bodies were dug up. A grand jury was empaneled in Lincoln County with instructions from the circuit judge to determine if any laws had been violated in digging up the bodies (Murton & Hyams, 1969). Members of the penitentiary board determined that there was a crisis in administration in the prisons and the board itself assumed leadership of the prisons, severely restricting Murton's authority.

Rockefeller indicated in a letter to the prison board that they were "under no commitment to retain Murton in any position whatsoever in the Arkansas Prison System" (Murton & Hyams, 1969, p. 199). Rockefeller continued that Murton was competent as a penologist but was "totally incapable of and insensitive to the requirements of operating in harmony with his associates in a governmental structure" (Murton & Hyams, 1969, p. 199). On March 7, 1968, approximately 5 weeks after the graves had been opened at Cummins, the prison board fired Murton. The official explanation of the incident was that the three bodies removed from Cummins prison were not those of inmates, but rather were individuals who had been buried in a paupers' graveyard that predated the prison.

Conclusion

The apparent success of Thomas Murton in effecting significant reforms at Tucker Farm did not translate into continuing success at the larger Cummins Farm. Why was Murton effective at Tucker but not at Cummins? Was it the size and scale of the two operations? Was it the differing racial makeup of the predominantly White Tucker and Black Cummins? Did Murton step on more politically connected toes at Cummins? These do not appear to be the likely distinguishing factors. It may be speculated that Murton's somewhat freelancing efforts in digging up "Bodiesburg" with no favorable outcome and the resulting embarrassment to the state and his former supporter, Governor Winthrop Rockefeller, are the most likely reasons for the fall from favor for Thomas Murton. Had Murton been more circumspect and cautious in his handling of the graveyard, he probably would have had more time to implement meaningful reforms at Cummins. But, the sordid "Bodiesburg" fiasco and resulting bad publicity and the firing of Murton did not halt the continuing progress of prison reform in Arkansas. The federal court was waiting in the wings.

REFERENCES

Associated Press. (1967, December 4). Prison panel says character injured, court suit readied. *Arkansas Democrat.*

Associated Press. (1968, February 10). Murton declares Rockefeller's aide approved grave digging in advance. *Arkansas Democrat.*

Board, governor impasse continues. (1967, December 7). *Arkansas Democrat.*

Buckley, B. (1968, January 30). 3 skelton's dug up in field at Cummins: Inmate leads search party to grave sites. *Arkansas Gazette.*

Convict says he buried "10 or 12." (1968, January 30). *Arkansas Democrat.*

Delay opening prison graves, WR is advised. (1968, February 15). *Arkansas Gazette.*

Donald, L. (1968a, January 19). He's been able to "stay on top" in move to Cummins, Murton says. *Arkansas Gazette.*

Donald, L. (1968b, January 21). Blunt memoranda describe takeover by Thomas Murton. *Arkansas Gazette.*

Douthit, G. (1967a, November 1). Bishop resigns, says his position made "impossible." *Arkansas Democrat.*

Douthit, G. (1967b, November 2). Maximum security complex at prison vital, Bishop says. *Arkansas Democrat*.

Douthit, G. (1967c, November 19). Death row prisoners enjoy new "freedom." *Arkansas Democrat*.

Douthit, G. (1967d, November 22). Murton choice of WR. *Arkansas Democrat*.

Douthit, G. (1967e, November 30). Board against Murton as prison chief. *Arkansas Democrat*.

Douthit, G. (1967f, December 28). Murton to head prisons. *Arkansas Democrat*.

Douthit, G. (1968a, January 30). Solons call for all-out grave probe. *Arkansas Democrat*.

Douthit, G. (1968b, February 2). Prison quiz pushed. *Arkansas Democrat*.

Douthit, G. (1968c, February 11). Tucker "social" is swinger. *Arkansas Democrat*.

Dumas, E. (1968, January 30). Murton quits prison post; he'll leave after session. *Arkansas Gazette*.

Espy, M. W., & Smyka, J. O. (1994). *Executions in the United States, 1608–1991: The Espy File* (No. 8451). Inter-University Consortium for Political and Social Research.

FBI asked to talk to former inmate who "saw deaths." (1968, February 7). *Arkansas Gazette*.

Fletcher says Murton's acts harmed state. (1968, February 14). *Arkansas Gazette*.

Forster, B. (1967a, October 31). Officials launch cleanup. *Arkansas Democrat*.

Forster, B. (1967b, December 4). Arts Center board upholds play delay. *Arkansas Democrat*.

Grand jury hears last testimony. (1968, March 1). *Arkansas Democrat*.

Hines, C. (1968). Close ties in a community evident in probe of graves. *Arkansas Gazette*.

Jury says Murton publicity seeker. (1968, March 9). *Arkansas Democrat*.

Lack of finances one problem of penal board. (1968, January 16). *Arkansas Democrat*.

Lemke, B. (1968, January 28). Daughters irked that mom's killer playing for dances. *Arkansas Democrat*.

Lewis, B. (1968, February 1). Memo by Murton about "resigning" stirs new doubts. *Arkansas Gazette*.

Murton, T. (1970). Too good for Arkansas: One year of prison reform. *Nation, 210*(1), 12–14.

Murton, T., & Hyams, J. (1969). *Accomplices to the crime: The Arkansas prison scandal*. Grove Press.

Murton applies for top prison office. (1967, November 21). *Arkansas Democrat*.

Murton indicates he won't quit yet. (1968, January 30). *Arkansas Democrat*.

Murton status haunts pen; check of skeletons slated. (1968, February 4). *Arkansas Democrat*.

Prison farm to be combed for graves. (1968, January 29). *Arkansas Democrat*.

Reform prison, Pryor warns. (1968, February 4). *Arkansas Democrat*.

Rockefeller mellows on Murton position. (1967, December 2). *Arkansas Democrat*.

Selection of Murton not assured. (1967, November 28). *Arkansas Democrat*.

Silverman, R. (Producer) & Rosenberg (Director) (1980). *Brubaker* [Motion picture]. United States: 20th Century Fox.

Slander suit names Murton. (1967, December 6). *Arkansas Democrat*.

Smith, G. (1968, February 10). Ex-convict tells senate prison rumors "vicious." *Arkansas Gazette*.

Valachovic, E. (1968a, January 31). WR displeased at publicity over skeletons. *Arkansas Gazette*.

Valachovic, E. (1968b, February 2). Inmate moved to Tucker. *Arkansas Gazette*.

Valachovic, E. (1968c, February 9). Governor orders no more digging until he says so. *Arkansas Gazette*.

Valachovic, E. (1968d, February 13). Report on skeletons doubts violent deaths. *Arkansas Gazette*.

Ward, J. L. (1978). *The Arkansas Rockefeller*. Louisiana State University Press.

KEY TERMS

Bodiesburg

Edward Barron

Prison dances

QUESTIONS

1. Discuss Dr. Edward Barron's concerns that shifted the focus on events and conditions at Tucker to Cummins Farm.

2. After Superintendent Bishop's resignation, Murton applied for the permanent superintendent's position. Discuss the various objections to his appointment by the prison board, Lincoln County residents, the inmate panel, and trusties.

3. Explain the controversy surrounding prison dances and how Murton demonstrated the legitimacy of the event.

4. What is Bodiesburg, and why did officials call for a complete investigation of the deaths and burials on prison grounds?

5. Discuss the outcome of the grand jury convened to investigate the operation of Cummins. How did Rockefeller respond to the grand jury's recommendations? Explain why.

FIGURE CREDITS

Fig. 4.1: Copyright © by Arkansas Department of Corrections. Reprinted with permission.

Fig. 4.2: Copyright © by University of Arkansas at Little Rock Center for Arkansas History and Culture. Reprinted with permission.

5 | Arkansas Prison Reform Goes to Court

Introduction

Significant progress was gained during Thomas Murton's brief tenure in Arkansas, but the state was still in the penological dark ages compared with more enlightened and modern systems. The Bodiesburg scandal overshadowed some of Murton's accomplishments, and the upcoming Arkansas State Police report of the matter was anxiously awaited. More adverse media attention was feared from the graveyard issue and other potential sources. The state had already experienced some level of federal court intervention, but much more was on the horizon.

ADC Chair Suggests Future Success; Others Call Prison Slave Camps

The Murton period was so dramatic and so eventful that the weeks after his departure presented yet another opportunity to reflect on the prison system and its future. John Haley, chairman of the Arkansas Department of Correction, publicly defended the system that had been subject to scrutiny and criticism for months. He assured his fellow Arkansans that prison reform was indeed in progress and that it would continue. He pointed out that reform efforts in recent years would not be reversed and would in fact expand. According to Haley, the Arkansas system had the potential of becoming one of the finest prison systems in the United States. The system would continue to emphasize economic self-support but at the same time would implement rehabilitation and vocational training ("Haley Asserts Prison System to be 'Finest,'" 1968).

Haley's remarks were in part directed at yet another blistering criticism of the Arkansas prisons. This time the source of the criticism was the Southern Regional Council, which released a report entitled "Delta Prisons: Punishment for Profit." The report described the prisons in Arkansas as an abhorrent consequence of a century of neglect (Farmer, 1968). "Self- supporting prisons," the report indicated, "must, in the end, become slave camps" (Farmer, 1968, p. 23).

To counter such charges, Arkansas officials indicated that considerable change had taken place in Arkansas after the report was written. For example, the number of state prison employees had, they said, tripled from about 35 to over 100 in 1 year. While this represented an effort by the state to reclaim its prison system, it in no way displaced the system's dependence on the trusty system. The majority of those attending staff meetings at Cummins or Tucker were still armed inmates ("Haley Asserts Prison System to be 'Finest,'" 1968). Furthermore, state officials continued to hold tightly to the idea that the prison can and must remain self-supporting.

Reorganized Arkansas Department of Correction

Other cited evidence of prison reform was a new law, Act 50 of 1968, creating the Arkansas Department of Correction. Thus, all parts of the system were formally placed under a single administrative unit. Additionally, courts by this time had declared unconstitutional the use of the strap and other forms of corporal punishment (*Jackson v. Bishop*, 1968). The U.S. District Court had abolished the use of the Tucker telephone, but it had allowed the continued use of the strap as a disciplinary tool with the condition that prison officials develop procedural safeguards for its use (*Jackson v. Bishop*, 1967). The 8th Circuit Court of Appeals took the next step and held that use of the strap was a violation of the cruel and unusual punishment prohibition of the Eighth Amendment (*Jackson v. Bishop*, 1968).

Drafting and debate of the reorganization of the prison system by Act 50 of 1968 presented an opportunity to revise and replace other obsolete provisions of prison law, such as those that required racial segregation. For example, prior to these revisions, statutes prohibited use by White inmates of bedding or clothes that had ever been used by Black inmates. Rather than reflecting this change in the new state law, corporal punishment was simply not mentioned (Steinmetz, 1969a).

Racial Segregation

Despite revisions in prison law, the state's prison system remained largely racially segregated. In March of 1968 the U.S. Supreme Court upheld a ruling in an Alabama case that racial segregation in state prisons was a violation of due process and equal protection provisions of the U.S. Constitution (*Lee v. Washington*, 1968). At that time all Black inmates in Arkansas except those on death row were housed at Cummins, where they were segregated from White inmates ("Segregation in Penitentiary Called Illegal," 1968.) Cummins was predominantly Black, housing some White trusties and White ranked prisoners. Calls for desegregation were being heard in Arkansas ("LR Attorney Demands an End to Segregation in Prisons," 1968). The Board of Corrections directed the acting commissioner to develop a desegregation plan ("Segregation in Penitentiary Called Illegal," 1968). This became mandatory with the *Washington v. Lee* (1968) case.

Post-Murton Leadership

The new acting commissioner appointed to succeed Murton was Victor Urban. Murton and Urban had worked together in Alaska. Urban was employed by the Federal Bureau of Prisons prior to his being hired by Murton at Arkansas. Urban was a very busy man. In addition to serving as acting commissioner, he also was the director of pardons and paroles and was the superintendent of Cummins ("'I'm Here to Do a Job and I'll Get Along With Anybody,' New Prison Head Says," 1968). This job description in itself was some indication of the difficulty Arkansas was in. The state had committed itself to form a department of correction, but it had insufficient staff for its full operation.

After the skeletons were dug up early in 1968, the Arkansas State Police Criminal Investigation Division initiated an investigation to determine whether inmates had been wrongfully killed and buried on prison property. The FBI also participated in part of the investigation. By March the report was complete and had been submitted to the governor. Rockefeller announced that the report would be released to the public, but the report would be redacted so as to exclude almost all names. To mention names of individuals regarding these allegations would, according to Rockefeller, be unfair to both the living and the dead ("Public to Get Edited Report on ASP Probe," 1968).

Arkansas State Police Report on Bodiesburg

The primary sources of evidence used to develop the report were death records and interviews with inmates and former inmates. State officials did not dispute that brutality and killings had taken place in the past. John Haley, chair of the State Board of Correction, claimed that severe brutality and murder "ended around 1957" ("Haley Says Probe by Police Reveals Slayings at Prison," 1968). The report took issue with the accounts given by inmate Reuben Johnson regarding the identity and causes of death of the three bodies dug up at Cummins. While specific instances of deaths were described by inmates in which prisoners were killed by trusties and by state employees, the report said that the testimony was old, poorly or entirely uncorroborated, in some cases contradictory, and in many instances irrelevant since all parties to an incident were dead. The investigation did not include examination of physical evidence from graves in the inmate cemetery commonly known to inmates as Bodiesburg or "Bolix Burg." The existence of this cemetery and the free-world cemetery in the same general area that predated the inmate cemetery reportedly were common knowledge (Dumas, 1968a). Old maps of the area even marked the graveyard on the plantation that later became the prison farm. It was reported that the graveyard was an old paupers' or slave burial ground (Feeley & Rubin, 1998).

Arkansans had heard enough about killings and burial of inmates in their prisons. Most were ready to close the door on these unpleasant and embarrassing revelations. Even those who originally called for full investigation were becoming increasingly silent. Officials defended this recent Arkansas

State Police prison report as professionally researched and prepared and were in agreement that the matter did not require further investigation or official action. John Haley, as chair of the Department of Correction, denied Murton's charge that the Arkansas State Police report was a "fraud." He further stated that it had been clearly established that the unmarked graves were in a paupers' cemetery. No more graves, he continued, would be exhumed with the possible exception for movement to new graves ("Haley Defends Police Reports on Skeletons," 1968).

Inmate Strikes

The calm of Victor Urban's relatively brief tenure as commissioner of corrections was broken by simultaneous sit-down strikes at Cummins and Tucker. The incident began with a conflict between a rank inmate and a supervisor at Cummins in which the supervisor was hit by a tomato. Believing that the wrong man was about to be punished, 17 inmates began a sit-down strike. They were taken to the main prison compound where they were placed in a fenced pen in an open area. They were left there day and night until the strike was broken. The inmates slept on the ground and were given two meals per day. Fourteen inmates at Tucker also began a sit-down strike in sympathy for those at Cummins ("14 Tucker Inmates Join in Sit-Down; Those at Cummins Left in Wire Pen," 1968; "Conference Fails to End Sit-down at Cummins; 17 Stay Out a 2d Night," 1968). After 3 days the inmates, both at Cummins and Tucker, gave up their strike ("13 Strikers Return to Work at Tucker, 1968; "30 Prison Strikers Give Up in Sitdown," 1968).

Unfortunately, the next sit-down strike was not settled so peaceably. In October 1968, a group of about 100 Cummins inmates refused to go to work. After discussion with prison officials, about 25 decided to go to work. The remaining 75 inmates continued talking with Associate Superintendent Gary Haydis about their issues and complaints. Haydis ordered the inmates to move away from a fenced area where a large number of inmates would soon be returning from the fields for a meal. Upon their refusal, Haydis fired a warning shot into the air, which the inmates ignored. He then fired birdshot at the group of inmates from a distance of about 75 feet. Other free-world employees then also fired birdshot from a greater distance. Twenty-four inmates were wounded, most of whom had superficial flesh wounds. One, however, received a serious eye wound that eventually resulted in the loss of sight in the eye. Commissioner Urban defended Haydis's action stating, "No inmate is going to tell Mr. Haydis or I or the prison board that we should run the prison this way or that" ("Prison Chief Defends Use Of Shotgun," 1968). Governor Rockefeller announced his suspicion that the disturbance was politically motivated. The Corrections Board, after investigation and deliberation, concluded that the shooting was "altogether unnecessary" (Dumas, 1968b; "Farm Shooting 'Unnecessary,' Board Asserts," 1968; "Prison Revolt Was in Making, Governor Says," 1968; "WR Hints He Sees Opposition Influence in Trouble at Prison," 1968).

Rehabilitation as the Next Wave of Prison Reform

Economic realities of prison reform were slowly becoming apparent. Early in the Rockefeller years surplus from prison revenues was spent easily on prison improvements and new personnel (Douthit, 1968a). Members of the legislature became increasingly nervous when income from prison farming decreased and it became apparent that the prisons no longer could support themselves. Mechanization of farming seemed to be a way to keep farming operations profitable. It was also argued that time saved through improved farming technology would free inmates to pursue education or other rehabilitative pursuits. However, most legislators viewed the cost of such improvements as prohibitive (Douthit, 1968a).

When chair of the Department of Correction, John Haley, went before the legislative council to seek state funds to operate the prison, he was given little encouragement. Some members simply told him that the prisons were not likely to get funding (Douthit, 1968b). When asked what the consequences would be if funding were not forthcoming Haley replied that the majority of the employees at the state prisons would have to be dismissed and the prison would have to go back to its old methods where convicts essentially ran the prison as a profitable operation (Douthit, 1968b). To offset an anticipated shortfall the board considered, but did not implement, a plan whereby all Tucker inmates would be moved to Cummins so that Tucker could be leased to private parties (Ferguson, 1968a). The message from the legislature was becoming clear: "Reform the prisons all you want, but don't ask us to approve state funding to support those reform efforts. We still want to have a prison which supports itself" (Associated Press, 1968).

Just after the re-election of Governor Rockefeller in November 1968, C. Robert Sarver of Charleston, West Virginia, was hired as the Arkansas commissioner of corrections. Sarver became interested in prisons and prison reform following service as a prosecuting attorney (Feeley & Rubin, 1998). Sarver, a 38-year-old attorney, had served as the director of corrections for approximately 6 months in West Virginia. He was fired from that job following a disagreement with the state commissioner of public institutions ("Prison Chief is Hired," 1968; "West Virginia Lawyer Gets Correction Job," 1968).

Sarver made no secret of his commitment to rehabilitation. In early appearances in the state, Sarver explained that inmates were sent to prison *as* punishment, not *for* punishment. Prisoners, he said, were social rejects, and prisons, through rehabilitation, can give persons who regard themselves as a failure a chance to succeed and can provide them

FIGURE 5.1. Arkansas Department of Corrections commissioner, Robert Sarver.

an opportunity to restore a sense of pride and dignity (Ferguson, 1968b). The worth of a corrections system, Sarver indicated, is based on its final product, the inmate successfully returned to society. "If he is a person who is responsible, self reliant, self respecting [sic], then the system has done its job" ("Prison Chief Says Punishment Not Goal," 1968).

Sarver's office was established at the state Capitol Building in Little Rock, Arkansas, rather than at one of the prisons. Much of his attention soon became focused on the prison budget. On the job just a few days, Sarver went before the legislative council to present his case for the next prison budget (Ferguson, 1968b). The fact that he even appeared before them was noteworthy, since neither Murton nor any other prison official had ever done so (Douthit, 1968c). Nevertheless, the prison budget was problematic for many legislators. The cost of running the prison for that year was projected to be about $300,000 more than farm income.

Sarver was well received by legislators. Having considerable experience as a politician, he seemed at home in the political environment (Ferguson, 1968b). Sarver said the details of the prison scandals were shocking to him. It no doubt was a relief to state officials when he announced his intentions to concentrate on the future rather than the past. Sarver announced in a blunt double entendre, "I don't intend to waste my time pulling skeletons out of closets" ("Prison Chief Says Punishment Not Goal," 1968).

Having selected rehabilitation as the new direction for Arkansas corrections, Sarver and the board began to plan for the next wave of Arkansas prison reform. Existing policy was based on the premises of punishment with scant attention to the idea that inmates could respond to guidance and learning in preparation for their eventual release ("Reform Measures for Prisons Due, Haley Tells Group," 1969). Rehabilitation of those in the younger age categories became a high priority. Sarver announced plans to use Tucker as an "intermediate reformatory" for young persons and first offenders (Douthit, 1969a). This would make possible, for the first time, separation of young offenders from older prisoners and for a setting in which rehabilitation programs for younger offenders could be established (Steinmetz, 1969a). Cummins would be the site of a new maximum security unit for the incorrigible, while the rest of Cummins would become a medium security unit in which the principal activity would still be agriculture. What previously had been a training school facility in Monroe County would become a pre-release center to prepare inmates for reentry to the free world (Douthit, 1969b).

Sarver projected that the farm profits would fall short of funding the prison for the next 2 years. The prison budget for each of the next 2 years was $2.6 million. He estimated that the prison system would need about $850,000 each year from the state revenues to operate and to implement the planned reforms (Douthit, 1969b). The message from Sarver, with the support of his board, was clear: Prison reform that includes rehabilitation and staffing by state employees will have to depend on state revenue.

As the legislative session was finishing its business the following spring, it was apparent that the General Assembly did not intend to provide the funding needed to establish an intermediate reformatory at Tucker nor a maximum security unit at Cummins, much less provide support to hire more free-world guards or to pursue rehabilitative programming. Sarver and the Department of Correction Board indicated that reform could not move ahead without state funding. John Haley and other board members said that inmate lives would be lost and endangered in the prisons without the maximum security unit to seg-regate dangerous offenders and without the reformatory for younger prisoners (Douthit, 1969d). Just before the session closed the legislature appropriated funds for the maximum security unit but linked the actual funding not to regular state revenue but to income produced by the prison farms (Douthit, 1969d). Sarver hoped to lease most of the Tucker farmland, which he estimated would gener-ate about as much revenue as had inmate farming. That plan, however, was not approved by the legislature (Steinmetz, 1969a).

Murton Redux

If Arkansans thought they had heard the last of Tom Murton, they were mistaken. Murton was invited to appear before a U.S. Senate juvenile delinquency subcom-mittee investigating prison conditions. Murton used the hearing as a forum to express his ideas on prison reform and to describe his experiences and views on the Arkansas prisons ("Murton Tells Senators State Rejected Reform," 1969). The Arkansas prisons are, Murton explained to the assembled Senators, "an isolated remnant of an ancient philosophy of retribution, exploitation, corruption, sadism, and brutality. The sordid history of this penitentiary is indelibly recorded on the bodies of those citizens who had the misfortune to be committed to penal servi-tude in this barbaric system" ("Transcript of Murton's Prison Testimony," 1969). The system, said Murton, was a reflection of the social institution of slavery.

The public in Arkansas, Murton continued, does not care what happens with inmates. "Men in prison can be mutilated and punished and even killed because there is little outside control or supervision over the guard force." Murton explained that Arkansans spoke of wanting prison reform, but he doubted their sincerity: "But when I tried to overhaul the degenerate system at its very roots, the state failed to back me up." Murton maintained that the graves he dug up gave evidence that inmates had been brutally murdered. The investigation conducted on the matter was a "cover up" that "whitewashed" the system ("Transcript of Murton's Prison Testimony," 1969).

Murton suggested that since he was forced to leave, the prisons had reverted to their former practices, using the old punitive philosophy of imprisonment that "has proven unsuccessful and undesirable in nearly all other jurisdictions not for years or decades but for centuries." Such prisons turn men into wild animals, commented Murton, by treating them like wild animals: "Our prisons are, in varying degrees, monster producing factories" ("Transcript of Murton's Prison Testimony," 1969).

Murton's appearance before the U.S. Senate raised the ire of Governor Rocke-feller and other state officials. Perhaps part of the defensive reaction against Murton's testimony resulted from the fact that there was at least some truth to what Murton said. It clearly was the case, for example, that trusty inmates still were in a position to make life and death decisions about other inmates (Douthit, 1969d). Rockefeller nevertheless announced that the conditions Murton described were history and said it was "tragic" for Murton to bring such matters up again. Rockefeller invited members of the Senate subcommittee to come to Arkansas to inspect the prisons for themselves. He also asked Senator Thomas Dodd, chair of the hearings, to give Robert Sarver equal time for rebuttal of Murton's testimony ("WR Invites Probers Who Heard Murton to Inspect Prisons," 1969.)

Sarver's Rebuttal

Sarver did appear before the Senate committee and reported that Arkansas prison reform began before Murton came to Arkansas and was continuing after he left. Murton's recent testimony, claimed Sarver, was "replete with untruths, half-truths, innuendoes, and unwarranted conclusions." Sarver told members of the subcommittee, "We do not have all the answers to all the problems we face, ... but the people of Arkansas are making progress in the development of our correctional program" ("Sarver Sees Reform in State's Prison, Replies to Murton," 1969). Sarver also mentioned that he had in his possession a file that would raise doubts regarding the "competence and reliability" of Murton ("Sarver Sees Reform in State's Prison, Replies to Murton," 1969). Senator Dodd seemed unreceptive to and unpersuaded by Sarver's attempts at rebuttal ("Sarver's Arguments Fail to Sway Dodd," 1969). Rockefeller described Dodd's treatment of Sarver before the hearing as harassment and questioned Dodd's motives for inviting Murton ("WR Charges that Dodd was Harassing Sarver," 1969).

Continuing Inmate Complaints

While reverberations of Murton's bitterness and the Rockefeller administration's defensiveness continued to draw attention, complaints about the prison system were being raised on several fronts. Tucker Superintendent Jack Finch described the need for individual cells, particularly for young inmates between 14 and 17 years of age who were sentenced to the state penitentiary. He recounted a case of gang rape of a youth at Tucker. The victim, "a quiet sensitive boy," was taken to the hospital at Cummins to give him safety from other inmates. Finch said that no boy would be the same after a term at Tucker living in the current barracks arrangement ("Tucker Head Cites Separate-Cell Need," 1969).

In May of 1969, several hundred inmates signed and sent a petition to Governor Rockefeller protesting conditions at the prison and threatening a broadly based sit-down strike. The petition in part read, "Governor, we don't believe you are aware of the conditions existing here. For example, we are now working eleven hours per day, six days a week. The food being served is not sufficient to sustain men working that many hours. In fact most of the food is not fit for human consumption." The inmates described being served "rotten" and "diseased" chicken, which they found ironic since the farm raised more than enough food to feed its own population. The petition continued, "Also there are no laundry facilities for men of rank status. Our personal laundry must be washed in a sink. There is one sink in each barracks so you can imagine how difficult it is" (Douthit, 1969e).

Commissioner Sarver reported to the governor that the inmates "didn't ask for anything we hadn't been working on for weeks. Their complaints were justifiable, there's no question about that." Sarver also reported that immediate efforts had been implemented to begin improvements. "I think they know that we have made a tremendous effort. There is nothing that a little money won't take care of," Sarver said. The State Health Department's thorough inspection of Cummins food services resulted in a report of numerous deficiencies. Sarver ordered Cummins Superintendent Ralph Roberts to personally supervise food services until problems were corrected. One example of problems they discovered was that all milk produced at Cummins was being sent to the state hospital in partial payment for bills from the hospital to the prisons for medical services. Thus, no milk or milk products were available for prisoners (Douthit, 1969f).

Informal accounts regarding the women's reformatory at Cummins indicated that little if any permanent prison reform had been implemented there. The solitary confinement or "hole" located in small outbuilding cells with no bathroom facilities other than tin cans was still being used. Inmates complained of lack of medical services, poor food, and lack of meaningful activity other than sewing to manufacture uniforms for male prisoners (Francisco, 1969).

Judge J. Smith Henley

A number of inmate complaints about Arkansas prison conditions were finding their way to the desk of United States District Judge J. Smith Henley, who had for some time been hearing and ruling on Arkansas prison matters. As discussed in the previous chapter, it was Judge Henley who held hearings in 1965 on abuses of the use of the leather strap ("Sarver Says Hearing to Have Good Results," 1969; *Talley v. Stephens*, 1965). The new 1969 allegations came before the court as consolidated petitions from Cummins prisoners for writs of habeas corpus that challenged treatment and conditions in the isolation unit as well as prison medical care ("Convict Asks Judge to Send Full-Time Doctor to Prison," 1969; *Holt v. Sarver*, 1969).

FIGURE 5.2. Judge J. Smith Henley.

Judge Henley would soon mount a "frontal attack on the Arkansas prison system" in two cases that would come to be known as *Holt I* and *Holt II* (*Holt v. Sarver*, 1969; *Holt v. Sarver*, 1970) (Feeley & Rubin, 1998, p. 63). These cases would address overall conditions of confinement, including the notorious Arkansas system of trusty guards, and will be addressed in the following chapter.

Conclusion

In this phase of the history of prison reform in Arkansas, Governor Rockefeller brought in a new rehabilitation-minded correction commissioner, Robert Sarver. Some who had thought that the problems of the prisons were merely due to the abrasive and uncooperative style of former superintendent Tom Murton learned that prison reform was controversial in and of itself, apart from Murton's personality. Major disagreements, especially in regard to funding, were emerging between Commissioner Sarver and the prison board on the one hand and the legislature on the other. Sarver and the board insisted that more funding must come from state revenues to operate the prisons, while the legislators insisted that the prisons remain self-supporting. In the midst of this dispute, the power of the U.S. courts, under the direction of Judge J. Smith Henley, become yet another factor in prison reform. The court had issued a ruling that proclaimed aspects of Arkansas prisons to be in violation of the U.S. Constitution and conducted grand jury hearings that resulted in multiple indictments of 15 persons who had been in positions of responsibility in Arkansas prisons. The court was starting to get the attention of Arkansas officials, but this was just the beginning of the intrusion of federal courts into the Arkansas Department of Corrections.

REFERENCES

Strikers return to work at Tucker. (1968, June 28). *Arkansas Democrat.*

Tucker inmates join in sit-sown; those at Cummins left in wire pen. (1968, June 27). *Arkansas Gazette.*

Prison strikers give up in sitdown. (1968, June 29). *Arkansas Democrat.*

Associated Press. (1968, May 19). Prison report released. *Arkansas Democrat.*

Conference fails to end sit-down at Cummins; 17 stay out a 2d night. (1968, June 28). *Arkansas Gazette.*

Convict asks judge to send full-time doctor to prison. (1969, May 26). *Arkansas Democrat.*

Douthit, G. (1968a, May 19). Penal system still a mess. *Arkansas Democrat.*

Douthit, G. (1968b, June 13). Rehabilitation, prison farming system collide. *Arkansas Democrat.*

Douthit, G. (1968c, December 1). Sarver finds doors open. *Arkansas Democrat.*

Douthit, G. (1969a, January 20). Reformatory at Tucker under study. *Arkansas Democrat.*

Douthit, G. (1969b, January 29). New prison plan approved. *Arkansas Democrat.*

Douthit, G. (1969c, March 9). Larey solicits job, but doesn't push it. *Arkansas Democrat.*

Douthit, G. (1969d, April 10). Prison board sees a financial crisis. *Arkansas Democrat.*

Douthit, G. (1969e, May 21). Cummins inmates threaten sit-down in food protest. *Arkansas Democrat.*

Douthit, G. (1969f, May 22). Governor acts to avert a sit-down at Cummins. *Arkansas Democrat.*

Douthit, G. (1969g, May 27). Sarver says isolation cells necessary evil in prisons. *Arkansas Democrat.*

Douthit, G. (1969h, June 19). Prisoners told they must work. *Arkansas Democrat*.

Dumas, E. (1968a, May 19). CID says inmate wrong, then lists tales of the death. *Arkansas Gazette*.

Dumas, E. (1968b, October 16). Haley says inmate action required stern measures. *Arkansas Gazette*.

Farm shooting "unnecessary," board asserts. (1968, November 9). *Arkansas Gazette*.

Farmer, W. J. (1968). The Delta prisons: Punishment for profit. Southern Regional Council.

FBI ordered to investigate prison shots. (1968, October 16). *Arkansas Gazette*.

Feeley, M. M., & Rubin, E. L. (1998). *Judicial policymaking and the modern state: How courts reformed America's prisons*. Cambridge University Press.

Ferguson, B. (1968a, September 4). Corrections board discusses possible closing of Tucker. *Arkansas Democrat*.

Ferguson, B. (1968b, November 26). Server offers budget and some philosophy. *Arkansas Democrat*.

Francisco, M. (1969, June 29). For women convicts, prison life is grim and dry. *Arkansas Democrat*.

Haley assert prison system to be "finest" (1968, March 22). *Arkansas Gazette*.

Haley defends police report on skeletons. (1968, June 10). *Arkansas Gazette*.

Haley says probe by police reveals slayings at prison. (1968, March 29). *Arkansas Gazette*.

Holt v. Sarver I, 300 F. Supp. 825 (E.D. Ark. 1969)

Holt v. Sarver II, 309 F. Supp. 362 (E.D. Arkansas 1970)

"I'm here to do a job and I'll get along with anybody," new prison head says. (1968, March 21). *Arkansas Gazette*.

Jackson v. Bishop, 268 F. Supp. 804 (E.D. Ark. 1967)

Jackson v. Bishop, 404 F.2d 571 (8th Cir. 1968)

Lee v. Washington, 390 U.S. 333 (1968)

LR attorney demands an end to segregation in prisons. (1968, March 23). *Arkansas Gazette*.

Murton tells senators state rejected reform. (1969, March 4). *Arkansas Democrat*.

Prison chief defends use of shotgun. (1968, October 15). *Arkansas Gazette*.

Prison chief is hired. (1968, November 8). *Arkansas Democrat*.

Prison chief says punishment not goal. (1968, November 22). *Arkansas Gazette*.

Prison revolt was in making, governor says. (1968, October 18). *Arkansas Gazette*.

Reform measures for prisons due, Haley tells group. (1969, January 10). *Arkansas Democrat*.

Sarver's arguments fail to sway Dodd. (1969, March 12). *Arkansas Democrat*.

Sarver says hearing to have good results. (1969, May 26). *Arkansas Democrat*.

Sarver says prison panel opposes self. (1969, July 17). *Arkansas Democrat*.

Sarver sees reform in state's prisons, replies to Murton. (1969, March 11). *Arkansas Democrat*.

Segregation in penitentiary called illegal. (1968, April 17). *Arkansas Gazette*.

Steinmetz, T. (1969a, February 2). Legislators to get proposals for overhauling prison system. *Arkansas Democrat*.

Steinmetz, T. (1969b, May 27). Trusty asks return of strap in hearing. *Arkansas Democrat*.

Steinmetz, T. (1969c, May 28). Convicts end pleas; judge wants change. *Arkansas Democrat*.

Steinmetz, T. (1969e, June 21). State told to better prison conditions. *Arkansas Democrat*.

Steinmetz, T. (1969e, July 8). Grand Jury begins its prison inquiry as Henley presides. *Arkansas Democrat*.

Steinmetz, T. (1969f, July 12). Jim Burton indicted. *Arkansas Democrat*.

Talley v. Stephens, 247 F. Supp. 683 (E.D. Ark. 1965)

Transcript of Murton's prison testimony. (1969, March 6). *Arkansas Democrat*.

Tucker head cites separate-cell need. (1969, March 12). *Arkansas Democrat*.

West Virginia lawyer gets correction job. (1968, November 9). *Arkansas Gazette*.

WR hints he sees opposition influence in trouble at prison. (1968, October 19). *Arkansas Gazette.*

WR charges that Dodd was harassing Sarver. (1969, March 13). *Arkansas Democrat.*

WR hints he sees opposition influence in trouble at prison. (1968, October 19). *Arkansas Gazette.*

WR invites probers who heard Murton to inspect prisons. (1969, March 5). *Arkansas Democrat.*

KEY TERMS

Bodiesburg	Reorganization
Inmate complaints	Robert Sarver
Judge Henley	Sit-down strikes
Prison reform	Victor Urban
Racial segregation	

QUESTIONS

1. What were some of the rules and procedures that changed following the *Jackson v. Bishop* ruling?

2. Regarding racial segregation, in what ways did the 1960 civil rights movement affect revisions in prison law?

3. Compare the two sit-down strikes at Cummins. How has inmate unity evolved over time in the Arkansas prison system?

4. Sarver and the board insisted that more funding must come from state revenues to operate the prisons while the legislators were insisting that the prisons remain self-supporting. Do you think the state should provide funding for prisons? Why or why not? In what ways can prisons supplement funding?

5. What do you think about Robert Sarver's quote that "inmates were sent to prison <u>as</u> punishment, not <u>for</u> punishment?" How does this statement relate to four of the goals of criminal sentencing (rehabilitation, deterrence, incapacitation, and retribution)?

FIGURE CREDITS

6 | *Holt v. Sarver*

Introduction

In the decade of the 1960s, U.S. courts reversed a longstanding trend by becoming more involved in prison issues. Beginning with *Cooper v. Pate* (1964) the U.S. Supreme Court opened the door for federal courts to hear cases and consider existing prison operations and policies in light of constitutional principles. This chapter provides background on federal court intervention into state prison systems and on early federal cases concerning Arkansas prisons.

Hands-Off Doctrine

Prior to the 1960s, judges had little if anything to do with the internal administration of prisons. The courts categorized American prisoners as being almost nonexistent until the dramatic changes of the mid-1960s (Dilulio, 1990, p. 3). In an 1871 Virginia case, *Ruffin v. Commonwealth*, the judge, in dicta, stated, "[The prisoner] has, as a consequence of his crime, not only forfeited his liberty, but all his personal rights except those which the law in its humanity accords him. He is for the time being the slave of the state" (*Ruffin v. Commonwealth*, 1871, p. 796). Thus, whatever the state wanted to do or not do with its prisoners was virtually immune from interference by application of the U.S. Constitution and the protections mentioned in its Bill of Rights (Dilulio, 1990; Palmer, 2010).

The court practice of not participating in prison matters was commonly called the "hands-off doctrine." An example of the application of this doctrine appeared in a 1951 ruling by a federal circuit judge who declared, "We think it well settled that it is not the function of the courts to superintend the treatment and discipline of persons in penitentiaries, but only to deliver from imprisonment those who are illegally confined" (*Stroud v. Swope*, 1951, p. 852). Similarly, the 10th U.S. Circuit Court of Appeals stated that judges do not have the "power to supervise prison administration or to interfere with ordinary prison rules and regulations" (*Banning v. Looney*, 1954, p. 771). Inmates living under abusive circumstances or wretched conditions could not expect to find relief through the courts. The "hands off" doctrine effectively established an "impenetrable constitutional wall" between prison cellblocks and the judge's chambers (Dilulio, 1990, p. 4).

The courts used several approaches to justify the hands-off doctrine. They had determined that living circumstances in prison were simply a part of "necessary deprivations" in prison life in that they deprive inmates of comforts found in the free world (Parker, 1986, p. 4). It was argued that such deprivations were an essential ingredient of the sentence to which inmates were being punished. The courts further justified keeping hands off by arguing that prison administration was an executive rather than a judicial function, that operation of state prisons was a matter left to the states, that the judiciary had little expertise in prison administration, that judicial intervention would weaken discipline and control of prisons, and that once courts entertained prison complaints the courts would be hit by an avalanche of complaints (Palmer, 2010; Parker, 1986). Federal courts applied hands off to federal prisons as a separation of powers issue due to the fact that the prisons were part of the executive branch, where the courts were the judicial branch. Federal courts applied hands off to the state prisons by virtue of the 10th Amendment reservation of non-enumerated powers to the states (Palmer, 2010). The courts were saying that monitoring or administering prisons was not their responsibility, and they did not want it to be otherwise.

Cooper v. Pate Opens the Door to the Courthouse

Changes to this doctrine were slow in coming. One case that opened the door for a reversal of hands off was *Cooper v. Pate,* a 1964 U.S. Supreme Court ruling that extended protections of the Civil Rights Act of 1871 to prisoners in state and local institutions. Cooper, a prisoner in the Illinois State Penitentiary, sued for relief, claiming that he was denied access to religious materials due to his religion. The Court agreed with Cooper and held that such a claim stated a cause of action under federal law. This case made it possible for a state prison inmate to bring a claim in federal court under the Civil Rights Act of 1871 that has been codified as Title 42 of the U.S. Code § 1983. This law, commonly referred to simply as "Section 1983" is the vehicle by which a person may bring a civil suit in federal court against a state official who, acting under color of law, deprives the person of constitutional or other civil rights. Thus the Court recognized that inmates have rights protected by the Constitution, and these rights may be enforced in the federal courts. This principle was reaffirmed by Justice White who stated, "There is no iron curtain drawn between the Constitution and the prisons of this country" (*Wolff v. McDonnell*, 1974, pp. 555–556).

Based on the findings of *Cooper v. Pate* (1964), inmates were able to approach the courts with issues that had Constitutional merit, and for the first time those in charge of correctional systems had to anticipate the possibility of answering to a higher authority outside of their own state government for the way they were operating correctional facilities. The legal isolation that had given almost unlimited protection to the keepers at state prisons and had denied almost all protection to the kept was at last broken.

Given an opportunity to approach the courts with grievances, inmates approached indeed! What was first a trickle of cases soon became a stream and in time became a raging river. The number of prison cases pending in federal courts was 218 in 1966 but rose to 20,346 by 1987 (Clear & Cole, 1994). This trend continued with the number of prisoner lawsuits increasing to 24,843 in 1990, peaking in 1995 at 40,211, but plummeting to 25,505 in 2000 following the enactment of the Prison Litigation Reform Act (PLRA) in 1996 (Ross, 2018). The Supreme Court offered further support of inmate litigation by supporting the existence and the initiatives of jailhouse lawyers in *Johnson v. Avery* (1969) and by requiring prisoner access to law libraries in *Bounds v. Smith* (1977). The courts also expanded their interpretations of federal civil rights acts and the writ of habeas corpus, both of which increased federal court intervention (Ross, 2018; Shover & Einstadter, 1988).

This shift in the court was not specific to corrections, nor did it take place in a vacuum. The 1960s was a time of increased awareness of social issues and change-oriented social activism. The media, legislatures, the judiciary, and the public in general participated in a debate regarding such issues as poverty, racism, and war. While not at the center of the vast national dialogue on social issues, the law and policies of agencies that processed persons accused of crime came under unprecedented scrutiny and criticism. Prior to addressing the operation of state and local correctional facilities, the U.S. Supreme Court had already established a trend by requiring a stricter set of standards for criminal justice agencies and by expanding protection for persons accused of crime (Shover & Einstadter, 1988).

In addition, recommended standards were being developed regarding humaneness and prisoners' rights. The United Nations formulated "Standard Minimum Rules for the Treatment of Prisoners" that prohibited "all cruel, inhuman or degrading punishments" and elaborated guidelines for the treatment of inmates (Shover & Einstadter, 1988, p. 160). Also, in the early 1970s, the National Council on Crime and Delinquency developed the Model Act that delineated minimum standards for the protection of prisoner rights. Some standards explicitly addressed prohibiting "inhumane treatment." These standards addressed such matters as corporal punishment, excessive force, assaults, degrading practices, and discrimination (Shover & Einstadter, 1988).

Social Change and Prisoners' Rights

Perhaps part of the reversal of the hands-off doctrine could be explained by actions of the prisoners, who were becoming more assertive and aggressive in expressing and drawing attention to their complaints. The politicization of the "have-nots," demonstrated by the civil rights movement, was not lost on the inmates. Inmate strikes, confrontation of authorities, internal inmate organization, as well as riots and rumors of riots were all part of a shift in political expression by inmates (Parker, 1986). Seeking to be treated fairly and humanely, inmates were abandoning silent and passive acceptance of brutality and abuse, which had been an institutionalized aspect of correctional practices for generations.

The courts' entrance into prison reform at this point has been described as having produced "a legal revolution ... unprecedented in the annals of Anglo-American penal history" (Shover & Einstadter, 1988, p. 161). Although the doors had been opened for correctional litigation in federal courts, the actual impact on correctional policy and operation was dependent on the particular facts and the particular points of law brought in the numerous cases before the courts.

Early Arkansas Cases

Some of the early cases challenging old boundaries and testing newly emerging boundaries of correctional litigation were Arkansas cases. Three early cases challenged conditions in Arkansas prisons during the period of 1965 through 1969. These cases have been mentioned earlier but will be elaborated in the present context of Arkansas prison litigation.

Talley v. Stephens came before the United States District Court for the Eastern District of Arkansas in 1965. Three inmates at Cummins initially filed this case as a pro se petition with the assistance of "jailhouse lawyers, or 'writ writers,' at Cummins" (Feeley & Rubin, 1998, p. 55). The petition claimed cruel and unusual punishment and deprivation of the right to petition the court for redress of prison grievances (*Talley v. Stephens*, 1965). The case was heard by Judge J. Smith Henley, who was later to preside over *Holt v. Sarver*. Judge Henley appointed two prominent Arkansas attorneys, Louis L. Ramsay, Jr. and Bruce T. Bullion, to represent the prisoners on a pro bono basis (*Talley v. Stephens*, 1965). Under the direction of the appointed attorneys, the case was reframed as a civil rights case for violation of the 8th and 14th Amendments under 42 U.S. Code § 1983 (Feeley v. Rubin, 1998). The case was not filed as a class action, but the court indicated that the consequences of the case would "have a collateral effect on the future treatment of other inmates" (*Talley v. Stephens*, 1965, p. 692, footnote 3).

The judge's opinion reflected ambivalence regarding the review of cases regarding prison conditions. On the one hand, Judge Henley stated without hesitation that incarcerated inmates retained certain rights

> among which were the right to be free from cruel and unusual punishment, the right to be free from invidious discriminations, and the right of reasonable access to the courts for the purpose of testing the validity of their confinement or protecting other constitutional rights (Spiller, 1975, p. 6).

Even in this 1965 case, Judge Henley showed both an inclination and a willingness to stretch interpretation beyond traditional limits. However, Henley also expressed reluctance to become heavily involved in prison administration: "The courts cannot take over the management of prisons, and they cannot undertake to review every complaint made by a convict about his treatment while in the prison" (*Talley v. Stephens*, 1965, p. 686).

The complaints regarding cruel and unusual punishment were that the work expectations of inmates exceeded their physical and/or medical capabilities, inmates received corporal punishment with a leather strap without benefit of procedural protection, and medical resources and procedure were so inadequate that they essentially denied medical treatment to inmates (Parker, 1986).

The judge found that the complaints regarding working conditions at Cummins had merit. Arkansas officials admitted that two inmates (Hash and Sloan) were required to work beyond their abilities. Both had serious disabilities and were classified by physicians as being in poor physical condition. The judge's opinion stated,

> the Court has no difficulty with the proposition that for prison officials knowingly to compel convicts to perform physical labor which is beyond their strength, or which constitutes a danger to their lives or health, or which is unduly painful constitutes an infliction of cruel and unusual punishment prohibited by the Eighth Amendment to the Constitution of the United States (*Talley v. Stephens*, 1965, p. 687).

However, this did not result in a ruling that working conditions constituted cruel and unusual punishment because the respondent (Cummins Superintendent Dan Stephens) admitted error prior to the trial and consented to injunctive relief, moving inmates Hash and Sloan to light work assignments (Parker, 1986; *Talley v. Stephens*, 1965). The State of Arkansas still had fresh memories of the bad publicity that resulted from the state resistance to desegregation of Little Rock Central High School in 1957 that required federalization of Arkansas National Guard troops by President Dwight Eisenhower. As a result, prison officials changed the work assignments of these inmates, took steps to move the inmates who filed the suit into better living conditions, fired the worst of the brutal free-world guards, and agreed to establish procedural safeguards for the use of the strap (Feeley & Rubin, 1998).

The court heard testimony of several inmates and one of the assistant wardens regarding the petition of inmate Talley. Before the trial resumed with testimony related to the petitions of inmates Hash and Sloan, the state filed pleadings that consented to judgment in favor of the latter two inmates (*Talley v. Stephens*, 1965). The court based its decision on the testimony and suggested findings of fact and law proposed by the two sides. Little was said in the decision regarding specific shortcomings of medical facilities. The court granted injunctive relief with the consent of the state, requiring the state to provide adequate medical attention for inmates (*Talley v. Stephens*, 1965).

Corporal Punishment

The issue of corporal punishment received more attention. The primary form of punishment on the prison farms was by blows administered with a leather strap, which was about five feet long, one-fourth inch thick, four inches wide, and attached to a wooden handle. An assistant warden normally whipped the offending inmate. The assistant warden typically required the inmate to lie down facing the ground in order to be struck by the whip on the buttocks. Although authorized at this time by legislation, there were no rules describing behavior that would result in using the whip or regulating its administration. The discretion of prison officials in using the whip was virtually without limit. There was an informal norm that no inmate was to receive more than 10 blows for any one offense. It was reported that the use of the whip frequently was prompted by an offense reported by a trusty guard (*Talley v. Stephens*, 1965; Spiller, 1975).

The court did not rule that corporal punishment or that the use of the whip were per se cruel and unusual punishment (*Talley v. Stephens*, 1965), but the court clearly was uncomfortable with corporal punishment, as it existed in the Arkansas prison (Parker, 1986). The formal ruling stipulated a moratorium on corporal punishment pending the establishment of "appropriate safeguards." Although the court's ruling did not dictate the safeguards, the judge did not hesitate to provide guidance for their content:

> [Corporal punishment] must not be excessive; it must be inflicted as dispassionately as possible by responsible people; and it must be applied in reference to recognizable standards whereby a convict may know what conduct on his part will cause him to be whipped and how much punishment given conduct may produce (*Talley v. Stephens*, 1965, p. 689).

Finally, the court addressed inmate access to the courts. The evidence on this issue was mixed. At times inmates had "reasonable and adequate access to the courts" (Spiller, 1975, p. 8). On the other hand, inmates described a pattern of discouragement, harassment, and occasionally the use of corporal punishment on prisoners for approaching courts with their grievances. The institutional practice of censoring mail to the courts and threats of reprisal to inmates was particularly problematic for the court (Parker, 1986). The court did note that the more aggressive impediments to prisoner lawsuits were prior to Superintendent Stephens's assuming control of Cummins. The judge ordered access to the courts for all inmates and enjoined reprisals against inmates for petitioning the courts (*Talley v. Stephens*, 1965).

The *Talley v. Stephens* (1965) case did not end the state's involvement with the federal courts and prison operations. To the contrary, "the small victory in *Talley* encouraged the growing group of writ writers to file still more petitions with the federal courts" (Feeley & Rubin, 1998, p. 56).

Jackson v. Bishop (1967)

The second early case brought before the U.S. District Court in Arkansas was *Jackson v. Bishop*. This 1967 case, like *Talley*, consolidated three separate suits brought against the superintendent of the Arkansas penitentiary (Spiller, 1975). Unlike *Talley*, these cases had been assigned to two different U.S. District Court judges who heard the cases together as a two-judge panel. The inmates contended that corporal punishment was cruel and unusual punishment per se; that the use of the strap under any circumstances was cruel and unusual; that rules and regulations would not make use of the strap constitutional; that rules for administering corporal punishment "do not adequately protect prisoners from unconstitutional treatment"; and that existing rules had been violated (*Jackson v. Bishop*, 1967, p. 806).

The court reiterated the *Talley* ruling in *Jackson*. The court held, as in *Talley*, that corporal punishment in itself was not unconstitutional. Nevertheless, the court did find that some forms of corporal punishment practiced in Arkansas prisons were unconstitutional. These were the Tucker telephone, which administered electrical shocks to the genitals of the inmate, the teeter board, which required inmates to remain uncomfortably balanced for long periods, and use of the whip on bare skin (Feeley & Rubin, 1998; *Jackson v. Bishop*, 1967; Parker, 1986).

The court agreed with the inmates that the rules to regulate corporal punishment by prison officials were totally inadequate. The judge further reprimanded the penitentiary board for its failure to comply with *Talley*. The court again temporarily prohibited use of the strap until adequate guidelines were in place. In the *Jackson* case the court included specific corporal punishment safeguards: The decision to use corporal punishment should not be made by one person, any accusation of one inmate by another must not be accepted at face value, and higher prison officials should participate in or review any decision to use corporal punishment (*Jackson v. Bishop*, 1967; Parker, 1986).

Jackson v. Bishop (1968), 8th Circuit Review: The End of the Strap

This time, the Arkansas inmate petitioners appealed to the U.S. Court of Appeals for the 8th Circuit. They sought review of the constitutionality of corporal punishment and the use of the strap in Arkansas prisons. The appellate court agreed with petitioners, thus reversing the district court, that use of the strap was unconstitutional regardless of regulatory safeguards. Potential for abuse and corruption, difficulty of enforcement, negative psychological and social consequences, and public opinion were all cited as supportive of the strap as being cruel and unusual punishment (Feeley & Rubin, 1998; Parker, 1986). Judge Harry Blackman (later to become U.S. Supreme Court Justice Blackman) of the 8th Circuit explained,

> We have no difficulty in reaching the conclusion that the use of the strap in the penitentiaries of Arkansas is punishment which, in this last third of the 20th Century, runs afoul of the Eighth Amendment; that the strap's use, irrespective of any precautionary conditions which may be imposed, offends contemporary concepts of decency and human dignity and precepts of civilization which we profess to possess (*Jackson v. Bishop*, 1968, p. 579).

The case just prior to the historic *Holt* cases was *Courtney v. Bishop* (1969). This complaint contended that the inmate was arbitrarily placed in isolation as punishment at Cummins. The inmate charged that while in isolation cells he was denied access to medical and psychiatric treatment, received inadequate and unsanitary food, and was beaten by prison officials.

The inmate's contentions were rejected at both the trial court and appellate levels. The district court ruled that neither due process nor cruel and unusual punishment provisions had been violated. The ruling indicated that the petitioner had not been arbitrarily confined in prison and that it was not necessary to have a hearing before administering punishment. The court held that complaints regarding food and medical care were not proven (*Courtney v. Bishop*, 1969).

The importance of the *Courtney* case is not so much in the specific allegations or the ruling. *Courtney* did, however, reveal issues that soon would be successfully raised in *Holt*. Specifically, *Courtney* was an example of how the focus shifted from a particular constitutionally objectionable aspect or incident of prison administration to an "overall aura of unconstitutional conditions within the prison system" (Parker, 1986, p. 151). It was in *Holt* that the overall conditions became the paramount consideration.

The *Holt* Cases

Judicial review of Arkansas prisons continued in *Holt v. Sarver I* and became much stronger and expansive with *Holt v. Sarver II*. Although Arkansas prison litigation was to continue for many years, these two cases were an important contribution to an expanding body of law in prison litigation. *Holt II* established precedent for later federal court review of other state prison systems. The two *Holt* cases began in the U.S. District Court for the Eastern District of Arkansas, where they were heard by Judge J. Smith Henley. Each case gained access to the court by means of 42 U.S.C.A. § 1983, the then recently established gateway to federal courts for prison inmates. Plaintiffs in the *Holt* cases were prison inmates represented by court-appointed attorneys, Steele Hays and Jerry D. Jackson (Feeley & Rubin, 1998; *Holt v. Sarver*, 1969; Parker, 1986; Spiller, 1975). Hays later went on to a distinguished career on the Arkansas Court of Appeals and the Supreme Court of Arkansas. The defendant was Commissioner of Corrections Robert Sarver. Both cases consolidated individual inmate complaints relating to the constitutionality of conditions and practices of the Arkansas prisons.

Conditions of Confinement and Inmate Safety

Holt v. Sarver I was reviewed and decided in 1969. This case considered petitions from three inmates with related grievances regarding the Arkansas prisons. The principal issues were whether confinement at the isolation unit constituted cruel and unusual punishment, whether inmates received proper medical attention, and whether constitutional rights of inmates were violated through lack of protection from assaults from other inmates.

The opinion by Judge Henley stated that the courts were not interested in a general way in the policy and administration of the prisons, but rather in whether convicts collectively or individually were being deprived of federal constitutional rights (*Holt v. Sarver I*, 1969). Should such unconstitutional practices be found, the court "may and should intervene to protect those rights" (*Holt v. Sarver I*, 1969, p. 827). The opinion continued by stating that the state must not only avoid imposing cruel and unusual punishment, but also "owes to those to whom it has deprived of their liberty an even more fundamental constitutional duty to protect their lives and safety while in prison" (*Holt v. Sarver I*, 1969, p. 827).

The court did not find merit to the claims that medical and dental care, or the food, unappetizing as it was, was in violation of inmate constitutional rights. Nor did the court find that the state had failed to protect inmates from assault by employees and guards.

The Trusty System and Inmate Safety

The court did agree with the petitioners that the safety of the inmates and the conditions of the isolation cells were below acceptable constitutional levels. The court recognized that a new maximum security unit was to become operational in about 1 year. This unit would probably remove the unconstitutionalities in question. However, the court ruled that inmates were entitled to injunctive relief prior to the completion of the new unit.

In regard to safety, the court was disturbed by the conditions in which inmates lived and slept while not performing their work assignments. Instead of cells and cellblocks commonly found in other U.S. prisons, Arkansas still used large open barracks to house inmates. At Cummins there were two barracks for trusties and two for "do-pops" (half trusties) and rank men (*Holt v. Sarver I*, 1969). At Cummins about 17 free-world armed guards were available who shared security duties with trusties. However, at night no free-world guards were on duty in the sleeping area that contained the rows of cots on which the prisoners slept (*Holt v. Sarver I*, 1969). Judge Henley's opinion described the sleeping situation of inmates:

> Since the inmates sleep together in the barracks, an inmate has ready access to any other inmate sleeping in the same barracks. Many of the inmates have weapons of one sort or another, and the evidence indicates that in spite of efforts to do so it is impossible from a practical standpoint to prevent inmates from having small weapons such as knives or scissors in their possession.
>
> At times deadly feuds arise between particular inmates, and if one of them can catch his enemy asleep it is easy to crawl over and stab him. Inmates who commit such assaults are known as "crawlers" and "creepers," and other inmates live in fear of them. The court finds that "floorwalkers" are ineffective in preventing such assaults (*Holt v. Sarver I*, 1969, p. 830).

The record showed that such incidents were rather common. During the 18 months prior to the ruling in *Holt I* there had been 17 stabbing incidents at Cummins, four of which resulted in death. All but one occurred in the barracks. Commissioner Sarver indicated that with existing facilities and staff there was little if anything they could do to prevent such violence (*Holt v. Sarver I*, 1969, p. 831).

Clearly violent incidents, wrote Henley, occur in even in prisons that are well managed, staffed, and equipped. However, in such institutions one finds "reasonable precautions" in place designed to provide protection to inmates from being the victim of violence at the hands of other inmates. At Cummins such precautions are virtually nonexistent. The section of Henley's opinion dealing with safety of inmates in the barracks concluded with the bold and dramatic statement:

> The Court is of the view that if the State of Arkansas chooses to confine penitentiary inmates in barracks with other inmates, they ought at least to be able to fall asleep at night without fear of having their throats cut before morning, and that the State has failed to discharge a constitutional duty in failing to do so (*Holt v. Sarver I*, 1969, p. 83).

Isolation

The court also regarded the isolation cells as problematic. Isolation cells had become the major sanction for disciplinary violations since the strap was no longer used (Feeley & Rubin, 1998). The court recognized the need for strong security and disciplinary measures and described the prisoner population as follows:

> Many of the inmates are psychopathic and sociopathic; some of them are aggressive homosexuals. Many of the inmates are hardened criminals and some of them are extremely dangerous to society in general, to their keepers, and to fellow inmates. Many of them are malingerers and will go to any lengths to avoid work. Many are prone to destroy State property, even items designed for their welfare and comfort (*Holt v. Sarver I*, 1969, pp. 829–830).

In addition to confining inmates who violated prison rules, isolation cells also accommodated persons in protective custody, those regarded to be security or escape risks, and those awaiting trial for new criminal charges. There were far too few cells to meet this demand, thus the cells were chronically overcrowded. In some instances as many as 10 or 11 men were confined in a single cell (*Holt v. Sarver I*, 1969). Additionally, the cells were poorly equipped and unsanitary. It was not uncommon for persons with infectious diseases to be confined in the same cell with others. Some men were confined in the isolation cells 24 hours a day (*Holt v. Sarver I*, 1969).

Counsel for the petitioners, Jerry Jackson, explained to the court that inmates were not claiming that solitary confinement itself was unconstitutional, but rather that isolation as it was then conducted at Cummins constituted cruel and unusual punishment. Inmate Harold Cranor testified that he had been placed in isolation 15 days for refusing to work. During that time he said he was allowed to shower and shave only once and was not provided adequate food (*Holt v. Sarver*, 1969). The food prepared for inmates in isolation, called grue, was a meat and vegetable combination baked and cut into four-inch squares (Steinmetz, 1969). Inmate Lawrence Holt described unsanitary conditions in isolation cells and of not being given access to medical treatment ("Convict Asks Judge to Send Full-Time Doctor to Prison," 1969). He also complained that untrained persons were dispensing medicine and providing other care that should be provided by a physician (Steinmetz, 1969). Two inmates also testified that they had been beaten by prison staff (Steinmetz, 1969).

Judge Henley wrote that it was to be expected that confinement in isolation for disciplinary violation, in order to serve intended purposes isolated confinement

> must be rigorous, uncomfortable, and unpleasant. However, there are limits to the rigor and discomfort of close confinement, which a state may not constitutionally exceed, and the court finds that those limits have been exceeded here. The Court finds that the prolonged confinement of numbers of men in the same cell under the conditions [...] that have been described is mentally and emotionally traumatic as well as physically uncomfortable. It is hazardous to health. It is degrading and debasing; it offends modern sensibilities, and, in the Court's estimation, amounts to cruel and unusual punishment (*Holt v. Sarver I*, 1969, p. 833).

Sarver defended the use of isolation as a necessary evil to maintain order and security at the prisons. Sarver said that it was his intention to use isolation only for those who are a security risk and those who were simply incapable of co-existing with other inmates in the general population. Most infractions, according to Sarver, could be controlled by good time policy, but in some instances inmates had to be segregated. He agreed with many of the inmate allegations and maintained that most of the complaints could be addressed with the addition of a maximum security building (Steinmetz, 1969).

Inmate Safety

As discussed above, a major allegation of inmates was that they are subject to attacks from other inmates with knives or other weapons in the barracks at night (Steinmetz, 1969). The consequences of these attacks obviously could be very serious (*Holt v. Sarver*, 1969). Records were introduced of four violent deaths and seventeen assaults at Cummins in the previous 18 months, with all but one of the assaults occurring in the barracks (*Holt v. Sarver*, 1969).

Sarver testified before the court that the Department of Corrections was hampered by lack of funds and personnel. Recognizing that attacks in the barracks were a major problem at Cummins, Sarver pointed out that there was little that could be done to prevent such attacks with only 17 paid security guards and no maximum security facility (Steinmetz, 1969). Sarver reported that although prospects for funding were improving, the prisons had completely run out of money and were operating on borrowed money (Steinmetz, 1969).

Judge Henley's Order

Judge Henley's ruling was strongly worded and direct. Arkansas prisons have conditions, said the ruling, in violation of the constitutional prohibition of cruel and unusual punishment. Much of his opinion was addressed to conditions found in isolation cells. The isolation cells, wrote Henley, "are dirty and unsanitary" and "are substantially overcrowded" with each 8' × 10' cell holding on average about four men with often as many as eleven per cell (*Holt v. Sarver*, 1969, pp. 832–833). Henley pointed out there is nothing wrong with isolation cells used as a disciplinary measure being "rigorous, uncomfortable, and unpleasant" (*Holt v. Sarver*, 1969, p. 833). He also noted that the elimination of the strap meant that the only meaningful form of discipline was the isolation unit. However, there are constitutional limits that must not be exceeded, and "The court finds that those limits have been exceeded here" (*Holt v. Sarver*, 1969, p. 833). Henley elaborated,

> The court finds that the prolonged confinement of numbers of men in the same cell under conditions that have been described is mentally and emotionally traumatic as well as physically uncomfortable. It is hazardous to health. It is degrading and debasing; it offends modern sensibilities, and, in the court's estimation, amounts to cruel and unusual punishment (*Holt v. Sarver*, 1969, p. 833).

Henley's ruling also held constitutionally objectionable the matter of inmates being vulnerable to physical assault from other inmates. State officials, he declared, have "failed to discharge a constitutional duty" to protect inmates from assault and injury or death at the hands of other inmates (*Holt v. Sarver*, 1969, p. 831). The court's opinion noted that many inmates had weapons, as is common in many prisons. Critical in the Arkansas case, however, was the fact that many inmates were living in a common area and had access to each other. Henley continued,

> The court is of the view that if the State of Arkansas chooses to confine penitentiary inmates in barracks with other inmates, they ought at least to be able to fall asleep at night without fear of having their throats cut before morning (*Holt v. Sarver*, 1969, p. 831).

Judge Henley's ruling required that the state begin immediately to correct unconstitutional conditions, including revision of practices regarding the use of isolation, ensuring inmate safety, and maintenance of sanitary living conditions. Sarver was directed to submit a report to the court in 30 days with his plans for effecting changes in the prison (*Holt v. Sarver*, 1969).

The court expressed hesitance to become involved in the administration of the prison in a manner that would interfere with the authority and flexibility needed to operate a prison in an orderly manner. Also, it was recognized that many of the problems were due to budget limitations and a general lack of resources. Thus, the court did not require specific remedial action. It did, however, provide several suggestions for correcting constitutional deficiencies. Major suggestions were hiring additional staff to improve the safety of inmates, transferring inmates between Cummins and Tucker to draw on the resources of both units more effectively, minimizing the number of inmates in isolation cells, and improving conditions in isolation cells (Feeley & Rubin, 1998; *Holt v. Sarver*, 1969; Parker, 1986).

State Response: Be Self-Supporting

Sarver and other officials had little immediate response to the court ruling. Sarver did say that the ruling on isolation cells "slapped our hands rather hard." He also said that meeting the requirement to provide inmates' protection from each other would be very difficult, given current staff. On most nights only three state employees were on duty in Arkansas prisons to ostensibly supervise the 900 inmates at Cummins and the 300 at Tucker. Both prisons depended on trusty guard "floor walkers" to provide some order inside the barracks. Sarver said the trusty system is "replete with evil," but the state did not have money to replace it with state-employed guards ("Slapped Rather Hard, Sarver Says of Ruling," 1969).

Shortly after the federal court ruling was issued, members of the Legislative Council Penitentiary Committee announced they would be making a trip to Cummins. Their primary concern was not to develop means of complying with mandates of the U.S. court, but rather to investigate problems with harvesting crops. With the new emphasis on rehabilitation, more inmates were being paroled, which left fewer men available for fieldwork. Since the prison farms were still relying on farming by hand rather than modern farm technology, there was a shortage of field hands. State officials went to Cummins accompanied by agricultural experts to determine how to improve efficiency and effectiveness of the harvest to maintain state income from the farm. Just before leaving Cummins, committee members also looked at the isolation cells and questioned some of their occupants (Douthit, 1969a).

This legislative council prison committee issued a report after its visit to Cummins, which stated that the Board of Corrections should do all it could to make the prisons self-supporting. Other programs, the report indicated, should be adjusted to avoid interference with convicts working on the farm. Sarver pointed out that this report was the opposite of a report issued by the same body in 1967 ("Sarver Says Prison Panel Opposes Self," 1969).

The economic cost of operating a prison system other than as farming for profit was becoming clear to the legislature. The marching instructions were clear to Sarver: "Get this prison system on a self-supporting basis. That is what we have had in the past and that is what we want now. Downplay rehabilitation or anything else that interferes with the cash crop operation." The committee report did not address the federal court ruling or even acknowledge that one had been issued (Douthit, 1969b).

Sarver's Report to the Court

Sarver did submit a report that outlined steps he proposed to correct deficiencies. These steps included the following:

1. Renovated disciplinary barracks
2. Establishment of an inmate council at Cummins Farm to address inmate concerns
3. Training program for the benefit of free-world guards
4. Reduction in overcrowding by a transfer of inmates between Cummins and Tucker
5. Improved sanitary conditions
6. Installation of a more effective inmate classification system (Feeley & Rubin, 1998; Parker, 1968)

Sarver reiterated that there were severe limitations for hiring new employees and making improvements given current budgets. He indicated to the court that the prison was essentially without funds and unable to hire free-world guards to replace the trusties (Feeley & Rubin, 1998; Parker, 1968).

Sarver's report was to have little impact in regard to settling the constitutionality of Cummins. Judge Henley recognized the restraints on Sarver imposed by governmental resistance. In fact, Judge Henley continuously commended Sarver for his efforts to comply with constitutional requirements and improve conditions in the Arkansas prisons. New cases continued to be filed, and Judge Henley decided to further broaden the court's review of Arkansas prisons by accepting additional petitions that were to provide the basis of *Holt v. Sarver II* (Feeley & Rubin, 1998; Parker, 1986).

Sarver seemed to have been aware that, as a result of federal court intervention, a cobra had bitten the prison system, while other officials appeared to hope that it was just a mosquito bite. It is true that earlier federal court intervention in the Arkansas prisons had been relatively innocuous, at least in the sense that what the courts demanded was not so far from what the state was ready to do. In 1965, Judge Henley had ruled that the use of the strap was unconstitutional unless its use was accompanied by procedural safeguards (*Talley v. Stephens*, 1965).

Federal Court Intervention Intensifies

The federal courts in general were becoming more interested in and more assertive with prison cases during this period. This was also true of Judge Henley in his application of the U.S. Constitution to Arkansas prisons. The June 1969 ruling was just the start of federal court involvement in the affairs of Arkansas prisons that would last more than a decade. Only days after he issued his ruling on conditions in Arkansas prisons, Judge Henley seated a grand jury to investigate further allegations regarding the Arkansas prisons. Henley described the objectives of the grand jury in very broad terms: "to hear evidence as to certain alleged practices and conditions said to have existed in the Arkansas

Penitentiary" and to determine whether any officials of the penitentiary, "acting under color of law, had violated or conspired to violate any of the criminal statutes of the United States designed to protect the civil rights of citizens" (Steinmetz, 1969).

After meeting 4 days the grand jury returned 46 indictments against 15 persons. Those accused included Jim Bruton, a former assistant superintendent at Tucker, four former prison employees, five former trusty guards, two current Cummins employees, and three persons who had been or were then employed at county penal farms. The indictments involved incidents that went back to the 1966 Arkansas State Police investigation. The specific accusations included fatal and non-fatal beating of inmates, use of the Tucker telephone and other devices designed to administer pain and suffering, and the firing of buckshot into the 100 striking inmates at Cummins in 1968 in which several inmates were injured, one seriously (Steinmetz, 1969).

Holt v. Sarver II

In April 1969, Judge Henley consolidated eight class action petitions filed on behalf of inmates from both Cummins and Tucker units of the Arkansas Department of Corrections. Little Rock attorneys, former prosecutor Jack Holt, Jr. and experienced civil rights lawyer Philip Kaplan, were appointed to represent the interests of the inmates. (Holt later served as chief justice of the Supreme Court of Arkansas, and Kaplan has had a long and distinguished career as a civil rights attorney.)

Three major issues were presented to the court. First, inmates contended that "the forced, uncompensated farm labor exacted from Arkansas convicts for the benefit of the State is violative of the Thirteenth Amendment" (*Holt v. Sarver II*, 1970, p. 364). Second, they maintained that the conditions and practices of the Arkansas prisons amounted to cruel and unusual punishment. Third, they contended that unconstitutional racial segregation remained in the system (*Holt v. Sarver II*, 1970).

A full listing of the complaints brought by the petitioners is found in the published decision of the court:

> The actions of defendants have deprived members of the plaintiff class of rights, privileges and immunities secured to them by the due process and equal protection clauses of the Fourteenth Amendment to the Constitution of the United States, including (a) the right not to be imprisoned without meaningful rehabilitative opportunities, (b) the right to be free from cruel and unusual punishment, (c) the right to be free from arbitrary and capricious denial of rehabilitation opportunities, (d) the right to minimal due process safeguards in decisions determining fundamental liberties, (e) the right to be fed, housed, and clothed so as not to be subjected to loss of health or life, (f) the right to unhampered access to counsel and the courts, (g) the right to be free from the abuses of fellow prisoners in all

aspects of daily life, (h) the right to be free from racial segregation, (i) the right to be free from forced labor, and (j) the right to be free from the brutality of being guarded by fellow inmates (*Holt v. Sarver II*, 1970, p. 364).

Holt II differed considerably from previous federal cases brought against Arkansas prisons. Clearly, this case was dealing with broader and more numerous issues. Apparently, Judge Henley in his work on *Holt I* become aware that the few issues targeted in that case did not begin to address the range of constitutional issues involved in the state's prison system. Additionally and simultaneously, the volume of formal complaints increased enormously. The scope of issues raised the possibility of a broad-based challenge on a prison system. Henley noted in his *Holt II* opinion, "As far as the court is aware, this is the first time that convicts have attacked an entire penitentiary system in any court, state or federal" (*Holt v. Sarver II*, 1970, p. 365).

The trial included numerous witnesses who described the horrific conditions found in the prisons. Expert evidence included testimony by James Bennett, former director of the Federal Bureau of Prisons, and a report by Austin McCormick who was the chief consultant to the Penitentiary Study Commission that was created by the Arkansas General Assembly in 1967 (Feeley & Rubin, 1998; *Holt v. Sarver II*, 1970). Director Bennett testified that the trusty system leads to "corruption and deplorable conditions." He pointed out that the trusty system had been abolished in Florida, Texas, and Georgia due to abuse and misuse of power by trusty inmates. The system leads to antisocial and degrading behaviors and influences. Of the trusty system Bennett testified, "I don't think it has any correctional value" (Dunn, 1970).

Thirteenth Amendment

The court rejected the claim that work required of inmates in Arkansas prisons was a violation of the 13th Amendment, which prohibits slavery and involuntary servitude except as punishment for criminal conviction. The petitioners in *Holt II* claimed that prisoners in Arkansas work long hours in the fields for no pay and that the state profited improperly from their work.

In *Holt II* the court granted that working conditions could not be regarded as attractive or even "humane by modern standards" (*Holt v. Sarver II*, 1970, p. 372). Prisoners assigned to fieldwork were required to work 6 days a week in difficult conditions. The only weather that kept men from the fields was below freezing temperatures in winter. Excessive heat in the summer and wet weather was not a bar to work. The court concluded that the working conditions were "arduous" (*Holt v. Sarver II*, 1970, p. 370). Nevertheless, the opinion continued, such conditions did not constitute slavery in that the state made no claim to own the inmates. On the other hand, the prison work did constitute servitude that was no doubt involuntary. However, the court indicated that such servitude was imposed as a condition of sentence on persons who had been convicted of crime, which is specifically permitted in the 13th Amendment. It was also noted that leasing of prisoners was not at all uncommon at the time of the ratification of the 13th Amendment following the Civil War. This fact makes the exception for forced labor as a part of a criminal sentence all the more salient. Thus, the court rejected the 13th Amendment claim (*Holt v. Sarver II*, 1970). Judge Henley discussed the profit-making focus of correctional policy in Arkansas, but it appears not to have had any influence on his adjudication of the 13th Amendment arguments (Feeley & Rubin, 1998).

Conditions and Practices

The court was persuaded by the arguments and evidence presented that Arkansas prisons were constitutionally unacceptable on the issue of cruel and unusual punishment. *Holt II* offered a new interpretation of cruel and unusual punishment in that it was applied to the entire prison system rather than to a particular objectionable feature of the prison, such as solitary confinement, the strap, the Tucker telephone, and abusive working conditions. Judge Henley describes his reasoning on this point:

> It appears to the Court, however, that the concept of "cruel and unusual punishment" is not limited to instances in which a particular inmate is subjected to a punishment directed at him as an individual. In the Court's estimation confinement within a given institution may amount to a cruel and unusual punishment prohibited by the Constitution where the confinement is characterized by conditions and practices so bad as to be shocking to the conscience of a reasonably civilized people even though a particular inmate may never personally be subject to any disciplinary action. To put it another way, while confinement, even at hard labor and without compensation, is not considered to be necessarily a cruel and unusual punishment, it may be so in certain circumstances and by reason of the conditions of confinement (*Holt v. Sarver II*, 1970, pp. 372–373).

All potentially constitutionally objectionable practices, wrote Henley, must be considered together.

> The distinguishing aspects of Arkansas penitentiary life must be considered together. One cannot consider separately a trusty system, a system in which men are confined together in large numbers in open barracks, bad conditions in the isolation cells, or an absence of a meaningful program of rehabilitation. All of those things exist in combination; each affects the other; and taken together they have a cumulative impact on the inmates regardless of their status (*Holt v. Sarver II*, 1970, p. 373).

Trusty System Challenges

One of the challenged practices related to overall prison conditions was the continued use of the trusty system. The court targeted the trusty system as a major contributor to systemic unconstitutionality. While many other American prisons granted trusty status to inmates, Arkansas had taken the concept of trusties to an extreme. Armed trusties at this time still made up the majority of the guard force. Commissioner Sarver testified that trusties carried out over 90% of prison functions relating to inmates. The court commented that the few state employees "are only nominally in command of the situation at Cummins, and the trusties could take it over in a moment" (*Holt v. Sarver II,* 1970, p. 373). At Cummins only two free-world guards were on duty at night to contribute to the security of about 1,000 men.

The court recognized the danger of excessive reliance on trusties. Trusties without doubt are capable of "abuses" of the authority inherent in trusty status. Obviously there is potential for abuse when some inmates are armed and are given the responsibility to guard other inmates.

When all is said and done, the fact remains that a trusty is a convict, and many trusties will on occasion act like felons and thieves. They will take bribes, they will engage in extortion, they will smuggle contraband, and they will connive at violations of prison rules. Opportunity for abuse is particularly present where, as in Arkansas, trusties have access to prison records pertaining to themselves and to other inmates. A trusty with such access can remove damaging material, such as a detainer, from an inmate's file; he can insert improper material; or he can impart to other inmates confidential information that ought not be imparted. The undesirability of having prison telephone communications with the outside world in control of trusties, as it is in Arkansas, is too obvious to require description (*Holt v. Sarver II,* 1970).

The potential for abuse with the trusty system in place has few if any limits. Judge Henley described the trusty system at one point: "Just about every abuse which the system is capable of producing has been produced and is being produced in this State" (*Holt v. Sarver II,* 1970, p. 374).

Free-world personnel ostensibly determine the selection of trusties, but as a practical matter who becomes a trusty is usually based on the recommendation of other trusties. Few if any identifiable criteria are used for selection, and those criteria that can be identified have little to do with responsible supervision of prisoners. Apparently, one major factor taken into consideration was whether the candidate was prepared to shoot to kill other inmates. While all guards must be prepared for such eventualities, the basis on which trusties were selected was not balanced with skills or justifications for protecting inmates. "A trusty is not expected to take any steps to protect an inmate from violence at the hands of another inmate, and the trustees do not do so" (*Holt v. Sarver II,* 1970, p. 374).

Trusties literally have the power of life and death over other inmates. As Judge Henley's opinion in *Holt II* put it,

> It is within the power of a trusty guard to murder another inmate with practical impunity, and the danger that such will be done is always clear and present. Very recently a gate guard killed another inmate "carelessly." One wonders. And there is evidence that recently a guard on night duty fired a shotgun into a crowded barracks because the inmates would not turn off their television set. In any event, the rankers live in deadly fear of the guards and entertain deadly hatred for them, and their feelings are reciprocated fully (*Holt v. Sarver II*, 1970, p. 375).

The trusties control so many aspects of institutional structure and operation that they are in a position to "make or break" the other inmates. Many amenities are available at the discretion of trusties, all of which come at a price. Work assignments and tools, drugs, liquor, weapons, food, clothing, beds, and almost any imaginable favor were available for a price. Trusties could easily and routinely steal food from the institution and sell it to inmates. Trusties were in a position to leave the prison to buy liquor and other items that they would sell at the prison for an enormous profit.

Trusty inmates often were very successful in this climate of brutal capitalism. They were able to accumulate money and material goods, they ate and drank well, they had authority over others, and as trusties enjoyed privileges, opportunities, and safety, which undoubtedly were denied to their fellow inmates of rank status. Judge Henley commented that some trusties do so well that they do not want to leave the institution (*Holt v. Sarver II*, 1970).

One of the most troubling features of the trusty system to the court was the discretion trusties had in granting or denying inmates access to institutional services and resources. Whether an inmate gains access to needed services generally depends on whether the inmate has money to pay the trusties or is regarded favorably enough among trusties to gain access without the usual extortion. Additionally, access to free-world personnel was often available only at the "good will, whim, or caprice" of trusties.

> If a ranker can pay or is on good terms with the trusties, he can get what he needs when he needs it; he can get to the infirmary when the doctor is there; he can get prescribed medications. If he cannot pay or does not get along with the trusties, the case is far otherwise (*Holt v. Sarver II*, 1970, p. 375).

The discretion of trusties also extended to determining whether the rank inmates should be disciplined. Since trusties were the immediate supervisors of rank inmates, it was trusties who would "write an inmate up" for such infractions as unsatisfactory work or refusal to work. The free-world prison employees who had final responsibility for determining disciplinary sanctions routinely took the reports of trusties at face value (*Holt v. Sarver II*, 1970).

Physical and Sexual Assaults of Prisoners

Having discussed living conditions in barracks in *Holt I, Holt II* observed that there was little change following the earlier ruling. *Holt II* elaborated on homosexuality in the barracks of Arkansas prisons. Part of the problem was architectural. The barracks, being a large caged dormitory with virtually no security, provided no protection of inmates from predatory sexual attack from other inmates.

> An inmate who is physically attractive to other men may be, and frequently is, raped in the barracks by other inmates. No one comes to his assistance; the floorwalkers do not interfere; the trustees look on with indifference or satisfaction; the two free world people on duty appear to be helpless (*Holt v. Sarver II*, 1970, p. 377).

Due to the violence in the barracks, sexual and otherwise, some inmates came to the front of the barracks where they would cling to the bars all night in fear. That practice, called "grabbing the bars" by the inmates, may have been largely symbolic since it offered little actual protection. Of equally dubious protectional value was the assignment of young men to cots nearest the front bars to keep them safe from sexual assault (*Holt v. Sarver II*, 1970).

At times drugs and alcohol became available to the extent that many of the inmates in a given barracks became simultaneously intoxicated. The subsequent disorder was predictable, but the ability to control such situations in Arkansas prisons was totally lacking. Free-world employees were too few in number and inadequately prepared to respond. Trusties would not and were not expected to respond. Apparently such binges simply played out until the drugs and alcohol ran out and exhaustion set in (*Holt v. Sarver II*, 1970).

Holt II noted that the overcrowding of isolation cells described in *Holt I* had been improved. Other areas in Cummins had been converted for use as isolation cells. Nevertheless, other conditions such as filth and lack of sanitation remained. The court recognized that at least some of the conditions complained about in the isolation cells were brought about by the inmates who resided there. Commissioner Sarver told the court that the Arkansas prisons could not assure inmates of safety. In some instances inmates could be placed in protective custody to remove them from the general population. However, being placed in "protective custody" placed inmates in the same crowded area that housed inmates found guilty of disciplinary violations. Sarver pointed out that inmate retaliatory measures could be so severe that "if the victim does not die ... it is not the fault of the aggressor" (Dunn, 1970).

A case in point regarding inmate safety was close at hand. Two inmates who had agreed to testify in the *Holt II* hearings later refused to do so because they had been told that they would be killed by inmates if they testified. They subsequently testified after being assured that they could serve the remainder of their sentences under the custody of the state police rather than return to Cummins (Dunn, 1970).

The court indicated that while problems still remained with isolation cells, other aspects of the penitentiary were of greater constitutional concern (*Holt v. Sarver II,* 1970).

Absence of Education and Rehabilitation Programs

The petitioners also contended that the lack of a rehabilitation program was an interference with their constitutional rights. It was possible to find token efforts to implement legislation designed to establish training and rehabilitation programs in the prisons of Arkansas. For example, intelligence and aptitude tests were given to inmates upon arrival at the penitentiary. However, no use was made of the test results for classification and programming. Inmates viewed the tests as useless (*Holt v. Sarver II,* 1970).

The court recognized that providing inmates with education and skills could give them an improved chance of staying out of prison in the future. The court observed that the premodern unmechanized farming methods that inmates were forced to use meant that there were no skills learned by inmates that would be transferable to potential employment in the community upon release. However, the fact that rehabilitation may be a legitimate goal for incarceration did not, in the view of the court, mean that it had "ripened" into a constitutional issue. The court was not willing to declare that the lack of a rehabilitation program rendered confinement in a penal institution unconstitutional (*Holt v. Sarver II,* 1970, p. 379).

However, Judge Henley wrote that the absence of a rehabilitation program might have constitutional relevance in circumstances where the general conditions and practices of the prison operate against reform and rehabilitation. This was the condition of Cummins and to a lesser extent of Tucker. Except in extremely unusual circumstances, inmates were not improved for having been an inmate in Arkansas prisons. Under such circumstances lack of rehabilitation programming "remains a factor in the overall equation before the Court" (*Holt v. Sarver II,* 1970, p. 379).

> Living as he must under the conditions that have been described, with no legitimate rewards or incentives, in fear and apprehension, in degrading surroundings, and with no help from the State, an Arkansas convict will hardly be able to reform himself, and his experience in the penitentiary is apt to do nothing but instill in him a deep or deeper hatred for and alienation from the society that put him there. And the failure of the State to help him become a good citizen will be compounded by the ever-present willingness of his fellow inmates to train him to be a worse criminal (*Holt v. Sarver II,* 1970, p. 379).

The court mentioned other prison conditions, which, like the lack of a rehabilitation program, were not unconstitutional in and of themselves, but nevertheless added to the totality of defects and deficiencies. Medical and dental services were lacking for many inmates, often due to the fact that trusties controlled access to medical and dental treatment. A medical witness for the prisons introduced evidence that the sanitary conditions in the Cummins kitchen were deplorable. It became clear through testimony in the court that inmates at Arkansas prisons were supplied with only the "bare necessities of life." While the court in no way argued for providing comfort to the inmates, such conditions clearly added to the overall depiction of conditions in the prisons.

> A man who ... is supplied with no towels, and with insufficient socks and underclothing, and who is required to sleep night after night on filthy bedding is certainly not stimulated to take any pride in himself or to try to be a good inmate of the Penitentiary to say nothing of being a good citizen in the free world when he is released (*Holt v. Sarver II*, 1970, p. 380).

"Banishment From Civilized Society to a Dark and Evil World"

The court detailed the meaning of the concept of "cruel and unusual punishment," stating that its meaning is flexible, depending on expanding and shifting social interpretations of decency, dignity, and humanity. Judge Henley continued,

> Generally speaking, a punishment that amounts to torture, or that is grossly excessive in proportion to the offense for which it is imposed, or that is inherently unfair, or that is shocking or disgusting to people of reasonable sensitivity is a "cruel and unusual punishment." And a punishment that is not inherently cruel and unusual may become so by reason of the manner in which it is inflicted (*Holt v. Sarver II*, 1970, p. 380).

Upon conviction for a felony in Arkansas, the offender is sentenced to prison, but in Arkansas, wrote the judge, "he receives much more than that." What he receives in addition is immersion in the prison conditions described in this case, conditions about which even the judge and jury who help decide his fate may be ignorant (*Holt v. Sarver II*, 1970, p. 380). In a frequently quoted passage from *Holt II*, Henley elaborates on conditions an inmate faces upon being sent to the Arkansas prisons:

> For the ordinary convict a sentence to the Arkansas Penitentiary today amounts to a banishment from civilized society to a dark and evil world completely alien to the free world, a world that is administered by criminals under unwritten rules and customs completely foreign to free world culture (*Holt v. Sarver II*, 1970, p. 381).

In such conditions, the court points out, regardless of how cooperative or inoffensive an inmate might be, "[he] has no assurance that he will not be killed, seriously injured, or sexually abused" (*Holt v. Sarver II*, 1970, p. 381). As they operated at that time, the Arkansas prisons could not offer protection from such dangers.

In addition to physical danger the convicts lived in circumstances the court described as degrading and disgusting. Further, the treatment an inmate received had no logical relationship to the seriousness of one's offense. Indeed, a person convicted of a serious violent crime may very well receive better treatment than a first offender convicted of a relatively minor property crime (*Holt v. Sarver II,* 1970).

Judge Henley declared,

> It is one thing for the State to send a man to the Penitentiary as a punishment for a crime. It is another thing for the State to delegate the governance of him to other convicts, and to do nothing meaningful for his safety, well being, and possible rehabilitation. It is one thing for the State not to pay a convict for his labor; it is something else to subject him to a situation in which he has to sell his blood to obtain money to pay for his own safety, or for adequate food, or for access to needed medical attention. However constitutionally tolerable the Arkansas system may have been in former years, it simply will not do today (*Holt v. Sarver II,* 1970, p. 381).

Racial Segregation

Regarding the 14th Amendment equal protection clause as it applies to racial segregation, the court fully recognized that racial discrimination is prohibited in prisons. Desegregation was already in place at Tucker. However, the court agreed with the respondents that immediate desegregation of the barracks at Cummins might be counterproductive at the present time in terms of order and control, making a bad situation even worse. The court discussed the difference in desegregation of schools, restaurants, theatres, and other places of public accommodation from such a transition in a prison environment. Desegregation at Cummins should take place at Cummins, but it should, according to *Holt II,* be part of an overall transition to an acceptably constitutional system (*Holt v. Sarver II,* 1970).

In regard to relief granted, *Holt II* concentrated on class relief from the overall unconstitutionality of the prisons. Specific relief to any individual petitioners was not granted. Judge Henley was seeking changes in the prison system itself to benefit all inmates subject to unconstitutional practices (*Holt v. Sarver II,* 1970).

The petitioners in *Holt II* sought both declaratory and injunctive relief. Regarding declaratory relief the court ruled that confinement in the Arkansas system under existing conditions amounted to cruel and unusual punishment. The court also declared that racial segregation in the prisons, including segregation of inmates, was unconstitutional as a violation of the due process clause (*Holt v. Sarver II,* 1970).

Injunctive Relief

The court had no hesitation in addressing the matter of injunctive relief. As in *Holt I,* the court recognized that Arkansas has the right within constitutional limits to operate its criminal justice system as it chooses and noted that the prisons do not have unlimited financial resources. Those with responsibility for the Arkansas prisons were directed in *Holt II* to make a "prompt and reasonable start" at eliminating the conditions, which rendered the prisons system unconstitutional. Diligent efforts must continue until the conditions were corrected. Judge Henley pointed out that the stakes were high:

> The lives, safety, and health of human beings, to say nothing of their dignity, are at stake. The start must be prompt, and the prosecution must be vigorous. The handwriting is on the wall, and it ought not to require a Daniel to read it. Unless conditions at the Penitentiary farms are brought up to a level of constitutional tolerability, the farms can no longer be used for the confinement of convicts (*Holt v. Sarver II,* 1970, p. 383).

The court struggled with the question of timing. "What must be done in the immediate future, and how long should Respondents be allowed to achieve their ultimate objective?" (*Holt v. Sarver II,* 1970, p. 383). The court noted that the state on its own had made some progress in correcting prison conditions. The court also recognized that it takes time to make state funds available. Additionally, the court mentioned that time would be necessary to hire and train new personnel and that care must be taken so that trusties are not replaced with "venal, corrupt, sadistic, and underpaid civilian employees" (*Holt v. Sarver II,* 1970, p. 383). While the court was willing to allow "reasonable" time for making modifications, the expectation was clearly expressed that progress must be prompt, and efforts must be unrelenting. Of the period of transition Henley wrote, "[It] is going to have to be measured in months, not years" (*Holt v. Sarver II,* 1970, p. 383).

Holt II required state officials to develop a plan to eliminate unconstitutional practices and procedures. This plan was to elaborate what they intended to do and how long it would take. While the court did not impose a plan on the state, it did offer guidelines.

One guideline offered by the court was that trusties must be deprived of their authority over other inmates. "Trusties, whether guards or not, are going to have to be stripped of their authority over the lives and living conditions of other inmates" (*Holt v. Sarver II,* 1970, p. 384). This did not mean that the court was prepared to order the complete elimination of the trusty system, but simply that the system must be overhauled in such a manner to delegate to free-world employees much of the power and discretion that trusties had at their disposal. Trusties must not be in a position to promote or demote other inmates, control access to free-world staff and medical treatment, steal items for resale, extort other inmates, have access to the pharmacy, and so on.

Trusties may continue to serve as guards in a limited capacity while under proper supervision. The court had no particular problem with trusties serving as tower and picket guards but was convinced that service as gate guards and as field supervisors must be terminated (*Holt v. Sarver II*, 1970, p. 384).

The conditions in the barracks and in the isolation cells had to be remedied. Some construction and remodeling was necessary to solve problems of space and distribution. Particular attention was to be given to keeping order in the living areas and to protecting inmates from violence. All inmates had to be given adequate food and sanitation.

The court recognized that many of the problems were interconnected, and that solution of some could have consequences for others. The court expressed the opinion that if proper attention were given to the trusty system, the barracks system, inmate safety, the isolation cells, and racial segregation, it was likely that many of the other problems would take care of themselves.

The court suggested that a good target date for complete removal of unconstitutional conditions was the time the new maximum security unit was to be opened in 1971. State officials were to make a report to the court by April 1 of 1970 indicating progress and plans for complying with the requirements of the court. But regardless of circumstances there had to be change that had the purpose and the results of making the Arkansas prisons constitutional. Judge Henley concluded his opinion in *Holt II* with the strong and resolute statement, "If Arkansas is going to operate a Penitentiary System, it is going to have to be a system that is countenanced by the Constitution of the United States" (*Holt v. Sarver II*, 1970, p. 385). The relief ordered by Judge Henley's district court decision was affirmed by the 8th U.S. Circuit Court of Appeals but remanded for Judge Henley to require a further report of progress made by the state in curing the defects found by the trial court (*Holt v. Sarver*, 1971).

With the delivery of his opinion in *Holt II*, Judge Henley had struck a strong blow against the way prisons had been run in Arkansas for many decades. The court's ruling was aggressive and thorough. Judge Henley was not asking for a minor adjustment of the system but had tapped into the heart of the system and was demanding major renovation. Held up to standards of the U.S. Constitution, the prison system was found to be seriously deficient. As much as the state might like to do so, it would find that the court would not be ignored. Thus, Arkansas prison reform shifted into a higher gear.

Conclusion

The early Arkansas prison court cases took tentative steps to correct abuses such as initially requiring some procedural safeguards on the use of the strap as a form of discipline (*Talley v. Stephens, 1965*) and later an outright ban on the strap and the most atrocious forms of corporal punishment such as the Tucker telephone (*Jackson v. Bishop*, 1968). With corporal punishment forbidden, the Arkansas prison officials had only the use of isolation as a meaningful form of discipline. Judge Henley was sympathetic to the plight of Commissioner Sarver in his efforts to affect reform in the Arkansas prisons but was insistent that the state bring its correctional practices into compliance with federal constitutional provisions.

Holt I required the state to address conditions of isolation units and take steps to better ensure the safety of inmates (*Holt v. Sarver I*, 1969). This case did produce some improvements, but prisoners continued to file civil lawsuits seeking further relief. *Holt II* went much further and took aim at the prison system as a whole, finding that the Arkansas prison system was itself a violation of the Eighth Amendment prohibition against cruel and unusual punishment (*Holt v. Sarver II*, 1970). The remedial steps in *Holt II* included protection of inmates from harm at the hands of other inmates, elimination of racial segregation of inmates, and severe limitations on the power of inmate trusties. Judge Henley recognized that the state would need a reasonable period of time to implement the necessary reforms but stressed that the time allowed be in "months, not years" (*Holt v. Sarver II*, 1970, p. 383).

REFERENCES

Banning v. Looney, 213 F.2d 771 (10th Cir. 1954)

Bounds v. Smith, 430 U.S. 817 (1977)

Clear, T., & Cole, G. (1994). *American corrections.* Wadsworth.

Convict Asks Judge to Send Full-Time Doctor to Prison. (1969, May 26). *Arkansas Democrat.*

Cooper v. Pate, 378 U.S. 546 (1964)

Courtney v. Bishop, 408 F. 2d. 1185,1186 (8th Cir. 1969)

Dilulio, J. (1990). *Courts, corrections, and the constitution.* Oxford University Press.

Douthit, G. (1969a, June 27). Overcrowding likely to continue for year in cells at Cummins. *Arkansas Democrat.*

Douthit, G. (1969b, July 19). Sarver says U.S. court order bars discipline as suggested. *Arkansas Democrat.*

Dunn, M. (1970, January 26). Trusty system said to lead to "corruption." *Arkansas Democrat.*

Feeley, M. M., & Rubin, E. L. (1998). *Judicial policymaking and the modern state: How courts reformed America's prisons.* Cambridge University Press.

Holt v. Sarver I, 300 F. Supp. 825 (E.D. Arkansas 1969)

Holt v. Sarver II, 309 F. Supp. 362 (E.D. Arkansas 1970)

Holt v. Sarver, 442 F.2d 304 (8th Cir. 1971)

Jackson v. Bishop, 268 F. Supp. 804, 806 (E.D. Arkansas 1967)

Jackson v. Bishop, 404 F.2d 571 (8th Cir. 1968)

Johnson v. Avery, 393 U.S. 483 (1969)

Palmer, J. W. (2010). *Constitutional rights of prisoners.* Matthew Bender & Company.

Parker, M. L. (1986). *Judicial intervention in correctional institutions: The Arkansas Odyssey* [PhD Dissertation, Sam Houston State University].

Ross, D. (2018). *Civil liability in criminal justice* (7th ed.) Routledge.

Ruffin v. Commonwealth, 62 Va. 790 (1871)

Shover, N., & Einstadter, W. (1998). *Analyzing American corrections.* Wadsworth.

Slapped rather hard, Sarver says of ruling. (1969, June 21). *Arkansas Democrat.*

Spiller, D. (1975). *After decision: Implementation of judicial decrees in correctional settings.* American Bar Association.

Steinmetz, T. (May 27, 1969). Trusty asks return of strap in hearing. *Arkansas Democrat.*

Stroud v. Swope, 187 F. 2d. 850 (9th Cir. 1951)

Talley v. Stephens, 247 F. Supp. 683 (E.D. Arkansas 1965)

Wolff v. McDonnell 418 U.S. 539 (1974)

KEY TERMS

"Creepers and crawlers"	Constitutional wall
"Do-pops"	Isolation
"Grabbing the bars"	Pro se petition
Bill of Rights, hands-off doctrine	8th. U.S. Circuit Court of Appeals
Buckshot	10th Amendment
Civil Rights Act of 1871	13th Amendment

QUESTIONS

1. To justify the hands-off doctrine, courts determined that living circumstances in prison were simply a part of "necessary deprivations" in prison life in that they deprive inmates of comforts found in the free world. Currently, in many U.S. prisons, inmates receive health care, housing, job opportunities, recreational activities, and so on. Do you think our current prison system is too soft? Why or why not?

2. Many inmates suffered from mental issues, with untrained persons dispensing medicine and providing other care that should be provided by a physician. How was this counterproductive to the role and responsibility of prison systems?

3. The removal of the strap as corporal punishment was replaced with isolation cells. Do you think this change was effective or ineffective in punishing inmates? Why?

4. Sarver submitted a report that outlined steps to correct deficiencies at Cummins. Which step do you find most important and why? Which was the least important?

7 | News Media Response to Federal Court Intervention

Crisis, Scandal, or Exaggeration?

Introduction

Apart from the actual litigation in the *Holt* cases, the prisons continued to receive media attention and obviously remained on the minds of Arkansans. The full extent of the prison problems was still being revealed and debated. Some called it a crisis or scandal, while others continued to defend the prisons and dismiss many of the revelations as exaggeration. Some who learned about the prisons saw no reason for change, but others continued to be embarrassed by the prison imbroglio and wanted reform.

An indication of the attention focused on prisons, and an indication of how prisons were being defined and redefined can be found in what state newspapers were writing about the prisons during the time of the Holt litigation (*Holt v. Sarver*, 1969, 1970, 1971). Without doubt, the prison situation provided many stories for news writers, often major stories, found either on the front page or in a prominent space in the state news sections. Editorial writers also directed their attention to prison issues. This chapter describes what Arkansas citizens were reading during this period when major court rulings were beginning to impact Arkansas prison reform.

An important transition is reflected. Many of the early news stories of this period report a defense of the old ways of operating the prisons and deny the reality represented in the *Holt* testimony and findings. Gradually, however, the reality of these rulings and their impact begin to provide a new philosophical underpinning for prison operations. Whether this new orientation was appreciated was debatable and debated. The important point is that apparently it was slowly being accepted, whether it was welcomed with open arms or not. It was definitely being implemented; the court saw to that.

Early Reactions

Just before the *Holt I* opinion was released, the prison board was wringing its hands over budget concerns. The prison farm income was not keeping up with prison expenditures as it had in the past. The payroll for free-world staff added in recent years, various repairs, and improved provisions for inmates all were placing an enormous strain on the prison budget. In early June 1969, the board chairman indicated they currently had a deficit of $194,537 ("Haley Says Prisons Still in the Red, No Solution at Hand," 1969). The proposed solutions were to look to farm production to solve the problem. Nevertheless, the outlook for breaking even looked bleak (Douthit, 1969a).

The farm crops looked good that summer but the prisons faced a labor shortage. Commissioner of Corrections Robert Sarver indicated that 300 workers were needed for fieldwork at Cummins but only 100 were currently available. Others could be made available, but only by taking them away from their current jobs that provided needed, if not essential, services for running the prison. Such a shift would require reducing security, food services, maintenance, gardening, and laundry operations (Douthit, 1969b).

Much of the problem could be traced to a lower prison population. In years past it was not uncommon to have over 2,000 inmates. By the summer of 1969, the count was closer to 1,000. The difference was traced largely to the "new philosophy" for running the prisons that, in part, made much greater use of parole (Douthit, 1969b). Ironically, Arkansas prisons at this time were losing money by paroling inmates. Other systems then and later were using parole to keep costs down and avoid the expense of expanding prisons. Inmate manpower was clearly seen as an essential element in maintaining the prisons. Haley and Sarver met with inmates to tell them that "the institutions's money is in the ground" and that every prisoner was expected to do his full share in getting it out (Douthit, 1969b).

In June of 1969, the opinion of *Holt I* was released. The opinion ruled that the isolation cells and lack of inmate safety were in violation of the Constitution prohibitions of cruel and unusual punishment. The court required that prison officials develop a plan for correcting these constitutional shortcomings. Judge Henley recognized that much of the problem was due to lack of funds (*Holt v. Sarver*, 1969; Steinmetz, 1969a). The court made it clear that lack of resources could not be used to justify operation of a prison system in an unconstitutional manner (*Holt v. Sarver*, 1969; Steinmetz, 1969a).

When the *Holt I* ruling was issued, Sarver and the board were focused primarily on the shortage of farm hands and how to get the prison farm crops harvested. Sarver recognized the potential impact of the federal court ruling. He described the court decision as having "slapped our hands rather hard." He confirmed the court's finding that it was not possible to give inmates improved safety without a major overhaul of the security force ("Slapped Rather Hard, Sarver Says of Ruling," 1969). Sarver elaborated,

> We have had, as the Judge pointed out, 17 stabbings in the last 18 months at Cummins alone. We don't have the free-world men to guard. The judge has suggested free-world people replace the [trusty] night floorwalkers. We don't have the money to do this ("Slapped Rather Hard, Sarver Says of Ruling," 1969).

Shortly after the ruling was issued, a delegation of legislators, members of the Legislative Council's committee on penal institutions (the Charitable, Penal, and Correctional Institutions Committee) visited Cummins. Their primary concern was to investigate why there were not enough inmates available at Cummins to complete the farm chores, particularly the harvest. The prison's financial condition had deteriorated to the point that they were going to have to borrow money to meet payrolls. Legislators were depending on the sale of crops to alleviate the financial conditions ("Slapped Rather Hard, Sarver Says of Ruling," 1969).

Having spent most of the day investigating the crops and farm manpower, members of the committee briefly examined the Cummins isolation cell building just prior to departing from the prison. The legislators found five Black prisoners confined in one 8' × 10' cell, an example of the overcrowding targeted by the federal court (Francisco, 1969a). Responding to the court's ruling was regarded as considerably less worthy of attention and comment than was the matter of farm production for supporting the prison budget.

A snapshot of how the field labor shortage was defined from two perspectives is found in an editorial that appeared in the *Benton Courier* shortly after legislators visited Cummins. State Senator Virgil Fletcher of Benton was one of the legislators who made the trip. He complained that only 300 inmates were available for harvesting crops. As quoted by Harrison (1969), the Senator recalled that farming was different on the family farm on which he grew up: "His father got 100 per cent participation of the family youngsters in the field work and did it through the use of 'a switch.'" Fletcher indicated that this approach should work at the Arkansas prisons and pointed out that the prisons use inmate labor since this has been accepted as the best way to run prisons in the poor state of Arkansas. Jack Harrison, the editorial writer, countered,

> This may be correct. But how can they expect all of the inmates to be out in the field picking squash when most of them are needed to tote the shotguns, peel the potatoes, and type the reports? If legislators like Senator Fletcher want to see all inmates in the cucumber patch making a profit for the state, then perhaps they can find a way to hire a few guards and other employees to fill the jobs the inmates now handle (Harrison, 1969).

Under the July heat an inmate harvesting crops collapsed and later died of an apparent heat stroke. After complaining to a guard that he felt sick, he was given lighter duty but remained in the field. This came at a time when prison officials reported they were "pushing as hard as [they could] to get a crop because if [they] didn't], the prison [wouldn't] have any money th[at] fall." Sarver indicated that they were "scraping the bottom of the barrel" to get enough field hands to keep the prison self-supporting. This included using inmates with serious mental and physical disabilities (Douthit, 1969c).

Federal Grand Jury

Regardless of what the Legislative Council's penal institutions committee regarded as high priority items, Judge J. Smith Henley's U.S. District Court kept the spotlight on the Arkansas prisons system. Henley seated a grand jury "to hear evidence as to certain practices and conditions said to exist or to have existed in the Arkansas Penitentiary" (Steinmetz, 1969b). At least 35 inmates and former inmates were subpoenaed to provide testimony regarding whether trusties or free-world employees had, in the performance of their duties, violated the civil rights of prisoners (Steinmetz, 1969b). Henley indicated that the grand jury was summoned at the request of the U.S. Department of Justice, which sent the FBI to investigate the shooting incident in which a Cummins associate superintendent fired birdshot into a group of striking inmates. One inmate lost an eye as a result of the incident ("20 On Hand to Testify on Prisons," 1969).

In his opening remarks to members of the grand jury, Henley indicated that the jurors would hear testimony regarding a shooting incident, the use of the leather strap, the isolation cells, and devices such as the Tucker telephone used in the punishment of inmates (Steinmetz, 1969b). Although Henley charged the grand jury not to indict anyone unless it was warranted, "on the other hand," Henley elaborated, "it is not your function to whitewash any institution or any individual" ("20 on Hand to Testify on Prisons," 1969). It became clear that the grand jury was investigating matters that went back in time as far as the incidents and prison conditions covered in the 1966 Arkansas State Police investigation.

The grand jury returned 46 indictments against former Tucker assistant superintendent Jim Bruton and 14 other persons. Bruton himself was indicted on 19 counts involving alleged brutality to inmates. Others indicted included former and present prison employees and trusties, along with four employees of county prison farms (Steinmetz, 1969b). Although Bruton and other staff had faced charges on the 1964–1966 incidents previously on the state level, the charges were dismissed following a ruling by state Circuit Judge Henry W. Smith that the statute under which they were charged was vague and unconstitutional. The state supreme court upheld the ruling by Judge Smith (*State v. Bruton et al.* 1969; Steinmetz, 1969b).

The indictments in federal court stemmed from incidents that were familiar to persons who followed Arkansas news. The Tucker telephone was an electric generator connected to the genitals and foot of an inmate in order to deliver electric shocks for punishment and to extract information. The leather strap was the primary method of inmate discipline. The current indictments indicated that the strap was used in such a way as to leave the bodies of inmates bleeding and bruised. There was testimony that assaults had taken place with blackjacks, pliers, hypodermic needles, and broom handles (Steinmetz, 1969b).

Sarver and the Legislature

If he ever enjoyed a honeymoon with the Arkansas legislature, Robert Sarver found that it had come to an end by the summer of 1969. The penal oversight legislative committee that visited Cummins that summer issued a report that recommended that the Board of Corrections do all it could to return the state prisons to a self-supporting basis through farm income. It further recommended that any other prison programs "be adjusted" so as not to interfere with convict farm work. Sarver pointed out to them that the same committee 2 years earlier had recommended more prison expenditures from state general revenues to increase rehabilitation programs. The committee, Sarver pointed out, opposed itself with its new directive ("Sarver Says Prison Panel Opposes Self," 1969).

The committee report also suggested that the "farm situation" could be improved by closer cooperation between the parole board and the Board of Corrections. Without explicitly saying so, this implied that any paroles should be delayed depending on the need for farm labor. Sarver pointed out that it would be devastating for morale to delay the release of parole-eligible inmates simply to have enough farm workers in busy times such as the harvest (Douthit, 1969c).

The Board of Corrections had assured the legislature that the farms could become more productive with modern farming equipment (Douthit, 1969c). Requests for funds for modernization had been presented to the legislature, but no appropriations were forthcoming.

Sarver offered to appear before the committee to discuss their findings but was refused. The committee report criticized discipline at the prisons and found fault with prison management in regard to agricultural productivity. A member of the committee suggested in a televised interview that they "keep a strap hidden down there somewhere and use it cautiously." Sarver pointed out that this would place the prison in violation of the orders of the federal court and expressed his frustration at trying to reform the system without legislative support ("He's 'Burning Out,' Sarver Says in Wake of Prison Criticism," 1969; Douthit, 1969d). He indicated that he and his superintendents had given all they could to the system and recognized that he was "burning out" ("He's 'Burning Out,' Sarver Says in Wake of Prison Criticism," 1969).

In a letter to the chairman of the Legislative Council, Sarver questioned whether prison reform was on the legislative agenda for Arkansas: "I am in somewhat of a quandary, however, as a result of what appears to be an inconsistency or conflict in the stated legislative purpose concerning the directions and goals of the department" (Douthit, 1969d). Not only is there no effective rehabilitation or treatment, wrote Sarver, there is no funding to purchase shoes, adequate clothing, kitchen equipment, or to improve deplorable living conditions. "Do we want a self-supporting, farm-operated prison or do we want rehabilitation treatment-oriented system which will restore adult offenders to useful law abiding citizens? … We cannot have both" (Douthit, 1969d).

In a speech to a Little Rock civic organization, Sarver reiterated his interest in rehabilitative efforts that he saw as a most challenging task: "The legislature and society have asked us to take these people and return them to society as law-abiding citizens." On continuing farming Sarver commented, "I am not altogether opposed to farming." However, he did tell the audience that Tucker could be leased for more income than the farm was producing with inmate labor ("Leasing Cummins Farmland Urged," 1969).

In a later television interview Sarver suggested leasing not only Tucker but also the farmland at Cummins in order to direct attention to changing inmates. "We're either going to be farmers … or we are going to run correctional institutions" ("Leasing Cummins Farmland Urged," 1969). Existing legislation allowed leasing, and Sarver argued that others could operate and farm more easily and efficiently than has been the case with the prison operation. An outside person "c[ould] provide the necessary machinery, hire trained people who know what they are doing and [wouldn't] have to guard them while they work. Also he [wouldn't] have to feed them, clothe them, give them medical care, and rehabilitate them" ("Sarver and Attorney General to Study Prison-Lease Details," 1969).

At the Crossroads

The prisons of Arkansas were still at the same crossroad that presented itself 3 years earlier when the prison scandals were revealed. Although some citizens and even some legislators were concerned, there was no grassroots movement to make significant reforms in the prisons. A constituency prepared to do the work to produce significant legislative initiatives did not back up the campaign interest in prison reform that helped to elect Rockefeller. Murton had expected that through exposure of the prison operation and conditions, public sentiment would be aroused sufficiently to produce an overwhelming demand for change. Thus far, even graphic and detailed revelations had not, in themselves, produced much change. They had brought embarrassment, talk of change, and damage control efforts, but not much change. The key to serious prison reform was held by the legislature, which thus far showed little interest in voluntarily embracing prison reform, and which thus far had not recognized that their journey to prison reform was about to be launched by the federal courts (Feeley & Rubin, 1998).

The words of *Arkansas Democrat* writer George Douthit's editorial captured the essence of where the state stood on prison reform in late July 1969:

> A Democrat reader asked last week: "Is there no resolving of the prison situation in Arkansas?"
>
> The answer to the question is *it will be resolved when the Arkansas legislature wants to resolve it and not before* [emphasis added]. The indictments returned recently by a federal grand jury against former employees and convicts of the prison is indicative of what still remains to be.
>
> We would say that the indictments against the individuals actually were against the system that the state has been so proud of for so many years. That included a long leather strap for punishments, farm crops that produced a self supporting [*sic*] institution, and trusties who formed their own "establishment of power" within the prison. …
>
> Legislative Council just a few days ago adopted a report which said that the farm should be made as self-supporting as possible.
>
> This is simply a step back toward the old days. …

What does it add up to? We have people in the legislature who claim they favor prison rehabilitation, but they don't really. Their actions indicate they want the old system back. The federal court has made it plain it is not coming back, so the legislators may as well make up their minds that Arkansas is in for prison reform (Douthit, 1969e).

A reminder of the old days presented itself as Carter Doze, a former inmate, went before the State Claims Commission to seek compensation for physical disabilities he received as a result of a beating he received in October 1964. He said a trusty in charge of the vegetable house where he worked at Cummins beat him. Doze testified that he lost an eye and partial use of his right hand and suffered brain damage. The reason given for the beating was that he carried a pocketful of peanuts away from the field. After the beating he was treated by a trusty "doctor" and later by a Pine Bluff physician (Associated Press, 1969a).

Additionally, crowding problems continued in isolation cells. This served as evidence that no movement toward significant reforms was occurring. At Tucker the only cells available to use for punitive isolation were the death row cells. Use of the death penalty in America was in a steep decline in the late 1960s, with no executions carried out anywhere in the United States in 1968 (Banner, 2002). Since no death sentences were being carried out, the number of death row inmates was increasing. In the first 9 months of 1969, five additional inmates were added to death row. Isolation in these same cells became the chief form of prison punishment since using the strap had been declared unconstitutional. This situation routinely created crowding in the death row cells. The Tucker superintendent found himself in the position of having to release inmates from isolation to make room for newly arriving inmates with death sentences (Douthit, 1969f).

Among all the media attention given to the Arkansas prisons in the fall of 1969 were stories of complaints filed against the Arkansas prisons on behalf of several inmates, including Joseph Holt, Robert Courtney, and Thomas Hildebrandt. All three were being held in isolation cells at Cummins (McIntyre, 1969). This was the beginning of the lawsuit that was to be referred to as *Holt v Sarver II*. The inmates alleged mistreatment with the Tucker telephone and by being beaten, kicked, and otherwise abused. They claimed that the conditions had not improved at the prisons since the court made its rulings in the previous spring. These complaints were joined with similar complaints from Tucker inmates who filed a petition written on toilet paper. The Tucker inmates claimed that they were subjected to cruel and unusual punishment due to conditions of the prison, including food and living circumstances ("Six File Toilet-Paper Petition," 1969).

Fletcher's Trial

Additional support for the picture being painted of the Arkansas prisons came from testimony in the trials of prison officials charged with depriving the civil rights of prisoners to be free from cruel and unusual punishment.

In the trial of Ernest Fletcher, a former Tucker employee, Jerry Dean Ivens, a former inmate at Tucker, described circumstances that led to his being whipped by Fletcher:

> Ivens said that he dropped a letter in a mailbox but that later in the day an inmate who works in the mail room brought the letter back to him, explaining that it would not be advisable to send out a letter critical of the prison system. Ivens told him that what he said in the letter was true and that the letter should be mailed.
>
> About 6 p.m. that day, Ivens said, former Tucker Supt. Jim Bruton, Fletcher and two trusties called him out of his barracks. According to Ivens, Bruton read the letter and asked if he had written it. When he said he that he had, Bruton told him to lie face down on the concrete floor and then told Fletcher to give him five lashes with the strap, Ivens said.
>
> According to the testimony, Fletcher gave "at least 11" lashes. Ivens said he stopped counting at 11 because he knew that the 11th lash was illegal. At that time, prison rules forbade more than 10 lashes to the same inmate in any 24 hour [sic] period.
>
> Ivens told the court that because he had been at Tucker only a few days he was not familiar with the custom the inmates hollered "Oh Captain" after each lash in order to assure the prisons officials or trusties that the whipping was hurting. ...
>
> Ivens ... said that he was wearing only his shorts and that the beating left bruises and lacerations (Hackler, 1969a).

In addition to Ivens, the jury also heard testimony from another inmate that corroborated Ivens's story of the beating. Fletcher's defense attorney told the jury that they should believe a church-going man like Fletcher rather than the testimony of two "thugs." Fletcher's attorney continued that rather than finding Fletcher guilty, the jury "ought to give the man a medal" for trying to corral the prisoners and "trying to make them earn their living." The jury apparently agreed and found Fletcher not guilty ("Ex-Warden Acquitted," 1969).

Murton and Sarver

The citizens of Arkansas were treated to another prison sideshow as Thomas Murton, former superintendent, agreed to return to the state for a speaking engagement at the University of Arkansas in Fayetteville. Sarver also agreed to be on the program. The two had not previously had an opportunity to meet and exchange views. Although not a formal debate, some differences between the two emerged, particularly in response to questions from members of the audience, some of whom were previously inmates at Tucker. Murton mentioned that he would do two things differently if he could do it over again: "I would have fired the remaining 39 employees I let stay, and I would have dug up the other 197 bodies." The 39 employees were those he retained at Cummins when he took over there, and the bodies were those of inmates he said were murdered and quietly buried in unmarked graves on the Cummins grounds (Douthit, 1969g).

Murton said that it was "pure fiction" that Governor Rockefeller did not have prior knowledge about digging up the bodies. "He [Rockefeller] is the one who agreed we needed something to jolt the people of Arkansas and to put down the Knox Nelson myth that this is the best prison system in the United States" (Douthit, 1969g). Murton described a discussion in the parking lot of state Board of Correction Board Chair John Haley's law office. Present at the meeting were Bob Scott (an assistant to Governor Rockefeller), Haley, Dr. Edwin Barron (former prison physician who had publicly criticized prison conditions), and Murton. Murton maintained that "Bob Scott knew that we were going to dig ... and Scott said go ahead and dig" (Douthit, 1969g).

> In his remarks Murton mentioned that prison reform had digressed since his departure, that inmates were being abused, and that prison officials had "sold out." Sarver claimed that progress was being made in Murton's absence. Sarver also took issue with Murton's indication that some "Mickey Mouse" regulations are to be ignored. Said Sarver, "The Mickey Mouse rules are designed to protect the taxpayer. ... If I fly in the face of the Legislature I will be in the same position Mr. Murton is in. ... I've got first of all to survive so that I can make inroads. ... I don't consider that selling out" (Douthit, 1969g).

In a final volley between the two before Murton left the state, Murton announced after touring the prisons that he found them in worse condition than he expected ("Murton Says He Found Prisons Bad," 1969). He later said that the brutality in the Arkansas prisons continued. Sarver was angered by Murton's comments and stated, "I guess he would rather sit back and make noise." Sarver was miffed because he wanted to consult with Murton regarding the present status of Arkansas prisons. When Murton failed to appear for an appointment with Sarver, Sarver questioned Murton's sincerity: "We were going to get his reaction to the institution. ... Apparently he is not very sincere. ... I wouldn't trust that man any further [sic] than I could throw him" (Associated Press, 1969b). The following year Murton (1970) stated his view of Arkansas prison reform was "that the flickering light of hope we had ignited had been extinguished" (p. 17).

Since money was running short in the prison budget, it was not unusual to have to wait until the last minute to place orders for such items as food and clothing. That, coupled with delays in filling orders, at times left the prison short on essential items. In October 1969, Sarver reported that the prison was completely out of shoes and some inmates were shoeless. At that same time the prison also ran out of bread and had to place emergency orders ("Prisoner at Cummins 'Shoeless,'" 1969).

Sarver's tension with the legislature continued. In November 1969, the Legislative Joint Auditing Committee criticized bookkeeping practices at both Cummins and Tucker as a result of a July audit. The committee mentioned that there had been improvements in bookkeeping but that there were still weaknesses. George

Tannous, a fiscal administrator hired to overhaul the prison business operation, said that many of the problems mentioned by the committee had already been corrected. Tannous mentioned that when he took over, six inmates were working in the business office handling accounts. At that time he found that some ledgers were incomplete and others had been lost completely. It was almost impossible to hire and retain qualified business office personnel given the low pay and working conditions in the prison business offices (Hackler, 1969b).

Another wave of Arkansas prison news during this critical period came from the release of Tom Murton's book, which described his experiences in the Arkansas prisons. The title of the book was *Accomplices to the Crime: The Arkansas Prison Scandal.* Excerpts of the book printed in state newspapers served as a reminder both of prisons' conditions as Murton saw them and of Murton's derogatory interpretation of the state's prison reform efforts (Douthit, 1969h). Governor Rockefeller's impression of the book was that much of it was "simply a reflection of the former superintendent's ego" (Douthit, 1970a).

Bruton's Trial

Meanwhile, back in U.S. District Court, the trial of Jim Bruton, a former assistant superintendent of state prisons, was underway. Opening statement by Assistant U.S. Attorney Robert Fussell stated that Bruton was the overseer of the most vicious, sadistic, and inhumane treatment of prisoners since that of Alolph Hitler. He promised the jury that they would be so shocked by the testimony that they would never forget it, including ordering and use of such instruments of torture as the Tucker telephone, hypodermic needles, broom handles, pliers, and other such tools. Bruton's attorney, R.A. Eilbott, countered by indicating that it was the system that was at fault rather than Bruton. Bruton, Elibott argued, merely inherited, but had not created, the brutality of the Arkansas prison. Given a system founded on the use of the strap and the trusty system, things happened that would seem like a "nightmare" to average citizens. With only four state employees other than Bruton to keep order and farm for profit, said Eilbott, it was necessary to use force at Tucker to operate the prison. Otherwise, inmates would be "taking over south Arkansas" (Hackler, 1969c).

Testimony in Bruton's trial recounted familiar themes and details regarding Arkansas prisons. One inmate, Carl Dean Mosley, told the jury that trusties, on orders from Bruton, had forced a confession from him regarding a rumored escape plan by beating him with a blackjack, sticking hypodermic needles into the ends of his fingers, and pulling his genitals with wire pliers. Although he was not able to read or write, he signed a confession prepared for him to stop the beating. Mosley vowed to beat or murder the trusties if he found them. Mosley reported that as a result of the violent efforts to make him confess, "his head was swollen, he had bruises all over his body, his fingers were swollen, and his knees were so enlarged from the beating that he could barely pull his trousers over them" (Hackler, 1969d).

Another inmate, Charles Kennedy, testified that Bruton and trusties beat him after he tried to kill an inmate who was trying to extort money from him.

He said that he figured that if he killed one or two of the inmates who were trying to extort money from him "they would get off my back." According to his testimony he was then beaten many times over a 6-day period with broom handles and a rubber hose. During this period Bruton joined in the beatings, at one time using the leather strap, but rather than striking him with the leather end, he struck him with the wooden handle. Upon receiving a gash in the leg as a consequence of the beating, he was taken to the inmate "doctor" who sewed him up without use of anesthetics. He was forced to tell the "doctor" that it felt good after each stitch (Hackler, 1969d).

Still another inmate, Gordon Ray Ross, testified that he had tried to kill a fellow inmate in order to be transferred from Tucker to Cummins. As punishment for this attempt, Bruton ordered that he be "rung up" on the Tucker telephone. Ross testified that two trusties restrained him by taping his hands and legs to a hospital bed. They then attached one wire to his penis and another to his big toe. When signaled to do so by Bruton, one of the trusties, William Morgan, began turning the crank that generated the electricity that ran through the body of Ross. Ross was questioned about the experience.

When asked what it felt like, Ross said, "It feels like your muscles are being torn out of you, with pain throughout the body." He said that Morgan would crank the instrument as long as Ross screamed and would quit only when Ross stopped screaming to gasp for air. Morgan continued this "three or four times," Ross said (Hackler, 1969e).

Trusty inmate William Morgan testified that he had "rung up" Ross and other inmates with the Tucker telephone upon being ordered to do so by Bruton. His description was consistent with that of Ross. Morgan, the inmate "doctor" at Tucker, said he learned how to use the Tucker telephone from a free-world physician, Dr. R.A. Rollins, who used to practice part time in the prison system. Morgan said that Rollins had told him that he had invented the instrument. Morgan testified that the telephone was used on inmates who were not afraid of the leather strap. He further stated that the instrument had never been used to his knowledge without a violation of prison rules and that the instrument left no permanent damage. He said Bruton would have him stop cranking to ask the inmate if he would stop doing whatever it was that brought on the punishment. If Bruton was not "satisfied," the cranking would continue (Hackler, 1969e).

When asked to describe life at Tucker, Morgan gave the following account:

> There were only five paid employees to guard 400 men at Tucker.
> Trusties, the more trustworthy inmates, guarded the prison. The trusties could buy civilian clothes—some even wore alligator shoes—and could eat meat with their meals. "Rank" inmates could not.
> Young inmates were raped by older inmates when they were brought to the penitentiary "unless they were exceptionally tough." Homosexuality was rife. There were frequent fights over who owned a "boy's girl" and men were "stomped and raped" at night in the barracks.

Men worked from dawn until early dusk and got no meat with
their meals.

There was no physician to attend Tucker inmates (Hackler, 1969e).

Morgan also testified that he delivered to Bruton between $10,000 and $12,000
in a 1-year period. The money, which came from inmates and family of inmates,
was passed to Bruton in exchange for a promise of a better job for inmates.
Morgan was told by Bruton that taking care of these transactions would "help
[him] get out of the penitentiary" (Hackler, 1969f).

In his closing arguments, Bruton's attorney, R.A. Eilbott, said that Bruton was
being singled out for practices that had become routine through the years in
Arkansas prisons. Bruton was placed in a very difficult position to operate such
a prison with few free-world employees, no state funding, and the requirement
that the prison generate revenue. Eilbott argued that it was unfair to hold Bruton
responsible for doing this job as others had done it for years (Hackler, 1969g).

Apparently, the jury agreed with the arguments on Bruton's behalf, returning
a verdict of acquittal on nine of the ten counts against Bruton. The jury was
unable to agree on the 10th charge. Robert Fussell, the assistant U.S. attorney who
prosecuted the case, said of the verdict, "I can't comprehend how some people
in this state would condone the use of an instrument like the Tucker Telephone
as punishment when the evidence presented was undisputed to its use" ("Bruton
Freed of 8 Charges," 1969). Bruton subsequently pleaded *nolo contendre* to the
remaining charge and was sentenced to 1 year in prison and a $1,000 fine. Judge
Henley suspended the prison term because he believed that prisoners would kill
Bruton before completing his sentence (Dunn, 1970a).

The Haydis Trial

The U.S. District Court for the Eastern District of Arkansas in late 1969 tried
Gary Haydis for violating the civil rights of inmates over the incident in which
Haydis fired a shotgun into a group of inmates. Twenty-four inmates were injured,
one of whom lost an eye. The incident began as 80 inmates, in October 1968,
refused to go to work in the fields. After talking with the inmates for several hours
regarding inmate grievances, several inmates still refused to move and were fired
upon ("Trial Set for Prison Employee Who Fired Birdshot at Inmates," 1969).

In the trial, argument and testimony were presented on Haydis's behalf, indicating that it was not he who fired directly into the inmates, that a warning shot
was fired, and that his motive for firing and ordering others to do so was to quell a
situation that could have become a prison riot. After hearing the evidence, Judge
Henley directed an acquittal of Haydis. Henley announced that the evidence failed
to show that Haydis had acted with bad purpose or evil intent in his actions.
Although the judge did not think that firing into inmates was appropriate, Haydis
was under duty to "do something" (Francisco, 1969b).

Ironically, within days of this firearms incident being settled in court, a
21-year-old inmate was killed in a shooting incident at Tucker. Jerry Don Houk
died on the way to a hospital after being shot in the stomach with a shotgun held
by a trusty. Robert Sarver said that the 19-year-old trusty "was playing with the

gun, fooling with it" when it discharged, striking Houk, who was described as a good inmate who never caused trouble ("Trusty's Gun Kills Convict at Tucker," 1969). Sarver said that there had been at least four violent deaths in the last 15 months at the prisons and that the system, the legislature, and the public were responsible for these deaths. Sarver said "we would not have had a weapon in the hands of a nineteen-year-old trusty if we had enough money to pay for supervision by people from the free world." In addition to the violent deaths there are "innumerable assaults" ("Trusty's Gun Kills Convict at Tucker," 1969).

Sarver also revealed that liquor and illegal drugs continued to be smuggled into Arkansas prisons. Although he was able to halt some of the trafficking, he reported that it was "still going on." It was quite common for inmates to use amphetamines in the barracks of Cummins and Tucker. A closer watch of inmates in visiting hours was initiated, but still security left much to be desired. The bulk of the security system still was in the hands of the trusty inmates. Sarver commented, "I think a great deal of the evil of our prisons lies with the trusty guard system" ("Sarver Says LSD, Liquor, Other Drugs Smuggled at Prison," 1969).

Holt v. Sarver II

As discussed in the previous chapter, in January of 1970, Jack Holt and Philip Kaplan, Little Rock attorneys appointed by the court to represent interests of the inmates, filed a revised complaint in federal court on behalf of inmates. While the inmates filed specific complaints regarding constitutional issues, Judge Henley indicated that he was interested in broader issues regarding the prison system, including the use of trusty guards. This was the official beginning of *Holt v. Sarver II* and drew the attention of the national news media (Associated Press, 1970a).

The Attorney General's Office asked for dismissal of the case on the grounds that the suit was "against the State of Arkansas" and that relief can be sought only through the state itself, and not through federal courts. Thus they sought to have the suit dismissed on the basis of jurisdiction. The defendants claimed that the lawsuit was an "attempt to coerce the State of Arkansas and the General Assembly to provide additional funds for the operation and maintenance of the state penitentiary" ("Correction Lawyers Ask for Dismissal," 1970). Judge Henley did not dismiss the suit.

Just prior to the hearing of *Holt II*, representatives of both sides of the lawsuit were sharing thoughts and opinions regarding the upcoming hearing with reporters. Attorneys for the inmates speculated that the suit could result in an order to close the prisons or to prohibit further commitments to the prisons until improvements were made. Sarver admitted that the prison system had many problems, not the least of which was its trusty system. "This business of requiring one inmate to carry a weapon is more of a responsibility and a burden than the state has the right to put on any inmate." When called by a reporter for an interview one evening, Sarver and one assistant superintendent were the only free-world employees on duty at Cummins that at that time supervised about 1,300 inmates (Shaw, 1970).

Even in the face of media coverage of the *Holt II* trial the legislature was standing tough in its resistance to providing further prison funding. The legislature informed Commissioner Sarver that funds previously promised for a maximum security unit at Cummins would not be available anytime soon. Although the legislature appropriated money for the new unit, it would only become available in the event of a surplus in the state budget, which did not happen. Funding the state prison continued to be a low priority with legislators ("Appeal Seen for Funds for Prison," 1970). The legislature refused to provide funds to retain state employees hired in recent years to improve the prisons. During 1969, 28 employees were cut from the payroll ("Sarver Displeased With WR's Budget for Special Session," 1970).

Sarver shocked the legislature by expressing the need for more than $3 million from an upcoming special session of the legislature. Sarver said that even that estimate was not sufficient to solve the problems of the prison but "it certainly w[ould] help." During Sarver's appearance before a newly formed committee to investigate prison problems, members of the committee constantly questioned him about the use of trusties at the prisons and why he thought replacing them with free-world people would improve conditions. Sarver reiterated his criticism of the trusty system and told legislators that it would be necessary to hire 226 guards and 28 supervisors to replace the inmate security force at Cummins and Tucker ("Legislators Question Sarver, Schedule Visit to Prison Farms," 1970).

The actual request that went before the special session of the legislature was considerably less than what Sarver had wanted. The governor requested $828,447 in operating funds for the remainder (about 5 months) of the fiscal year, and $1,086,761 for the fiscal year beginning on July 1, 1970. These two requests included about $595,000 for construction. Sarver, in expressing his disappointment, said that this budget would not allow for replacing inmate guards with state employees or for creating a substantial probation and parole program ("Sarver Displeased With WR's Budget for Special Session," 1970).

Members of the committee formed to investigate prisons visited Cummins and reported that conditions were not as bad as one would expect from press accounts. Committee members reported that the barracks and the kitchen were in good shape. Representative Ray Smith of Hot Springs agreed that the prison conditions were not as bad as had been described in testimony before Judge Henley (Douthit, 1970b).

On February 18, 1970, Judge J. Smith Henley announced his decision in *Holt II*. Existing conditions at Cummins and Tucker were declared "cruel and unusual punishment" by the court. The opinion also stated that continuing segregation was unconstitutional. Commissioner Sarver was directed to provide a report by April 1 of plans to remedy the unconstitutional conditions. Henley stopped short of declaring the trusty system unconstitutional, but his opinion showed that many of the unconstitutional conditions followed from abuses and corruption inherent in the trusty system. Henley pointed to the power of the trusties and to the fact that the prisons were simply not in the control of state officials. The opinion was the first time that a prison system in its entirety was ruled to be cruel and unusual punishment (Dunn, 1970b; *Holt v. Sarver II*, 1970).

Initial Response to *Holt II*

Initially, the ruling received both acceptance and praise. Attorney Philip Kaplan, who, along with Jack Holt, represented the inmates, said that the ruling went "even further than we thought it would go." John Haley, chairman of the Board of Corrections, stated that the opinion "points out some conditions that we have maintained all along should be abolished." Commissioner Sarver commented, "This is the first real major step toward prison reform" ("Attorneys Satisfied," 1970). Murton, contacted by phone in Alaska, said that Judge Henley should be commended for having the courage to declare the Arkansas prisons unconstitutional (Douthit, 1970c).

The response from the legislature was not so favorable. Senator Knox Nelson said he was not surprised by the ruling but stated, "It's regrettable that the federal judge didn't appropriate some money to take care of this." According to Nelson, the state did not have "the money or the means to fulfill the dictates of the court." Nelson's suggestion for prison reform was "entering into a contract with some other state or the federal government to take our prisoners and take care of them" ("Attorneys Satisfied," 1970).

Sarver and Attorney General Joe Purcell disagreed about appealing *Holt II*. The Attorney General's Office wanted to appeal the decision. In Purcell's opinion, the federal court "exceeded its power and jurisdiction in detailing specifically the manner in which the state correctional institutions must be administered." He elaborated by stating,

> I recognize that the courts have a right to prohibit unconstitutional acts and practices, but I question the right of a federal court or the federal government to assume the role of supervisor of the internal affairs of a state penal institution by setting out directives to the Board of Correction, the governor and the state legislature on how we must operate the state penitentiaries ("No Appeal Decision," 1970).

Sarver, on the other hand, saw no reason to pursue an appeal. The Legislative Joint Audit Committee unanimously adopted a resolution urging the Attorney General's Office to appeal. Learning of the resolution Sarver responded, "These delaying tactics are not helping the situation a damn bit. We might as well go ahead and face the problem. We've played around with this thing for years and it is time we did something about it" (Associated Press, 1970b). Sarver also contended that an appeal could not take place without his consent since the suit was against him. "I am a lawyer and, as I recall, a lawyer cannot appeal a ruling without the consent of his client" (Associated Press, 1970b).

The Board of Correction was not entirely opposed to appeal, but according to chair of the board, John Haley, "Our board is not willing to do anything that would result in any delay in implementing prison reform. We have been working with the problem for years. We are frustrated and hampered by the lack of funds to implement the program … for years." Sarver said he was willing to risk being held in contempt of court if an appeal was likely to delay prison reform ("No Appeal Decision," 1970).

In discussing proposed new funding for Arkansas prisons, legislators were not reticent to express their views of federal court intervention. The following remarks were made on the Senate floor:

> Senator Robert Harvey of Swifton: "We have this court order and we are under the gun."
>
> Senator Morrell Gaithright of Pine Bluff: "The only damn thing this branch can do is pass the laws and appropriate the money. ... The federal courts have the power—whether it's right or not—they have the power of the U.S. Government—and I don't like it—to make us do what they order."
>
> Senator Carl Sorels of Atkins: "Why not turn it over to Judge Henley and let him enforce it?"
>
> Senator Virgil Fletcher: "I'd like for one time to call the hand of the federal court. I would like to have a showdown and determine if the federal courts are going to take over a state agency."
>
> Senator John F. "Mutt" Gibson of Dermott: "Until we find a constitutional means of discipline, it will cost us a great deal of money to keep those people."
>
> Senator Olan Hendrix of Prescott: "It is a bitter pill to take the money from general revenue, but it is something we have got to do" ("Irate Senators Inveigh Against Federal Ruling on Prisons," 1970).
>
> State Representative Thomas E. Sparks: Asserted that U.S. District Court hearing "was probably staged" ("Fordyce Lawyer Says Hearing on Prisons 'Probably Staged,'" 1970).

In spite of the resistance, the legislature at last began to provide money to change the prisons. In March, 1970, after Judge Henley's ruling but before the state was required to report its reform plan to the court, legislators appropriated about $2.3 million from the states general fund. Thus, it became possible to begin making changes required by the federal court. For many years the only money made available to the prisons was money, often only part of the money, which the prisons themselves generated.

Perhaps much of the motivation for the change of heart regarding legislative funding for prisons was well summarized in the words of State Representative H. Allan Dishongh, who indicated that if the conditions of the court were not satisfied "they [the Board of Correction] will receive unmitigated hell" from Henley. "I'm just sorry," said Dishongh, "that it came down to having a federal judge slap our hands and tell us to get our house in order" (Dunn, 1970c).

Conclusion

Continued pressure from the federal courts and the news media finally had some impact on the state legislature. While this pressure came from both the courts and the media, it is clear that the greater impact was the power of the federal courts to require that the State of Arkansas live up to its constitutional obligations to provide a correctional system that met the minimal standards that are set forth in the Eighth Amendment prohibiting cruel and unusual punishment. The news media could arouse public opinion opposed to the horrors of the Arkansas prison system. However, bad press found itself up against a fiscally tight-fisted legislature that continued to drag its feet on the prospect of spending substantial state funds at Cummins and Tucker. Not until the federal courts stood firm did more meaningful reform gain new traction.

REFERENCES

20 on hand to testify on prisons. (1969, July 9). *Arkansas Democrat*.

Appeal seen for funds for prison. (1970, January 30). *Arkansas Democrat*.

Associated Press. (1969a, September 5). Ex-inmate tells of beating. *Arkansas Democrat*.

Associated Press. (1969b, October 19). *Arkansas Democrat*.

Associated Press. (1970a, January 15). Revised complaint tests trusty system. *Arkansas Democrat*.

Associated Press. (1970b, February 21). Differ over appeal. *Arkansas Democrat*.

Attorneys satisfied. (1970, February 19). *Arkansas Democrat*.

Banner, S. (2002). *The death penalty: An American history*. Harvard University Press.

Bruton freed of 8 charges. (1969, November 22). *Arkansas Democrat*.

Correction lawyers ask for dismisal. (1970, Janurary 9). *Arkansas Democrat*.

Douthit, G. (1969a, June 13). Sarver seeks action on labor shortage. *Arkansas Democrat*.

Douthit, G. (1969b, June 19). Prisoners told they must work. *Arkansas Democrat*.

Douthit, G. (1969c, July 8). Convict, 50, died of heat stroke working at prison, Sarver says. *Arkansas Democrat*.

Douthit, G. (1969d, July 19). Sarver says U.S. court order bars discipline as suggested. *Arkansas Democrat*.

Douthit, G. (1969e, July 27). Pressure up on Sarver. *Arkansas Democrat*.

Douthit, G. (1969f, September 11). Death row bulging with the condemned. *Arkansas Democrat*.

Douthit, G. (1969g, October 14). Debate is enlivened. *Arkansas Democrat*.

Douthit, G. (1969h, December 1). Murton book printed. *Arkansas Democrat*.

Douthit, G. (1970a, Janurary 4). WR hits Murton's new book. *Arkansas Democrat*.

Douthit, G. (1970b, February 7). Turner finds prison scene was distorted. *Arkansas Democrat*.

Douthit, G. (1970c, February 21). Murton lauds judge. *Arkansas Democrat*.

Dunn, M. (1970a, January 16). Bruton pleads 'no contest.' *Arkansas Democrat*.

Dunn, M. (1970b, February 19). Conditions at prisons held illegal. *Arkansas Democrat*.

Dunn. M. (1970c, February 23). Prisons. *Arkansas Democrat*.

Ex-warden acquitted. (1969, October 9). *Arkansas Democrat*.

Fordyce Lawyer Says Hearing on Prisons "Probably Staged." (1970, March 1). *Arkansas Democrat*.

Francisco, M. (1969a, June 29). For women convicts, prison life is grim and dry. *Arkansas Democrat*.

Francsico, M. (1969b, December 18). Acquital of Haydis directed. *Arkansas Democrat*.

Hackler, T. (1969a, October 7). Lashings described. *Arkansas Democrat.*

Hackler, T. (1969b, November 14). Auditing committee is critical of books at Tucker, Cummins. *Arkansas Democrat.*

Hackler, T. (1969c, November 17). Bruton called overseer of sadism. *Arkansas Democrat.*

Hackler, T. (1969d, November 18). Convict vows vengeance on trusties. *Arkansas Democrat.*

Hackler, T. (1969e, November 19). Inmate says he used "Tucker telephone" on Bruton's orders. *Arkansas Democrat.*

Hackler, T. (1969f, November 21). Jury gets the case of Bruton. *Arkansas Democrat.*

Hackler, T. (1969g, November 22). Payments from convicts to get better jobs linked to Bruton. *Arkansas Democrat.*

Haley says prisons still in the red, no solution at hand. (1969, June 11). *Arkansas Democrat.*

Harrison, J. (1969, June 12). Prisoners can't farm and stand guard, too. *Arkansas Democrat.*

He's "burning out," Sarver says in the wake of prison criticism. (1969, July 18). *Arkansas Democrat.*

Holt v. Sarver, 300 F. Supp. 825 (E.D. Ark. 1969)

Holt v. Sarver, 309 F. Supp. 362 (E.D. Ark. 1970)

Holt v. Sarver, 442 F.2d 304 (8th Cir. 1971)

Irate senators inveigh against federal ruling on prisons. (1970, March 4). *Arkansas Democrat.*

Leasing Cummines farmland urged. (1969, September 1). *Arkansas Democrat.*

Legislators question Sarver. Schedule visit to prison farms. (1970, January 31). *Arkansas Democrat.*

McIntyre, C. (1969, September 18). "Tucker telephone" used at Cummins, inmate says. *Arkansas Democrat.*

Murton says he found prisons bad. (1969, October 18). *Arkansas Democrat.*

Murton, T. (1970). Too good for Arkansas: One year of prison reform. *The Nation, 210*(1), 12, 17.

No appeal decision. (1970, February 24). *Arkansas Democrat.*

Prisoner at Cummins "shoeless." (1969, October 20). *Arkansas Democrat.*

Sarver and attorney general to study prison-lease details. (1969, September 4). *Arkansas Democrat.*

Six file toilet-paper petition. (1969, October 3). *Arkansas Democrat.*

Sarver says prison panel opposes self. (1969, July 17). *Arkansas Democrat.*

Sarver says LSD, liquor, other drugs smuggled at prison. (1969, December 26). *Arkansas Democrat.*

Sarver displeased with WR's budget for special session. (1970, February 6). *Arkansas Democrat.*

Shaw, R. (1970, January 25). Hearing could close prisons. *Arkansas Democrat.*

Slapped rather hard, Sarver says of ruling. (1969, June 21). *Arkansas Democrat.*

State v. Bruton et al., 246 Ark. 293 (1969)

Steinmetz, T. (1969a, June 21). State told to better prison conditions. *Arkansas Democrat.*

Steinmetz, T. (1969b, July 8). Grand jury begins its prison inquiry as Henley presides. *Arkansas Democrat.*

Trial set for prison employee who fired birdshot at inmates. (1969, December 14). *Arkansas Democrat.*

Trusty's gun kills convict at Tucker. (1969, December 20). *Arkansas Democrat.*

CASES CITED

Holt v. Sarver, 300 F. Supp. 825 (E.D. Ark. 1969)
Holt v. Sarver, 309 F. Supp. 362 (E.D. Ark. 1970)
Holt v. Sarver, 442 F.2d 304 (8th Cir. 1971)
State v. Bruton et al., 246 Ark. 293 (1969)

KEY TERMS

Ernest Fletcher

Farm income

Federal grand jury

Gary Haydis

News media

Prison crowding

R.A. Eilbott

QUESTIONS

1. Sarver questioned whether prison reform was on the legislative agenda for Arkansas. What do you think was the original objective of the Arkansas prison system? How would reforming these prisons affect that objective?

2. R.A. Eilbott, the attorney of former assistant superintendent Jim Bruton, claimed there were five state employees overseeing the prison; therefore, in order to keep order and continuous farm profit, the use of force was required. What is your opinion on this statement? Do think hiring more state employees would have alleviated the necessity for excessive use of force? Why or why not?

3. Inmates lived in fear of being beaten, sexually abused, and of death. How did the prison facilitate this systematic use of fear to encourage corruption?

4. How did federal courts and news media impact the decision of state legislature to provide funding for the prison?

5. Which amendment do you think was most associated with the constitutional obligation to provide a correctional system that met the minimum standards of living in prisons? Why?

8 | State Response to Holt Rulings

Introduction

The State of Arkansas had faced public scandal and scorn following the Arkansas State Police investigation into conditions exposed at Tucker and the Bodiesburg fiasco at Cummins. The hiring of Thomas Murton marked the commencement of initial steps at reform. The *Holt* cases were instrumental in breaking the inertia of hidebound views of the role and responsibility of the state in prison operation and management in Arkansas. The entire prison system was found by U.S. District Judge J. Smith Henley to be a violation of the Eighth Amendment prohibition against cruel and unusual punishment. Yet, the legislature still seemed reluctant to fully recognize their position.

Denial and Irritation

During the months following the *Holt* rulings, the general reaction of many state officials to the federal court's involvement was denial and accusation. Legislators seemed upset that the authority for prisons had shifted to an arena over which they had no control. Having a federal judge tell them what to do with the prison system did not sit well with the senators and representatives. For decades most legislators expected the prisons to take care of themselves and were not enthusiastic about having to consider a series of bills designed to reform practices, which many saw little reason to reform. Being expected to generate financial support for this repository for convicted criminals was more than a small irritation to the members of the legislative bodies. Speculating on motives and casting blame were not uncommon reactions ("Prison Bills Are Approved in the Senate," 1970; "Sparks Draws Curt Reaction From Lawyers," 1970; Smith, 1970; "Sarver Will Seek Funds to Employ 83 More Persons," 1970; Smith, 1970d).

There was also consternation in the executive branch. Attorney General Joe Purcell and the state Board of Corrections continued to be at odds regarding whether to appeal the federal court decision. Purcell maintained that an appeal should be filed for purely legal reasons rather than as a challenge to the concept of prison reform. Sarver questioned the need for an appeal since the Corrections Board agreed with the court's decision. Sarver did not interpret the court ruling to mean that Judge Henley was seeking to run the prison system, as some had charged. The ruling, claimed Sarver, simply required that the state make changes, leaving the substance of those changes to the state (Smith, 1970a).

Attorney General Purcell at first took the position that he would not appeal unless the Corrections Board approved. Urged by a legislative joint auditing committee resolution and a resolution of the full senate, the board left the decision to appeal up to the attorney general's discretion. Purcell decided to appeal in order to resolve questions of federal-state relations. The key issue he wanted to address was to what extent the federal judiciary could regulate the day-to-day operations of a state prison system ("Purcell to Appeal Order Reform Arkansas Prisons," 1970; Smith 1970c).

Funding Reforms

Policymakers were far from enthusiastic but began to explore the necessity of providing additional funds for the prison system. Corrections officials told the legislative Joint Budget Committee that a minimum of $3.1 million was needed in the remainder of the biennium for prison improvement. This sounded too high to committee members who agreed to work with the Department of Corrections to reduce the budget requests to the $2.3 million supplemental appropriation recommended by the Legislative Council. Commissioner Sarver did not agree with the committee claiming that the $3.1 million budget was a "bare-bones" proposal already trimmed down from $4.1 million. According to Sarver, the $3.1 million would not even replace all of the trusty guards ("$3.1 Million Floor Asked For Prison Use," 1970).

Commissioner Sarver's budget request included a controversial work-release program. Work-release would permit selected inmates to work for pay at regular jobs outside the prison. Such a program could, according to Sarver, teach the inmates responsibility. Sarver's budget request also included provision to pay prisoners in jobs with high responsibility on the prison farm. The maximum pay was to be $.20 per hour ("Work-Release Prison Plan Explained to House Members," 1970). The federal minimum wage in 1970 was $1.45 (U.S. Department of Labor, n.d.). Neither the work-release program nor inmate pay was approved by the legislature (Smith, 1970d).

The legislature did pass bills to appropriate additional funds for the prisons. These bills provided $2.3 million for salaries and maintenance of the Corrections Department. Much of this was to hire 246 new employees, most of whom would serve as guards to replace trusty guards. The legislation also funded $350,000 for capital improvements, including construction of a new maximum security unit at Cummins, and $450,000 for farm mechanization and equipment replacement (Associated Press, 1970a; "Prison Bills are Approved in the Senate," 1970).

Thus, under pressure of the federal courts, additional funds were made available to the prisons. A report to Judge Henley indicated that funds from the legislative session made it possible to begin making improvements required by the federal court. For the fiscal year, beginning July 1970, about $1 million more would be provided for prison operation than had been available in the previous two fiscal years (Associated Press, 1970b).

The Arkansas legislature was unhappy with the exercise of power by the federal court, but when it came down to the issue of whether the requirements of the court would prevail, the legislature blinked. When it became known that Judge Henley intended to close the prisons should the state refuse to make changes, one legislator probably spoke for many in saying, "Let him. Then we will have a bigger mess than we have now" (Douthit, 1970b). The question was what would happen with the inmates if the prisons were closed. Apparently, the judge planned to send all inmates back to the county jails. Rather than face this unworkable prospect, legislators opted to approve financing to begin required reforms (Douthit, 1970b).

Additional funds were also made available through federal grants to assist with reform efforts. The U.S. Justice Department approved a $61,096 grant to complete the maximum security unit at Cummins. The U.S. Department of Labor granted $282,000 to help train 100 new prison employees ("Aid Seen in Prison Training," 1970; "Fire Sarver, Brothers Urge; Board Refuses," 1970).

Sarver the Reformer Versus the Legislature

Robert Sarver, as commissioner of corrections, was on center stage during this period of dramatic change in the prisons. Often he was seen as disloyal or bothersome by legislators because he seemed to be, and clearly was, as much interested in bringing about change as the federal court. His testimony in the *Holt* cases and his subsequent lack of interest in appealing the rulings contributed to legislators' growing displeasure with Sarver.

Sarver added to the tension between himself and the legislature by suggesting challenges to Arkansas laws (Arkansas Statutes Annotated § 46-804) that permitted women to be sentenced to prison for up to 3 years for drunkenness or drug addiction without having ever committed a felony. Sarver, himself an attorney, called such laws patently unconstitutional, if for no other reason than being discriminatory since men were not sent to prison for the same offenses. According to Sarver, women were the most neglected of all prison inmates in the Arkansas system ("Someone Should Challenge Laws to Imprison Women, Sarver Tells Club Group," 1970). This provision of the law was later revised so as to limit incarceration of females in the Arkansas Department to those convicted of felonies (Arkansas Code Annotated § 16-90-104).

Sarver's general approach to prison philosophy and operation continued to emphasize efforts to change inmates in a positive manner so that they could return to society more inclined to take care of themselves and less inclined to return to crime. Sarver believed that Arkansas could develop some of the best prisons in the country. The heart of Sarver's approach was to provide a setting where persons could learn responsibility, self-esteem, self-confidence, and self-control. "If you never give him any responsibility and just lock him up, then he's never going to learn" (Someone Should Challenge Laws to Imprison Women, Sarver Tells Club Group," 1970).

To promote his approach to dealing with inmates Sarver implemented an honor barracks for inmates who performed their duties satisfactorily and stayed out of trouble. He recognized the need for maximum security for some inmates but also wanted to provide alternatives to traditional imprisonment at Cummins and Tucker. He proposed community treatment centers and forestry camps and called for improved efforts to separate dangerous inmates from non-dangerous ones (Jordan, 1970).

An example of Sarver's becoming the center of controversy came in July 1970 when a meeting of the legislative committee on correctional institutions turned into a prolonged attack of Sarver. Sarver was criticized for approving an emergency furlough for an inmate to visit a sick child. Apparently, there was no sick child, the inmate did not return to the prison, and he committed another offense. Sarver admitted that he had made an error and had been "conned." Family members of the victim of the furloughed inmate called for Sarver's termination. Criticism then became more generalized regarding Sarver's approach to corrections and his ability to run the prisons. Criticisms were expressed regarding parole decisions being too lenient. One senator criticized the prison administration stating that in spite of increased expenditures on the prisons that there were more escapes, less work by inmates, and "more unrest and confusion in the operation of the prison than ever before." Another senator commenting on the prison situation told Sarver, "We're going to do something about it if you don't straighten out this mess" (Dumas, 1970).

Second Judicial Circuit Prosecuting Attorney Gerald Pearson criticized Sarver's administration. Pearson charged that forces of "extreme liberalism" were in control of the prisons, expressing particular concern regarding parole and furlough policies and the number of escapes. Sarver responded that escaping the prison was difficult to control and did not require "any ingenuity" since there were no fences or walls. Such escapes, he pointed out, were related to changes in progress, particularly the dismantling of the trusty system ("Prison Laxity Charged," 1970).

The prison system with regularity provided problems for Sarver and his staff to solve. One change that had to be addressed was how to respond to inmates who refused to work. In the past, use of the strap or other violent sanctions for refusal to work were routinely employed. Without violence, other techniques had to be developed. In the spring and summer of 1970, inmates who refused work were confined to a baseball field. Inmates remained there day and night unless it rained. An inmate petition to the federal court claimed that 35 inmates were left on the baseball field from May 14 to June 30. Sarver defended the practice: "It's a lot easier on Jackson than the men who are behaving themselves and are out in the hot sun and working all day" (Associated Press, 1970c).

Judge Henley reviewed the petition and denied relief, although he agreed to continue scrutiny of this and other prison practices as part of major litigation involving the Arkansas prisons ("Henley Indicates New Penal Scrutiny," 1970). Later federal Judge Oren Harris ruled that keeping inmates on the ball field for long periods was unconstitutional. He said that the practice was "inhumane" and that inmates should not be subjected to such treatment ("Ball Field Cruel,"

1970). Sarver was frustrated by the ruling, stating that "if prisoners refused to work and got away with it, [they] will have to give up on being self supporting [*sic*]." Sarver continued, "What the hell are we going to do now?" He pointed out that if one inmate refuses to work and is supported in any way, it encourages all other inmates to do the same (Douthit, 1970b).

Sarver the Voluntary Hostage

Another incident that seized Commissioner Sarver's undivided attention began in November 1970. About 17 inmates at Cummins held two free-world guards and two trusties hostage, threatening to kill them if their demands were not met. The Cummins Superintendent, Bill Steed, and Sarver exchanged themselves for two of the hostages. The initial demands were for a car and clearance past the main gate. The inmates, who were housed in the isolation unit at Cummins, armed themselves with weapons taken from guards. The hostages were obviously shaken and feared for their lives ("Inmates Hold Four Hostages at Cummins," 1970; Kirby, 1970; Smith, 1970e).

After 12 hours of negotiation with Sarver and Steed, the inmates ended the rebellion. Sarver reported that as soon as the inmates realized that their demand for transportation and clearance to leave the prison were not to be met, their complaints centered on prison conditions, including lack of clothing, sanitation, and eating utensils, as well as the frequency of the prison searches: "They are living in an unconstitutional system; they know that." No deals were made with the inmates (Kirby, 1970).

The Legislative Council called for a state police investigation of the incident, expressing interest in the punishment of those involved and concern about preventing such incidents (Parsons, 1970). This action angered Sarver who responded that he had little tolerance for "Monday-morning quarterbacking by an uninformed handful of Old Guard politicians." Most legislators, said Sarver, were genuinely concerned about prison problems and wanted to help, but some of the "Old Guard" insisted on interfering with the day-to-day operations. "We have virtually begged them [legislators] to provide funds to prevent placing our people in jeopardy. Except as required by federal court they have been unresponsive" ("Sarver Is Irked," 1970).

Sarver Goes on National TV

The tension increased between Sarver and the state legislature. Sarver was of the opinion that the legislature had not fulfilled its responsibilities in supporting Arkansas prison reform. In an appearance on the *Dick Cavett Show*, Sarver blamed much of the current problems in Arkansas prisons on lack of adequate funding by the legislature. Legislators were none too pleased to be accused on national television or to be labeled as Old Guard. Many were of the opinion that the continuing prison troubles lay not so much in funding as in management of existing resources. Legislators pointed to increased funding as evidence of legislative concern. Some were becoming more explicit in their criticism of Sarver.

State Senator Virgil Fletcher of Benton commented, "I just don't think he will get a salary next biennium. ... I just don't think the people of Arkansas will want to continue paying him to go around and give lectures about how poor Arkansas' system is. I think they've got a gut-full of him. I know I have" (Parsons, 1970c).

The conflict escalated as one legislator asked all members of the Board of Corrections to resign to allow Governor Bumpers the opportunity to appoint his own board. Members of the board indicated they were not inclined to resign ("En Masse Resigning is Sought," 1970). Sarver fired back at some members of the legislature for "meddling" in the affairs of the executive branch of the government. He called for an attorney general's opinion on whether the General Assembly or the Legislative Council could order or request the state police to investigate another department. Sarver said that some members of the legislature were more interested in personal politics than in the interests of the state and were not concerned for the lives of the people in institutions. "I have tried to get along with the legislature, and I think I do with the majority of them," said Sarver. However, he commented, "If the state ever gets a weak man in this post and a lily-livered board, we will be back where we were in 1965" ("Sarver Hits 'Meddling' of State Legislators," 1970).

Racial Unrest at Cummins

In the midst of this posturing and bickering between Sarver and the legislature, another incident at Cummins erupted. On November 20, 1970, fights broke out between Black and White inmates. At first the incident was limited to fistfights between a few inmates, but the fighting rapidly spread to other inmates who were arming themselves with anything they could find. Sarver described the situation as "extremely volatile and reaching riotous proportions." Black inmates were confined to the auditorium while Whites were held in the gymnasium ("Fight Breaks Out at Cummins; 'Black vs. White,' Sarver Says," 1970; "Guard Is Alerted on Prison," 1970; "Prison is Quiet as Convicts go Back to Work," 1970).

Both Whites and Blacks were demanding a return to segregation. Desegregation, initiated at Cummins the previous April, had been in effect only a few months. Sarver pointed out that the state was under court order to provide integrated facilities and that it was impossible to re-segregate work and living arrangements ("Guard Is Altered on Prison," 1970).

When fighting continued the next day, 100 heavily armed state troopers entered Cummins, and National Guard units were placed on alert. Persons identified as leaders of both Black and White inmates were separated from other prisoners. By Sunday, November 22, 1970, inmates were returned to their barracks. The disturbance was over, and State Troopers were withdrawn ("Fight Breaks Out at Cummins; 'Black vs. White,' Sarver Says," 1970; "Guard is Alerted on Prison," 1970; "Prison is Quiet as Convicts go Back to Work," 1970).

In his next appearance before the Corrections Board, Sarver waved an olive branch to the legislature and other state agencies. He apologized for his remarks about Old Guard members of the legislature "meddling" and "Monday morning quarterbacking" in the affairs of the prison system. He described his comments as inflammatory and a product of his frustration. He expressed hope that differences could be resolved so that prison reform could continue. He also expressed appreciation for the state police for assistance in dealing with the potentially explosive circumstances resulting from conflict between Black and White inmates (Parsons, 1970c, d, and e).

Phase Out of Trusty System

In addition to having difficulties adjusting to desegregation, the inmates simultaneously had to adjust to the phasing out of the trusty system. Although segregated facilities and the trusty system were judged to be lacking and were being replaced, both were institutionalized arrangements to which inmates had been accustomed for many years. Such changes, according to Sarver, had an impact that few could appreciate ("Armed State Police Move Into Prison as Fighting Flares," 1970).

The phase out of trusty status at Tucker began by abolishing the old inmate categories and their accompanying reward structure. The old three-tier categorization of rank men, do-pops, and trusty distinguished inmates not only by status but also by good time provision (reduction of sentence for good behavior) and other privileges. Rank men had been allowed only 5 days of good time per month while meritorious good time, better jobs, and other privileges were reserved for do-pops (sometimes called half-trusty) and trusties. Under the new

FIGURE 8.1. Armed inmate trusty guards, like those shown in this photo from 1971, were still in use despite federal court orders to phase out this practice in *Holt v. Sarver II* (1970). The inmates wore a different color to indicate their rank in the hierarchy, with trusty armed guards wearing khaki. The armed trusty guards were not eliminated from field supervision until 1972, as will be discussed in Chapter 9.

system all inmates were eligible to earn up to 13 days of good time each month (Parsons, 1970a).

This change did not mean that the state no longer used inmate guards. It simply meant that such jobs no longer carried the status and privilege that had so long accompanied them. Instead of being called trusties, the inmates who guarded others were called "security personnel." The changes also meant that fewer inmates were armed. Inmates found these changes confusing. Some who had been trusties saw no reason to accept the responsibility of guarding others if the privileges were removed. One inmate pointed out to the Tucker superintendent that it made no sense to carry the gun if he did not get anything for it (Parsons, 1970a).

Inmate responses to the unfolding events in Arkansas prisons varied considerably. Trusties who had enjoyed privileges that were suddenly being taken away were understandably threatened and were upset by losing the protection that higher status and weapons afforded them. Some were so threatened and fearful that they escaped. Others became hopeful that reforms would improve their circumstances. Still others remained cynical that nothing was changing or would change. One inmate, in a letter to the editor of a state newspaper, wrote that "things seem to be getting worse instead of better here at Cummins Prison" ("Mr. Sarver's Funny Farm," 1970).

There was no question that the inmates were aware of the action of the federal courts. In a few cases they legally tested the implications of Judge Henley's ruling. Shortly after announcement of *Holt*, inmates challenged being sent to an "unconstitutionally controlled and operated prison." One inmate who was given 8 years for robbery described the sentence as "a probable death sentence." Judge Henley was not moved by such pleas, indicating that while unconstitutionalities must be corrected, this did not forbid Arkansas from accepting new prisoners, nor did it require the release of current prisoners ("Prison Edict Fails as Grounds to Free 2 Cummins Convicts," 1970).

Rehabilitation Programs

Policymakers also gave attention to program expansion and change for inmates. Dr. Payton Kolb, secretary of the state Board of Correction, called for rehabilitative programs, training programs, and treatment programs. He recognized that such programs were not politically popular, but refusing to establish rehabilitative programs would doom Arkansas prisons to continue as little other than "crime colleges." He cited 40% to 50% of the inmates returning to state prisons as an indication of the need for teaching inmates new life skills. "We seem to get the idea that if a man is not working in the fields twelve to thirteen hours a day picking cotton in 103 temperature, he's not working." According to Kolb, an inmate who completes his sentence at Cummins or Tucker has little on which to draw for life survival other than his crime skills ("Prisons Are Called 'Crime Colleges,'" 1970).

There was more talk than action in regard to starting such rehabilitative programs. Little if any of the funding made available after the federal court rulings was dedicated to establishing or augmenting rehabilitation efforts. Indeed, virtually all funding that was available for new programming came from sources outside of prison budgets. The State Board of Education, for example, voted in March of 1970 to spend more than $200,000 to start a vocational education program for the state prison inmates ("Job Project for Inmates Established," 1970).

Another example of the development of a rehabilitative project came from the private sector. Several businesspersons, including Senator Oscar Alagood of Little Rock, developed the idea of a private corporation, Operation Useful Training, Inc., which would operate industries on site at prisons for the purpose of training inmates in legitimate occupations. Inmates were to be paid for their work while profits from the industries would revert back to the prison system. The major objective was to encourage and train inmates to continue working in similar occupations following their release from prison. This is also an example of a promising idea that never got much further than the early planning stage. Few inmates ever participated in the kinds of industrial programs envisioned by those who formed this corporation ("Job Project for Inmates Established," 1970).

Report to the Court

Meanwhile, the state of Arkansas was preparing its response to the federal court regarding unconstitutionalities. Judge Henley asked for a report from the state by April 1, 1970, to outline the plan to address deficiencies identified in the court's landmark February ruling (Douthit, 1970b). The state was required to develop specific plans to correct the general objections of unconstitutionally raised in the case. Thus, the court refused to accept responsibility for running the system for the state, but instead reserved the right to review changes and to reject any plans that did not meet criteria set by the court.

The state Board of Correction, in its initial report to Judge Henley, indicated that sufficient funds had been secured to remove major responsibilities for running prisons from trusty inmates and to assign them to state employees. According to the report, the Department of Corrections in the next fiscal year was planning to hire "sufficient personnel to place all critical areas in the hands of staff." While this would not completely replace the trusty system, it would double the current number of 86 free-world staff, giving priority replacing to the functional areas as control of records, medical and food services, job assignments, and key security positions (Associated Press, 1970b).

The court had expressed special concern regarding the living conditions and supervision of inmates. In his *Holt II* (1970) opinion Judge Henley stated trusties must "be stripped of their authority over the lives and living conditions of other convicts" (p. 384). The report described the plan of the state to hire persons to assure the safety, security, and control of inmates: "The Department considers constant free-world supervision over the barracks area a matter of immediate urgency." The report outlined plans to segregate high-risk inmates from others, temporarily in a separate barracks and subsequently in a maximum security unit under construction (Associated Press, 1970a).

Judge Henley accepted most of the Corrections Department's report, stating it showed "a prompt and reasonable start ... toward eliminating the unconstitutional conditions." Likewise, the judge expressed appreciation of the state's efforts to provide funding for prison reforms. However, the judge was less than pleased in one regard: The report indicated that the additional security personnel would be hired and in place by July 1, 1970. Judge Henley said the department must move more swiftly to ensure the safety of inmates, particularly from assaults in the barracks and adjoining areas. "It is small comfort to a barracks inmate," said the judge, "to know that he may expect to be safe sometime after July 1 if that safety depends on his being able to live that long" ("Prison Assaults Must Be Curbed, Judge Henley Says," 1970).

The judge asked for additional interim report on May 10 and July 10 ("Judge Henley Asks a Further Report on Prison Remedies," 1970; "Prison Plan Leaves Henley Dissatisfied," 1970). His response to the May report was that the Department of Corrections still has "considerable distance to go" before reaching constitutional tolerability. The court recognized that this was a period of transition but found through continuing inmate complaints that much change was still required ("Prison Plan Leaves Henley Dissatisfied," 1970).

The Trusty System Clings to Existence

In the July interim report the department reported that free-world employees had replaced trusties in key positions at Cummins and Tucker. At Cummins security persons had been hired to replace trusty guards at the main gate; in the barracks, non-inmate clerical workers for the first became available to manage prison records, including inmate records. Free-world employees also were placed in charge of the infirmary. Similar changes were instituted at Tucker (Garrison, 1970a).

The trusty system, however, was neither quickly nor causally dismissed. While new employees began to take over responsibilities previously held by trusties, officials reported in the summer of 1970 that trusty inmates were still depended on for major tasks, including work supervision of rank inmates and for prison security. Armed inmates still manned security towers and still occupied many of the guard positions within the prison compound (Garrison, 1970a).

On another aspect of the legal battles over Arkansas prisons, the Arkansas Attorney General Joe Purcell filed an appeal of the *Holt II* decision with the 8th U.S. Circuit Court of Appeals. The 8th Circuit affirmed Judge Henley's ruling that the Arkansas prison system as a whole amounted to cruel and unusual punishment in violation of the Eighth Amendment. The court noted that Arkansas officials were making progress, as evidenced by the periodic status reports filed with Judge Henley. It was observed that it would take some reasonable amount of time in order to revamp a practice such as the trusty system. Funds must be legislatively appropriated, new buildings constructed, and free-world guards hired and trained. The case was remanded to the trial court to continue its supervision and require such additional hearings and reports as deemed necessary (*Holt v. Sarver*, 1971). It would be more than 10 years before the federal courts released the State of Arkansas from supervision.

Governor Dale Bumpers and Prisons

The legislature postured with Governor-elect Bumpers regarding prison budgets prior to his actually taking office. The governor-elect asked for a prison operation budget of about $2.5 million for both fiscal years 1971–1972 and 1972–1973. The legislature talked of providing far less, but in negotiations Bumpers's budget, although reduced to about $2.2 million for each of the 2 fiscal years, ultimately prevailed (Parsons, 1971a). Additionally, the Corrections Board asked the legislature for $2.8 million in capital improvement funds to construct five new facilities, including a new women's facility (Parsons, 1971b).

The legislature was interested in working with the new governor on prison matters but remained skeptical regarding his approach to corrections. In the Senate Penitentiary Committee, Senator Carl Sorrels pointedly asked a colleague about Bumpers's correctional philosophy, whether "his thinking [wa]s in line with [thei]rs" ("Work-Pay Projects for Prisons Meets Senate Opposition," 1971). In response, one legislator told Sorrels that the governor was interested in taking control of the prisons and was trying to "listen to all sides" on the matter ("Work-Pay Project for Prisons Meets Senate Opposition," 1971).

Not only did legislators want to test the new administration regarding its intentions for the prisons, many were interested in raising the issue of retaining Sarver as the commissioner of prisons. Questions were raised regarding Sarver's input into budget requests (Parsons, 1971). The budget initially included controversial items such as community treatment centers, work-release programs, pay for selected inmates, and programs aimed at youthful offenders, items Sarver had promoted in the past ("Bumpers Gets Prison Plan," 1971).

Sarver Versus the Legislature

Thus began another round of tug of war between the administration and the legislature regarding support for prisons. In debate before the state House regarding pending prison budget appropriations, lack of confidence in the current prison leadership was expressed. To shouts of approval and applause Representative John Bethell called for a shake-up in prison leadership, asking that the Bumpers Administration fire those whom they couldn't trust in the prison system. Regarding such terminations Bethell continued by stating that if such terminations did not take place, "they should hold up the appropriations until they do put somebody out there [they] can trust" (Parsons, 1971b).

These threats against unnamed and untrusted persons in charge of the prisons became very explicit in late November 1971 as a petition circulated in the state House calling for Sarver to be fired or to resign. Should that not take place, according to the petition, the House would not be supportive of tax measures designed to provide funding for the prisons. Representative James Cole, one of the representatives circulating the petition, said he was not mad at Sarver but "the practical politics of it is that the people in the area [he] represent favor prison reform, but they have lost confidence in Sarver doing the job." Cole told newsmen that he had more than the required majority of the House support to pass the resolution calling for Sarver's termination ("Petition in House Seeks to Displace Sarver From Post," 1971).

Sarver first responded with a statement that he had no intention of resigning: "I was hired to do a job here, I'm doing it to the best of my ability, and I intend to continue doing it." Sarver continued, "I'm going on the assumption that the board's going to stay solid, and we'll just go right on." The position of commissioner of corrections was at the pleasure of the Board of Corrections and was not subject to termination by the governor ("Petition in House Seeks to Displace Sarver From Post," 1971).

Governor Bumpers objected to hiring and firing pressure from legislative resolutions. He maintained that newly developed state government reorganization was formulated to deal with just such matters and should be allowed to do so. One legislator, John Bethell of Des Arc, introduced a resolution to the House pointing out to the governor that the legislature did have an interest and authority in the matter of Sarver's tenure as superintendent based on the principle of checks and balances (Parsons, 1971c).

A few days after his initial response, Sarver offered to resign at the end of the legislative session if the legislature would approve the governor's prison reform program. In his statement Sarver recalled a remark that the Arkansas prison system "was a quagmire that sucks in and destroys people," a fact commonly known to prison administrators in the United States. He stated that his major regret in his tenure as commissioner of corrections was the inability to change the national image of the Arkansas prison system. Nevertheless, Sarver indicated that the state would be able to replace him with little trouble (Parsons, 1971c).

An editorial in the *Arkansas Democrat* congratulated Sarver for having "trumped the House's ace." The editorial pointed out that Sarver had made a skillful political move by using the legislature's keen interest in having him removed as superintendent to advance Arkansas prison reform. Sarver outdid the representatives at their own game when he said he would resign if the legislature would approve all Bumpers requested for the prisons, plus a million dollars for a new women's reformatory. Sarver indicated that he, unlike many politicians, was more concerned about the improvement of the prisons than he was about his personal ambition (McCord, 1971).

However, the legislature was not so easily out maneuvered. The consideration of appropriations continued to be influenced by the matter of Sarver's continuing as superintendent. When the appropriation was brought before the state Senate, senators took the floor to criticize Sarver in speeches described as "enraged." Sarver was described as a smooth-talking, unreasonable person who had harmed rather than helped the Arkansas prisons. He was accused of being a bad administrator and manager, as well as being incapable of successfully overseeing the farming operations. Some accused him of having staged the November 2, 1970, hostage incident at the prison for political purposes and as a "heroism stunt" ("Senators Blister Sarver, Refuse Funds for Prisons," 1971).

Sarver's Exit

As pressure to get rid of Sarver expanded, it became apparent that neither the governor nor the Board of Corrections intended to make heroic efforts to keep Sarver as superintendent. Too much was at stake. The legislature seemed intent on withholding prison funding depending on Sarver's removal. They wanted Sarver's resignation or termination before approving funding. Without funding approval, both the operation of the prisons and the relationship to the federal courts were jeopardized ("Pressure on Sarver Growing," 1971).

On March 29, 1971, the Board of Corrections met and announced their decision to fire Robert Sarver. Board Chairman John Haley made no secret of the fact that the immediate reason for the termination was the personality conflict between Sarver and the legislature that was hindering the Corrections Department's state appropriation. Governor Bumpers announced that he had asked the board to fire Sarver. According to Bumpers it was a difficult decision, but Sarver, in the governor's view, had lost his "effectiveness" (Kotok, 1971).

Conclusion

Thus, another prison reformer in Arkansas was ejected from the Corrections Department's chief administrative position. At one level the removal of Sarver, like that of Murton, could be understood as a product of personality conflict, political bickering, administrative style, or of competence. At a deeper level Sarver's firing was a consequence of his accepting responsibility for uprooting a firmly entrenched cultural tradition. Many Arkansans, particularly legislators, did not like being told by a federal judge or by Robert Sarver that their prisons had to change. There was little they could do to express their outrage to the federal judge, but Commissioner Sarver was another matter.

REFERENCES

$3.1 Million floor asked for prison use. (1970, March 3). *Arkansas Gazette.*

Aid seen in prison training. (1970, July 7). *Arkansas Democrat.*

Armed state police move into prison as fighting flares: Prisoners now locked in barracks. (1970, November 22). *Arkansas Gazette.*

Associated Press. (1970a, April 1). Prison document submitted. *Arkansas Democrat.*

Associated Press. (1970b, April 1). Trusties in critical jobs to be replaced at prisons, report from Henley asserts.

Associated Press. (1970c, July 12). Inmate who won't work lives on baseball field. *Arkansas Gazette.*

Ball field cruel: Harris orders Cummins to quit punishment of prisoner. (1970, July 24). *Arkansas Democrat.*

Bumpers gets prison plan. (1971, January 27). *Arkansas Democrat.*

Douthit, G. (1970a, January 4). WR hits Murton's new book. *Arkansas Democrat.*

Douthit, G. (1970b, March 15). Federal judge in prison case help whip hand. *Arkansas Democrat.*

Dumas, E. (1970, July 17). *Arkansas Gazette.*

Lawmakers blast Sarver; Firing demand is repeated. *Arkansas Gazette.*

En masse resigning is sought. (1970, November 20). *Arkansas Democrat.*

Fight breaks out at Cummins; "Black vs. White," Sarver says. (1970, November 21). *Arkansas Democrat.*

Fire Sarver, brothers urge; board refuses. (1970, July 9). *Arkansas Gazette.*

Garrison, J. (1970a, July 11). Key jobs filled by paid workers, prisons report. *Arkansas Gazette.*

Garrison, J. (1970b, August 6). 3 Inmates tell Judge Henley of supervisor selling vodka. *Arkansas Gazette.*

Guard is altered on prison. (1970, November 22). *Arkansas Democrat.*

Henley indicates new penal scrutiny. (1970, July 13). *Arkansas Democrat.*

Holt v. Sarver II, 309 F. Supp. 362 (E.D. Ark. 1970)

Holt v. Sarver, 442 F.2d 304 (8th Cir. 1971)

Inmates hold four hostages at Cummins. (1970, November 2). *Arkansas Democrat.*

Job project for inmates established. (1970, March 27). *Arkansas Democrat.*

Jordan, W. (1970, June 14). Delegating responsibility improves prisons, Sarver says. *Arkansas Gazette.*

Judge Henley asks a further report on prison remedies. (1970, April 15). *Arkansas Democrat.*

Kirby, M. (1970, November 3). Prison rebellion ends. *Arkansas Democrat.*

Kotok, D. (1971, March 30). Sarver out as director of prisons. *Arkansas Democrat.*

McCord, R. (1971, March 1). Sarver's trump. *Arkansas Democrat.*

"Mr. Sarver's funny farm." (1970, September 30). *Arkansas Democrat.*

Parsons, T. (1970a, October 15). No privileges for guards. *Arkansas Democrat.*

Parsons, T. (1970b, November 18). Prison inquiry ordered. *Arkansas Democrat.*

Parsons, T. (1970c, November 19). 'Monday morning quarterbacks.' *Arkansas Democrat.*

Parsons, T. (1970d, November 25). Sarver regrets reply to council as inflammatory. *Arkansas Democrat.*

Parsons, T. (1970e, November 26). State Police prison performance praised. *Arkansas Democrat.*

Parsons, T. (1971a, January 6). Bumpers' budget prevails. *Arkansas Democrat.*

Parsons, T. (1971b, January 10). $2.8 million for prisons. *Arkansas Democrat.*

Parsons, T. (1971c, February 23). House defeats emergency fund for state prisons. *Arkansas Democrat.*

Parsons, T. (1971d, February 26). Sarver says he'd resign job if money for prisons voted. *Arkansas Democrat.*

Petition in House seeks to displace Sarver from post. (1971, February 24). *Arkansas Democrat.*

Pressure on Sarver growing. (1971, March 27). *Arkansas Democrat.*

Prisons are called "crime colleges." (1970, April 16). *Arkansas Democrat.*

Prison assaults must be curbed, Judge Henley says. (1970, April 16). *Arkansas Gazette.*

Prison bills are approved in the Senate. (1970, March 6). *Arkansas Democrat.*

Prison edict fails as grounds to free 2 Cummins convicts. (1970, March 13). *Arkansas Democrat.*

Prison laxity charged. (1970, June 30). *Arkansas Democrat.*

Prison is quiet as convicts go back to work. (1970, November 23). *Arkansas Democrat.*

Prison plan leaves Henley dissatisfied. (1970, May 29). *Arkansas Gazette.*

Purcell to appeal order reform Arkansas prisons. (1970, March 6). *Arkansas Gazette.*

Sarver is irked. (1970, November 19). *Arkansas Democrat.*

Sarver will seek funds to employ 83 more persons. (1970, February 21). *Arkansas Gazette.*

Sarver hits "meddling" of state legislators. (1970, November 21). *Arkansas Democrat.*

Senators blister Sarver, refuse funds for prisons. (1971, March 26). *Arkansas Democrat.*

Smith, D. (1970a, February 25). Purcell endorses prison reforms, but asks appeal. *Arkansas Gazette.*

Smith, D. (1970b, February 26). Legislative panel asks prison board to back appeal. *Arkansas Gazette.*

Smith, D. (1970c, March 3). Senate tells Purcell to appeal decision on prison system. *Arkansas Gazette.*

Smith, D. (1970d, March 7). Legislature passes $2.3 million plan for state prisons. *Arkansas Gazette.*

Smith, D. (1970e, November 3). Cummins prisoners revolt for 13 hours: Sarver, Steed take place of hostages. *Arkansas Gazette.*

Someone should challenge laws to imprison women, Sarver tells club group. (1970, March 21). *Arkansas Gazette.*

Sparks draws curt reaction from lawyers. (1970, March 2). *Arkansas Gazette.*

U.S. Department of Labor (n.d.). *History of changes to the minimum wage law.* https://www.dol.gov/whd/minwage/coverage.htm

Work-pay project for prisons meets Senate opposition. (1971, February 16). *Arkansas Democrat.*

Work-release prison plan explained to house members. (1970, March 5). *Arkansas Gazette.*

CASES CITED

Holt v. Sarver II, 309 F. Supp. 362 (E.D. Ark. 1970)

Holt v. Sarver, 442 F.2d 304 (8th Cir. 1971)

KEY TERMS

Dale Bumpers

Good time provision

Rebellion

Security levels

Work-release program

QUESTIONS

1. Sarver hoped to teach the inmates responsibility and requested a controversial work-release program. How much were inmates expected to be paid? Was this program approved by the legislature? In your opinion, why or why not?

2. What was the most neglected populous in the Arkansas prison system, and why do you think that was?

3. In efforts to provide an alternative to traditional imprisonment at Cummins and Tucker, Sarver developed the need for varied security. Today, we

have several different security levels (minimum, low, medium, high, and administrative). How does separating inmates assist prison operatives?

4. Good behavior was recognized and rewarded by days of "good time provision." In the three-tier categorization of inmates, who received more good time and opportunities in the old system? Under the new system, who was eligible for good time and how much?

5. Arkansans and legislators fought Sarver relentlessly to preserve the traditional operations and methods administered within the Arkansas prison system. Why do you think traditional culture was important to the state, resulting in the removal of Sarver from an administrative position in the correctional department? Assessing Sarver's initiatives, was he overall effective or ineffective?

FIGURE CREDITS

Moving Beyond Crisis

1972–1974

Introduction

Beginning in 1972, the transition from the self-funded, informally operated prison system based on the trusty system to a more formalized and state-funded system was becoming apparent. There were still many problems and challenges, and the transition was far from complete, but the course had been set, and there was no turning back to the old system that had dominated corrections in Arkansas for so many decades.

Partial End of Armed Trusties and Increase in Funding

In January of 1972, corrections officials announced that there were no more armed trusties in the fields at Cummins and Tucker. Armed trusties still performed duty as tower guards, but even their duties were performed in conjunction with paid state guards. Funds made available to the state under the Federal Emergency Employment Act helped Arkansas replace the armed trusties in the fields with state employees. Thus, Arkansas rectified one of the major issues in the dispute, which had ultimately rendered the system out of compliance with the requirements of the U.S. Constitution ("Arkansas Prisons Clear the Fields of Armed Trusties," 1972).

In addition to relying on federal money to make changes, the state was dramatically increasing its own expenditures. In a January 1972 meeting the Board of Correction approved a staff recommendation to increase the budget for inmate care and custody from $580,943 to $1,012,825. Most of this increase came from an appropriation by the legislature to the governor to use as he saw fit on prisons (Kirby, 1972a). This is a dramatic change from the pre-Murton era when the state was not required to appropriate any funds for prison operations but was actually a moneymaking operation for the state (Feeley & Rubin, 1999).

On another front, reports on prison farming activity for 1971 showed income to be higher than for recent years. The total income for 1971 was $1,793,499 compared with income of $1,246,472 for 1970 and $1,076,343 for 1969. The new corrections commissioner, T. Don Hutto, attributed the increase to improved morale due to a liberalized "good time" policy that allowed prisoners to earn early release. Cotton and rice were the largest income-producing crops for 1971 (Associated Press, 1972, January 6).

Actual and Suggested Reforms

Apparently, as a result of litigation in the federal courts, members of the Board of Correction and correctional staff became more receptive to the complaints and concerns of Arkansas prison inmates. In a meeting with the inmate council of Tucker, Board Chairman John Haley told members of the Tucker inmate council that they could meet with the board whenever they chose to do so. Haley told members of the council, "You are in a good position to see problems and to suggest solutions that we might not even know about" (Kirby, 1972a).

In the same meeting, members of the inmate council complained about the disbursement of the Inmate Welfare Fund, which came primarily from the profits of the inmate commissary. Haley explained to the inmates that although the final decision on the use of these funds rested with the superintendent, inmates were to be given an opportunity to make suggestions and that the funds were always to be used for purposes of inmate welfare. This was distinguishable from practices in the old system in which prison officials could and did use these funds for purposes entirely unrelated to prison welfare. This is another example of how the state was beginning to pay attention to prison matters in ways that had long been ignored (Kirby, 1972a).

John Haley, who had been on the board for 5 years and chaired it for 4 turbulent years, announced his resignation in January of 1972. Governor Rockefeller had appointed Haley. Haley oversaw the board and sometimes the administrative details of the prisons during the Murton, Urban, and Sarver periods. Haley was also instrumental in the reorganization of the state prison system into the Arkansas Department of Correction by General Assembly Act 50 of 1968 that was then codified as Arkansas Statutes § 42–100. In his outgoing remarks Haley warned that Arkansas should not copy the blunders of other state systems and suggested particular points to be addressed by legislative action, such as the need for a budget item for a prison physician and more funds to improve the farming operation (Associated Press, 1972b; Kirby, 1972b).

Haley advocated alternatives to prison, such as work release programs, probation supervised by qualified probation officers, and community treatment facilities. This approach never gained much support in the state during Haley's term on the board. At one point Haley stated,

> The major obstacle to prison reform is getting people to realize that at least half of the people in our prisons don't belong there. We will have alternatives when the public accepts the fact that most convicts are no different from any other human being and represent little more risk, if any, to humanity than any man on the street. A lot of people get a knee jerk reaction from the word "convict." They think convicts ought to be in prison forever (Kirby, 1972b).

Early in 1972, Commissioner Hutto announced that an attorney would be hired by the Department of Correction to assist inmates with their legal problems. Additionally, legal reference books would be purchased and made available to the inmates. These actions came in response to requests from inmates through the Inmate Council for Legal Aid (Kirby, 1972c). This action by the department is noteworthy in that it predates the case of *Bounds v. Smith* (1977) in which the U.S. Supreme Court ruled that states must provide either legal services or a law library to ensure that inmates had access to the courts.

Reduced Institutional Violence

Evidence of increased order and lack of violence in the prisons came in a report to the board that no weapons had been fired at Cummins unit "for any reason" during calendar year 1971. Two shots were fired at the Tucker unit, one when a tower guard thought he saw movement and another as a warning to inmates who refused to stop fighting. This represented a rather remarkable shift from the day in which armed trusty inmates could and often did fire weapons for whatever reasons they deemed appropriate (Kirby, 1972b).

Similarly, Commissioner Hutto fired two supervisory members of the security staff for "indiscriminate shooting and the use of excessive force" in the apprehension of two escaping inmates. The two were attempting to escape through a window in the main administration building. Correctional staff had advanced warning of the escape attempt and had increased the number of guards on duty. First reports to Commissioner Hutto indicated that the two had been apprehended without serious injury. Later investigations showed that the two escapees were fired on by corrections employees from the tower and the parking lot and had been injured by the blows from employees, at least one of which was administered by the butt of a shotgun. One inmate sustained a broken jaw, a ruptured eardrum, and other minor injuries. The two supervisors were dismissed immediately (Kirby, 1972d).

Judge Henley asked Commissioner Hutto to make a "personal and thorough" investigation of the complaint of the two inmates involved in the aborted escape attempt. In a letter to Hutto, Henley wrote,

> It goes without saying that if prison personnel either at Tucker or Cummins are in fact beating or inflicting corporal punishment of inmates, they are in contempt of this court and are subject to being dealt with as the law provides (Associated Press, 1972c).

Hutto responded to the judge in part that the matter had been "handled with poor judgment" and by informing the court that in addition to the two dismissals that the associate superintendent and the chief of security had been demoted for their failure to take proper steps in response to the anticipated escape attempt (Associated Press, 1972c).

A New Dawn for Arkansas Prisons

Commissioner Hutto had numerous ideas and proposals for improving corrections through legislative action. In a March meeting of the corrections board, Hutto expressed interest in forming a "non-geographical" school district for the department, which would enable the prison system to establish a public school district that would function as other such districts in the state, with minimum funding, teachers, a superintendent, state programming, and so on. Hutto also proposed that Arkansas participate in the Interstate Correctional Compact, whereby states by mutual agreement would allow a person convicted in one state to serve the sentence in another, often so that he could be near family members (Kirby, 1972d).

At the same March board meeting, Hutto received permission to carry out a study of existing laws that forbade former inmates from holding certain licenses in the state. The board discussed applying for grants through the federal Law Enforcement Assistance Administration for such items as a diagnostic and classification center, pre-release programs, prison industry, work-study release programs, and other programs. It was announced that the state Bar Association had formed a committee to assist in meeting the legal needs of inmates. Others suggested an expansion of the use of volunteers in corrections and expressed the need to gather and preserve items of historical importance (Kirby, 1972d).

By the spring of 1972, corrections officials announced that all firearms had been removed from the prison compounds at Tucker and Cummins. Old pistols, shotguns, and rifles, carried for many years by inmate guards, were being cleaned, repaired, and stored for exhibition in a planned prison museum (Kirby, 1972h).

Thus began a new era of correctional administration. The days of the almost totally isolated and secretly operated prison system based on the trusty system, torturous corporal punishment, and economic self-sufficiency was giving way to a system administered by a professional staff, paid employees, policies and procedures, connections with other state entities, and even with other state departments of correction, and of course with the federal court, which continued to orchestrate many of these changes.

Another indication that the prison system was reaching some point of balance or normalcy was that Cummins and Tucker had each begun to produce an inmate newspaper. This not only was allowed by the board and prison administrators, but in the case of Cummins was at the request of the board. At Cummins, the paper had been suspended for more than a year. Its previous title was *Pea Pickers' Picayune* but the new publication was called the *Cummins Journal* and was to come out in a more expensive magazine format, including photographs, illustrations, and cartoons ("Cummins Revives Its Newspaper," 1972).

Continuing Allegations

Not all of the activity in the prisons was directed toward positive modifications. Some involved addressing long-standing problems while other efforts involved responding to new problems and issues that developed in this period of rapid change. An example of the daily flow of problems faced by Mr. Hutto and his staff was the complaint from six inmates that they had contracted tuberculosis as a result of unsanitary conditions at the prison. The inmates contended that they were healthy when they entered the prison. In a letter of complaint sent to a Little Rock newspaper, one of the inmates charged, "Never in my life have I had to live in such filthy conditions." Additionally, the inmates accused the prison system of ignoring valid medical complaints and providing inferior medical treatment (Kirby, 1972f).

Hutto responded to the charges by pointing out that one does not get tuberculosis as a result of unsanitary conditions, but rather by breathing air exhaled by a TB carrier. He also stated that the inmates had received standard medical treatment for their medical complaints and were given more aggressive treatment when the original treatment failed to correct the problem. Hutto did note, however, that the possibility of catching TB was greater in situations where large numbers of persons live in close quarters, and he confirmed that the men involved had been in good health when they entered the system (Associated Press, 1972d).

Evidence of discontent from the Sarver years surfaced in the form of a lawsuit that charged former prison officials, including Sarver, with neglect that resulted in an inmate injury in 1969. The inmate, James Moore, said that while he was sleeping another inmate cut his throat. Moore claimed the inmate who committed the assault had a history of violent behavior and should not have been confined in a barracks with other inmates. Moore claims that he could not work as a result of brain damage and other neurologic damage he sustained in what he described as a near decapitation ("Suit Names WR, Sarver," 1972).

Other legal action regarding the use of trusty guards continued to be filed. Andrew Kelly, a Cummins Prison inmate, testified before the state Claims Commission that a 20-year-old inmate guard accidentally fired a shotgun that hit Kelly in the lower back in 1971 ("Inmate Says He Had 3 Operations After Prison Shooting," 1972). Kelly spent 4.5 months in the hospital. The Claims Commission regarded the shooting to be "negligent" and awarded Kelly $20,000 ("20,000 Goes to Inmate Struck by Shotgun Blast," 1972). Another inmate, James Dixon, was awarded $6,500 by the Claims Commission for an incident that the commission regarded as an "unjustified" shooting of Dixon, which shattered his leg ("Panel Rules in Favor of Former Inmate," 1972).

New Women's Unit

Plans and discussion of a new women's facility accelerated in 1972 when money became available. The legislature appropriated $300,000 for the facility and an additional $616,000, according to Commissioner Hutto, was designated for the project from federal funds through the Law Enforcement Assistance Administration. A site given much consideration was a 365-acre tract of land at Camp Robinson, a military base that contained parts of buildings that were considered to have possible use for a women's reformatory facility (Kirby, 1972g).

The site at Camp Robinson later proved unfeasible following protests from the commander of the Arkansas National Guard and recognition that existing arrangements with the U.S. military would literally necessitate an act of Congress to make the property available for a state prison. Another site given consideration was the state's School for the Deaf facility on Madison Street in Little Rock. This site was abandoned due to protests from residents in the area (Kotok, 1972).

The site that gained favor and ultimately was selected for the women's reformatory was an 80-acre tract near the juvenile training school in Pine Bluff. Contrary to other possibilities, the people of Pine Bluff were enthusiastic about the possibility of being selected as the location for the women's unit. The Chamber of Commerce actively worked to sell the Corrections Board on the Pine Bluff location as they would in recruiting other industry to the city. Additionally, the city was offering the tract to the state at no cost (Kotok, 1972; "Prison Transfer Expected," 1972.)

Skeletons Return

Another old issue resurfaced in 1972 in a report regarding the skeletons that had been dug up near the end of Murton's administration of the Arkansas system. Dr. Clyde Snow, head of physical anthropology research at the Civil Aeromedical Institute of the Federal Aviation Administration in Oklahoma City, using anthropological research methods, analyzed the remains disinterred at Cummins prison farm in 1968. His major conclusion, following his work of more than 1 year, was that the bones most likely were the bones of prison inmates buried 50 to 70 years ago. Snow did say that the claim by inmate Ruben Johnson that the bones were those of inmates buried in the 1940s could not be correct. He also regarded it unlikely that the bodies were part of a pre-prison cemetery, as had been offered as an explanation in the heat of the controversy surrounding the bodies in 1968. Snow's research indicated that the cause of death of the three was uncertain. One of the skulls was fractured, but it was not clear whether this fracture was associated with the death or occurred later during a cave in. Snow indicated that many questions remained and probably would not be cleared up without more excavation in the same area where it appeared that several more persons were buried ("Suit Names WR, Sarver," 1972).

Commissioner Hutto Reports Progress

After about 1 year on the job as the correctional commissioner, T. Don Hutto reflected that progress made thus far in his administration was due to a shift in awareness and perception of the prisons. Hutto explained that he took over the leadership during a time when people were just beginning to recognize the problems of the prison system and were at the same time becoming willing to support change and to make financial resources available. Asked about what was taking place in the first year of his administration relative to recent leaders of the system, Hutto remarked, "It's hard to compare it because many of the things that have been accomplished couldn't have been done without financial support. … I had more financial tools than anyone before me has had" ("Hutto Hopes to Aid Prison Industry, Education Process," 1972).

This financial support made it possible, for the first time, to acquire a team of experienced administrators and other personnel that opened the door to the dismantling of the trusty system. "The biggest problem I faced was the lack of personnel in the department, which resulted from a number of other problems, but the basic problem was the small number of personnel and experience" ("Hutto Hopes to Aid Prison Industry, Education Process," 1972).

Hutto said that with the personnel in place his goal was to concentrate on prison programming, particularly education and prison industry. He envisioned a total education system for inmates, which would integrate an academic program with vocational training and on-the-job experience in prison industry. A similar approach in Texas, according to Hutto, was proving to be very successful (Associated Press, 1972e).

Hutto stated that prison living conditions had improved. "Prison is never a good place to be but it can be decent and humane and our prisons are definitely humane" ("Hutto Hopes to Aid Prison Industry, Education Process," 1972).

Federal Court Concerns in Post–*Holt I* and *II* Litigation: *Holt v. Hutto III* (1973)

Although progress was being made, the federal court was still less than satisfied with Arkansas prisons. Judge Henley criticized prison officials for interfering with inmate access to the courts. He was referring to numerous complaints the court had received from inmates regarding the conduct and attitude of prison personnel about inmate writ-writing (the filing of civil law suits in federal courts) activities. Inmates reported having been cursed, ridiculed, mocked, abused, and threatened in connection with their attempts to convey complaints to the court. One inmate described difficulty in getting writing materials to write to the court and in interference with his writing once the materials were received ("Prison Officials are Chastised by Judge Henley," 1972). Henley also recognized merit to the request from inmates that they be provided with a law library ("Henley Sees Merit in Inmate Petition," 1972; *Holt v. Hutto III*, 1973).

Having received a "constant stream of complaints" from inmates, Judge Henley announced his intention to hold a new hearing to determine if the changes ordered by the court were being carried out. In addition to the complaints alleging hindrance of inmate access to the courts, inmates charged that they were being forced to run to work in the fields and at other times during their work period; that inmates were being assigned duties beyond their physical strength; that homosexual assaults were being made on inmates; and that sentences to solitary confinement were being made in an arbitrary manner. Inmates testified that excessive force was still being used. One inmate claimed that he had been beaten and stomped by three wardens ("Prisoners' Complaints Continue in Federal Hearing," 1973). Henley acknowledged that inmates often make frivolous and unfounded complaints, but that it was important to hear the complaints and most importantly to see that the previous decrees of the court were being taken seriously and being implemented (*Holt v. Hutto III*, 1973; "Inmate Says Muslims Ignored," 1972).

One of the issues in the lawsuit filed in the federal courts alleged that the practice of the Muslim religion was being restricted in the Tucker unit. The suit contended that Muslims were not given adequate facilities to hold meetings and that staff harassed persons who attended the meetings. Further it was difficult to obtain and distribute Muslim literature, and visits by a Muslim minister were kept at a minimum (*Holt v. Hutto III*, 1973; "Inmate Says Muslims Ignored," 1972; "Prisoners' Complaints Continue in Federal Hearing," 1973).

In the hearing on the issue of religious freedom, Tucker Superintendent Robert Britton revealed that the names of inmates who attended Black Muslim meetings were given to the FBI. Having inmates who attended the meetings sign a register at each meeting developed the list of names. Asked why the list was kept since no similar list was kept for persons attending other religious services, Superintendent Britton dodged the issue by responding, "I don't think it needs to be known." Later he indicated that the FBI had requested information regarding who was participating in Muslim services (Fields, 1972; "Prisoners' Complaints Continue in Federal Hearing," 1973; *Holt v. Hutto III*, 1973).

Alvin X. Higgins, an inmate at Tucker who said he served as acting minister for Black Muslims at Tucker, testified that he had been told by the prison chaplain that Muslim services would not be permitted at the prison and that Muslim literature had been confiscated and destroyed by prison staff. Requests for cooperation with dietary requirements of the Muslim faith, said Higgins, had been ignored (O'Neal, 1972a and b). A Cummins inmate claimed to have been held in the maximum security unit for several months primarily because of his religion ("Complaints by Prisoner," 1972; *Holt v. Hutto III*, 1973). Judge Henley ruled Black Muslim prisoners may not be discriminated against due to their religion (*Holt v. Hutto III*, 1973).

FIGURE 9.1. Tucker unit warden, Lee Henslee, and trusty hold bloodhounds at the prison.

Henley concluded that Black Muslims constituted a valid religious sect and were entitled to protection under the free exercise of religion clause of the First Amendment. Judge Henley noted that one of the main problems faced by Muslim prisoners was dietary restrictions imposed on adherents to the Muslim religion (*Holt v. Hutto III*, 1973). Henley held that the impediments to free exercise of religion by Muslims had not been intentional by the prison officials, and he opined that these issues could be resolved administratively. Nonetheless, Judge Henley did "enjoin in general terms discrimination against the undue restrictions upon the Muslims" (*Holt v. Hutto*, 1973, p. 203).

There was testimony that free-world guards were seeking to stir up racial tension among inmates. Segregation of inmates by race was by then an uncommon practice in most living areas but remained in place at the Cummins maximum security area. Lieutenant John Ashley, security chief at Cummins, testified that occasionally Black and White inmates were placed in the same cells, but that the inmates decided they couldn't get along. Ashley testified that he had not been instructed to assign Black and White inmates to separate cells, but Black and White inmates just seemed to get along better with inmates of the same race. He also admitted that Blacks were at times referred to as "niggers" (Dean, 1973c). The prison officials denied any allegations of intentional racial discrimination. Department of Corrections officials said that they had leaned over backward to accommodate the needs of Black Muslim inmates ("Testimony Given for the Defense in Prison Case," 1973) and that one Black Muslim commended the department for its cooperation (Dean, 1973c).

The same hearings produced testimony from an inmate, corroborated by the testimony of another prison official, that Superintendent Britton had struck an inmate several times on the head. The incident occurred when the inmate, Johnny Cox, overstayed a furlough and was tracked down by dogs at a farm between Stuttgart and Dewitt, Arkansas. Bloodhounds trained and handled by inmates were often used to track down escapees. Britton admitted that he had struck the inmate with a "chop to the shoulders" but that it was the only time he had ever struck an inmate (Fields, 1972). In spite of inmate testimony to the contrary, Superintendent Britton and Associate Superintendent J.R. McClaren stated that neither they nor guards had abused inmates physically or verbally (O'Neal, 1972). Prison officials testified that much of what inmates claimed was incorrect, but some of what they said was true. Officials maintained that force was used in compliance with policy and law (Dean, 1973a), although Robert Britton, superintendent of Tucker, admitted that on one occasion he violated department policy by striking an inmate (Dean, 1973a). Judge Henley found that the prison administration had an appropriate use of force policy and only directed that any incidences of use of force on inmates be investigated immediately and that the inmate's version of the event be fairly considered (*Holt v. Hutto*, 1973).

FIGURE 9.2. Arkansas Department of Corrections Commissioner, Terrell Hutto.

Judge Henley heard testimony from Cummins inmates indicating that they were worked and forced to run until they collapsed, and that they were given inadequate medical attention. Representatives of the Department of Correction denied these and many other inmate allegations ("Workers Collapsed, Prison Law Library is Off Limits, Inmate Contends," 1972). The decision by Judge Henley found that there had been occasions when inmates were required to run to and from work, but that is was not a widespread institutional practice. It was also found that prison staff did use inappropriate language at times, but that it was no worse than what inmates used with each other. Judge Henley did find that such conduct by staff was inappropriate, unprofessional, and should be avoided, but did not rise to the level of a constitutional violation (*Holt v. Hutto*, 1973).

Cummins Superintendent A.L. Lockhart and Correction Board member Dr. Thomas Wortham told the court that medical and dental care were unsatisfactory. Inmates had testified that needed medication and medical treatment were not available. Wortham explained that the department was hiring a full-time physician and that additional medical facilities were being planned (Dean, 1973d). Lockhart also testified that prison barracks were extremely overcrowded. It was not uncommon for more than 120 men to occupy a barracks, which normally would hold 80 men (Dean, 1973b).

Commissioner Hutto and the board continued to make improvements to the prison system. A full-time physician was employed, and improved medical equipment was acquired (Dean, 1973d). Additional funds were appropriated to make improvements at Tucker and Cummins (Associated Press, 1973). The state developed a policy to provide educational assistance to all inmates who were not high school graduates ("Prisons to Implement Education Programs," 1973) and created an independent school district for the corrections department to implement those plans ("Important Correctional Law," 1973). Tests showed that the average educational attainment at Tucker was at the 6.4 grade level while that at Cummins was 5.0 ("Important Correctional Law," 1973).

One can sense that Judge Henley may have been growing weary of the continuing Arkansas prison saga when he said, "The Court hopes that this will be the last long opinion dealing with the Department that the Court will be called upon to write" (*Holt v. Hutto*, 1973, p. 216). Henley dismissed the petitions of the individual prisoners and ordered the limited injunctive relief, described earlier. The inmate petitioners then appealed the decision of Judge Henley to the 8th U.S. Circuit Court of Appeals. While the 8th Circuit did find that there had been significant improvement, the court found there was still much to be done.

Finney v. Arkansas Board of Correction (1974)

The prisoners appealed to the 8th Circuit Court of Appeals, which found that the Arkansas prison system was still unconstitutional, directed further corrective action, and remanded the case back to the district court for further proceedings (*Finney v. Arkansas Board of Correction*, 1974). The 8th Circuit observed that the current litigation had its origins with *Holt I* that was decided in 1969. *Holt II* in 1970 found the Arkansas prison system to be unconstitutional, directed certain remedial actions to be taken, and recognized practical limitations that would require some time to occur. The district court conducted multiple review hearings and noted substantial progress but also found continuing constitutional violations requiring further court supervision. Finally, as discussed, the district court determined that there was no need for further supervision (*Holt v. Hutto III*, 1973).

The 8th Circuit affirmed in part and reversed in part and remanded the matter back to the district court.

The 8th Circuit Court of Appeals agreed with the state that "there is no such thing as a 'perfect' prison system, but this does not relieve respondents of their duty to make their system a constitutional one in which the human dignity of each individual inmate is respected" (*Finney v. Arkansas Board of Correction*, 1974, p. 200). The 8th Circuit was specific in its ruling and provided clear guidance to the lower court and to prison officials as to how to proceed. The appellate court found several areas of continuing constitutional concern.

Conditions of Confinement/Rehabilitation

The court was particularly concerned with poor conditions and lack of security in the barracks living quarters of inmates. Each barracks housed more than 100 inmates with no system of classification other than race and rank and virtually no systems or procedures to ensure the safety of inmates. This problem was all the more pronounced because it had been previously addressed by prior rulings and had not been corrected even after more than a year and a half later. It was noted that some relief was on the way through the construction of new housing units that would reduce overcrowding. However, it was pointed out that any relief would be of limited duration because the inmate population was increasing each year. The court was also still concerned with the lack of resources to protect against inmate-on-inmate assaults (*Finney v. Arkansas Board of Correction*, 1974).

Conditions of confinement, including treatment of inmates by staff, working conditions, and disciplinary procedures, were of great concern to the court. Inmates who refused to work or worked too slowly faced loss of good time credit toward release dates or transfer to solitary confinement. Work on the hoe squads included assignments regardless of the inmates' physical condition or ability. Some inmates were also still forced to run to and from the fields. The 8th Circuit found the existing system to be unconstitutional and directed the district court to conduct further hearings to address these deficiencies (*Finney v. Arkansas Board of Correction*, 1974).

The lack of rehabilitation programs had been a part of the district court's decision in *Holt II* that the Arkansas prison system was unconstitutional. New programs had been implemented that included basic education and training in building trades. However, the court found these programs to be limited to a very small number of prisoners. The prison officials were directed to submit to the district court a comprehensive plan for education and rehabilitation of prisoners in compliance with the U.S. Supreme Court requirements of *Wolff v. McDonnell* (1974).

Maximum Security Units/Disciplinary Procedures

Holt I and *II* found the old maximum security units to be unconstitutional for a number of reasons, including overcrowding, sanitation, and nutrition. The court in *Finney* noted that a new maximum security unit greatly improved the problems of overcrowding and sanitation. However, the court still had concerns about the dietary practices employed in the maximum security unit. Inmates housed in this unit were fed grue, which is described as a "tasteless, unappetizing paste-like food which is served to prisoners in solitary confinement as a form of further punishment" (*Finney v. Arkansas Board of Correction*, 1974, p. 207). The district court held that this diet was sufficient to provide adequate nutrition. But the appellate court was not convinced and directed that the trial court "ensure that prisoners placed in punitive solitary confinement are not deprived of basic necessities including light, heat, ventilation, sanitation, clothing and a proper diet" (*Finney v. Arkansas Board of Correction*, 1974, p. 208).

The district court awarded injunctive relief to the petitioners regarding the disciplinary procedures employed by the Arkansas prisons. The trial court had required disciplinary hearings be conducted within 3 days between the hours of 6:00 a.m. and 6:00 p.m., and that the matters be documented in a form that would allow a reviewing authority to be aware of the findings and the process. The appellate court noted that, subsequent to the district court decision, the U.S. Supreme Court had announced its decision in *Wolff v. McDonnell* (1974) requiring 24 hours written notice of the allegations, the qualified right to confront and call witness, and a written statement of the decision and underlying reasons for the ultimate decision. The 8th Circuit directed that the district court follow *McDonnell* and also prevent the officer who raised the allegations against the inmate from acting as a decision maker in the disciplinary hearing (*Finney v. Arkansas Board of Correction*, 1974).

Trusty Guards/Juvenile Prisoners

The trusty guard system had been significantly reduced since 1969, but armed trusty guards still operated in the fields and the guard towers under the supervision of free-world guards. This remaining vestige of the trusty guard system was unacceptable to the appellate court. The remand to the district court included

FIGURE 9.3. Free-world guards on horseback observed inmates doing hand field work at Cummins in 1975. This is after trusty guards were removed from field supervision in compliance with federal court orders. As you can see, there are no armed inmates helping to supervise at this point.

directions for the trusty guard system to be completely ended "within a few months" (*Finney v. Arkansas Board of Correction*, 1974, p. 205).

Commingling of adult and juvenile prisoners was also an ongoing problem. Youthful inmates were housed at the Tucker Intermediate Reformatory. But those younger offenders who were disciplinary problems were transferred to Cummins where they would either live in solitary confinement or in the general prison population. These transfers were found to occur summarily with no regard to due process. The lack of procedural safeguards in transfers was problematic because the conditions of confinement and rehabilitative programs were much better at Tucker than at Cummins. The 8th Circuit enjoined further transfers of juvenile inmates to Cummins until such time as the other substantive constitutional deficiencies at Cummins were corrected (*Finney v. Arkansas Board of Correction*, 1974).

Health Care

Medical, dental, and mental health care was found to be a continuing problem since *Holt I*, and the improvements that had occurred were far from satisfactory. Facilities and staffing were both inadequate. The 8th Circuit was troubled with the lack of progress since the initiation of federal court involvement, observing that the State has

> achieved little more than a study and a hope to improve the present inadequate care. This court fully realizes, as did the district court, that this is a difficult problem for the Board of Correction and prison officials. In the meantime, however, 1200 inmates are continuously denied proper medical and dental care, and individuals with contagious diseases, as well as some who are mentally and emotionally ill, are at large in the general prison population (*Finney v. Arkansas Board of Correction*, 1974, p. 204).

The court observed that the system did not have a physician, dentist, or psychiatrist on staff, though there had been testimony at the trial that a full-time physician was being hired. The Arkansas Department of Health evaluated the healthcare facilities and found all areas to be lacking. Lab and X-ray services were very limited; there was no ambulance for transfers to state acute care units in Little Rock or Booneville. When a dentist did make an infrequent visit there were no restorative dental services provided. If dental work as serious as an extraction was necessary, the prisoner would be transported to Little Rock. The record indicated that none of the 1,200 Cummins inmates had been taken for dental work in the 8 months leading up to the hearing. The Department of Health concluded that the health care unit did not meet state standards for an infirmary or a hospital.

In short, even subsequent to the *Holt* cases, the requisite improvements to the prison healthcare system were woefully inadequate. The court, in its remand, required that the district court conduct additional hearings to establish specific goals and timelines for the provision of proper healthcare services to all prisoners.

Racial Discrimination

While the state had made progress with regard to racial discrimination since *Holt II*, the trial court still found problems and enjoined the state from continuing to segregate prisoners in the maximum security unit, interfering with Black Muslim religious activities, and discrimination against Black inmates in classification, job assignments, disciplinary procedures, and inmate privileges. The 8th Circuit found that the trial court did not go far enough in its directives. On remand the district court was to address the prisons' hiring practices, with a view to hiring more Black employees. With Black inmates making up 48% of the population, there were few Black employees and almost none of them were in a "position of control, influence or even persuasion" (*Finney v. Arkansas Board of Correction*, 1974, p. 210). The district court was directed to "amend its decree to include an affirmative program directed toward the elimination of all forms of racial discrimination" (*Finney v. Arkansas Board of Correction*, 1974, p. 210).

Inmate Mail

Complaints by prisoners about the handling of mail included the prisons' policy of opening and inspecting even privileged mail to and from attorneys and courts. Prisoners also challenged the mailing list policy of not allowing a prisoner to add a person to the list who had not previously consented. The 8th Circuit had the benefit of what has since been the seminal Supreme Court of the United States (SCOTUS) case on inmate mail. In *Procunier v. Martinez* (1974) SCOTUS held that inmates retain First Amendment protections and regulations regarding inspection and that censorship of inmate mail must be reasonable and necessary to maintain institutional security. The district court required only that privileged (legal) mail be opened and inspected in the presence of the inmate. The appellate court found the policy regarding pre-approval of persons for the mailing list was not reasonable. The district court was directed to review the inmate mail policies in a manner consistent with the 8th Circuit ruling and with the SCOTUS *Martinez* ruling (*Finney v. Arkansas Board of Correction*, 1974).

More Money and Further Progress

In spite of the continuing trial and appellate court action regarding the extent to which the prisons had conformed to expectations of the federal court and whether the requirements of constitutionality had been met, the day-to-day activities continued at Tucker and Cummins. Slowly, the framework and the details of a revised prison system were under construction, both within the prison system proper as well as outside the system through activities of the legislature and through public support.

In order to enact such changes it was necessary to increase state funding. In a September 1972 Corrections Board meeting, the board approved a budget that requested an increase of about $1 million over the previous budget request. The increases were primarily for expanding staff by 70 positions in order to continue the process of replacing inmate guards with state employees ("Prisons to Ask Extra $1 Million for Bigger Staff," 1972). Although these requests were trimmed when they got into legislative enactment, it was clear that the legislature and the governor were committed to support the reform being enacted in the Arkansas prisons (Tirey, 1972).

Conclusion

Arkansas had weathered the storms of scandal in its prison system and was on its way to building a reformed system. The new system under political and social construction was not considered the most advanced or progressive of the period, but was in sharp contrast to the system that had lasted so many years and had aroused such enormous controversy. With a push from the federal courts, Arkansas had greatly reduced the long defended trusty system and began developing correctional practices much more in harmony with correctional practices found elsewhere in the United States. Although it would take many more years of litigation, the Arkansas system was eventually declared to be consistent with the requirements of the U.S. Constitution.

REFERENCES

20,000 goes to inmate struck by shotgun blast. (1972, July 7). *Arkansas Democrat.*

Arkansas prisons clear the fields of armed trusties. (1972, January 5). *Arkansas Democrat.*

Associated Press. (1972a, January 6). Farm money at Cummins shows rise. *Arkansas Democrat.*

Associated Press. (1972b, January 18). Haley's work in corrections praised by Bumpers, Hutto. *Arkansas Democrat.*

Associated Press. (1972c, March 15). 2 prison officials at Tucker to be demoted. *Arkansas Democrat.*

Associated Press. (1972d, April 6). Hutto questions inmates' charges. *Arkansas Democrat.*

Associated Press. (1972e, July 23). Hutto to ask prison independent school system. *Arkansas Democrat.*

Associated Press. (1973, April 11). Bumpers vetoes item for prisons building. *Arkansas Democrat.*

Bounds v. Smith, 430 U.S. 817 (1977)

Complaints by prisoner. (1972, December 21). *Arkansas Democrat.*

Cummins revives its newspaper. (1972, April 9). *Arkansas Democrat.*

Dean, J. (1973a, January 5). Testimony of inmates is disputed. *Arkansas Democrat.*

Dean, J. (1973b, January 6). Condition at Cummins. *Arkansas Democrat.*

Dean, J. (1973c, January 9). Prison roommate policy. *Arkansas Democrat.*

Dean, J. (1973d, January 21). First full-time physician is hired by State Board of Corrections. *Arkansas Democrat.*

Feeley, M. M., & Rubin, E. L. (1999). *Judicial policy making and the modern state: How the courts reformed America's prisons.* Cambridge University Press.

Fields, A. (1972, November 13). Tucker "Muslims" listed. *Arkansas Democrat.*

Finney v. Arkansas Board of Correction, 505 F.2d 194 (8th Cir. 1974)

Henley sees merit in inmate petition. (1972, August 24). *Arkansas Democrat.*

Holt v. Hutto III, 363 F. Supp. 194 (E.D. Ark. 1973)

Hutto hopes to aid prison industry, education process. (1972, July 21). *Arkansas Democrat.*

Important correctional law. (1973, May 7). *Arkansas Democrat.*

Inmate says he had 3 operations after prison shooting. (1972, May 9). *Arkansas Democrat.*

Inmate says Muslims ignored. (1972, September 7). *Arkansas Democrat.*

Kirby, M. (1972a, January 9). Board may show change in attitude toward prisoners. *Arkansas Democrat.*

Kirby, M. (1972b, January 19). Haley hopes to continue his work. *Arkansas Democrat.*

Kirby, M. (1972c, February 13). State prisoners to get legal aid. *Arkansas Democrat.*

Kirby, M. (1972d, March 2). 2 Tucker employees are fired. *Arkansas Democrat.*

Kirby, M. (1972e, March 19). Schooling for Arkansas inmates. *Arkansas Democrat.*

Kirby, M. (1972f, April 5). 6 Cummins inmates blame prison for TB. *Arkansas Democrat.*

Kirby, M. (1972g, April 11). Probable prison site visited. *Arkansas Democrat.*

Kirby, M. (1972h, April 23). Guns out of prison compounds. *Arkansas Democrat.*

Kotok, D. (1972, May 19). Panel inspects Pine Bluff land for prison site. *Arkansas Democrat.*

O'Neal, R. (1972a, November 14). Abuse called "deliberate." *Arkansas Democrat.*

O'Neal, R. (1972b, November 14). Prison testimony ends. *Arkansas Democrat.*

Panel rules in favor of former inmate. (1972, June 7). *Arkansas Democrat.*

Prison officials are chastised by Judge Henley. (1972, August 7). *Arkansas Democrat.*

Prison transfer expected. (1972, June 26) *Arkansas Democrat.*

Prisoners' complaints continue in federal hearing. (1973, January 5). *Arkansas Democrat.*

Prisons to implement education programs. (1973, April 15). *Arkansas Democrat.*

Prisons to ask extra $1 million for bigger staff. (1972, September 24). *Arkansas Democrat.*

Procunier v. Martinez, 416 U.S. 396 (1974)

Suit names WR, Sarver. (1972, April 17). *Arkansas Democrat.*

Testimony given for the defense in prison case. (1973, January 8). *Arkansas Democrat.*

Tirey, B. (1972, December 20). 40 jobs added to corrections panel staff; Hutto's salary is raised. *Arkansas Democrat.*

Wolff v. McDonnell, 418 U.S. 539 (1974)

Workers collapsed, prison law library is off limits, inmate contends. (1972, December 20). *Arkansas Democrat.*

KEY TERMS

Inmate Council for Legal Aid

Inmate Welfare Fund

Interstate Correctional Compact

Law Enforcement Assistance Administration

Writ-writing

QUESTIONS

1. In January of 1972, corrections officials announced that there were no more armed trusties in the fields at Cummins and Tucker, but they still existed in towers. Discuss the obstacles that prohibited the officials from fully rectifying this major issue that rendered the system unconstitutional.

2. How did changes in the Inmate Welfare Fund and the Inmate Council for Legal Aid reveal that the Board of Corrections had become more receptive to the concerns of Arkansas prison inmates?

3. Explain why in 1972 Judge Henley criticized prison officials for failing to carry out the federal court's rulings as it related to interfering with inmate access to the court, freedom of religion, and access to medical care.

4. In *Finney v. Arkansas Board of Correction* (1974), the court found that the state had failed "to assume an obligation for the safekeeping" of prisoners. Discuss why the court ordered the state to be more aggressive in eliminating overcrowding and inhumane conditions, and other specified deficiencies.

5. What did the court in *Finney v. Arkansas Board of Correction* (1974) order the state to provide in reference to rehabilitation, due process in disciplinary hearings, protection of privileged correspondence with attorneys, and certain aspects of solitary confinement? Why?

FIGURE CREDITS

10 | *Finney I*

Introduction

As a result of improvements to the Arkansas prison system, in 1973 Judge Henley released the state from the ongoing court supervision from the then 3-year-old case that had declared the prisons unconstitutional (Dean, 1973; *Holt v. Hutto*, 1973). Henley wrote that although problems still remained, vast progress had been made since the original ruling in 1970. Judge Henley's order included the following statement:

> In view of the marked improvements that have been made in the Department and that are continuing to be made the Court does not consider it either necessary or desirable to retain further supervisory jurisdiction with respect to the Department and such jurisdiction will not be retained (*Holt v. Hutto*, 1973, p. 216).

The problems that remained were regarded by Judge Henley as more administrative in nature than constitutional (Dean, 1973; *Holt v. Hutto*, 1973). Prison officials were, according to the court's ruling, doing what they could to run a reasonably humane and constitutional prison system. Lower-level employees, however, tended to be poorly paid, undertrained, and unprofessional. The court found that most overt racial discrimination had been eliminated. Henley made specific orders to improve procedure regarding disciplinary hearings, mail, and transfer of inmates from one prison to another (Dean, 1973; *Holt v. Hutto*, 1973).

Hutto and others found the district court's announcement to release the case an occasion to reflect on the progress of the Department of Correction during the period the case had been under review. Only a few inmates were still serving as guards in towers. One hundred fifty free-world guards had been hired to replace inmate trusty guards. There had indeed been a changing of the guard in Arkansas prisons. The correction system had converted from a system that had almost no state employees to one that was for the first time run almost entirely by state employees. In 1966, there were about 40 employees in Arkansas corrections, and that number included all who were working in the parole division. In 1973, that number had grown to 369 state employees. Correctional budgets similarly increased. For many years, using the trusty system, the prison operated on a near self-sustaining basis. In 1970–1971 and 1971–1972, the legislature provided about $1.7 million in state revenue to the prison for care and custody of inmates. In 1972–1973 the appropriation was $2.5 million ("Hutto Cites Improvements in Arkansas Prison System," 1973). But, while Judge Henley found enough improvement and continuing momentum in reforms to close the case and bring an end to the continuing court supervision, the 8th U.S. Circuit Court of Appeals felt otherwise and, as discussed in Chapter 9, remanded the case back to the district court for continuing supervision and court hearings (*Finney v. Arkansas Board of Correction*, 1974).

State Efforts to Comply With Court Requirements Pending 8th Circuit Appeal

Even before the court of appeals sent the prison cases back to the district court for further proceedings, the Arkansas Board of Correction continued to hammer away at the task of meeting the expectations and orders of the court. A policy prohibiting racial discrimination was implemented, along with requirements that disciplinary hearings be held within 72 hours of charges of when an inmate had violated prison rules. Regulations were implemented to protect communication between an inmate and his attorney ("Correction Board Sets Desegregation of Cells," 1973).

Reminders of problems associated with the old trusty system occasionally surfaced. An example was a claim to the Arkansas State Claims Commission filed by an inmate, Kenneth Odom, who was shot in the stomach by a trusty tower guard in 1970. Odom was seated in bleachers at the baseball field during a noon break and was not involved in any behavior that violated the law or prison regulations. State police investigating the incident determined that the bullet that hit Odom ricocheted off the ground where the trusty guard fired shots in the direction of inmates who were not following orders regarding their movement. Odom filed his suit for $200,000 with the State Claims Commission, claiming disability and physical suffering ("Former Inmate, Shot Accidentally, Files $200,000 Suit," 1973). The commission awarded Odom $43,250 in 1974, which was the largest award decided against the prison system at that time ("Ex-inmate is Awarded $43,250," 1974).

Prison Reform Growing Pains

Although much of the dramatic post-*Holt I* and *II* transition from the old prison system to the new went smoothly, there were growing pains. Early in 1974, State Senator Knox Nelson announced that he had become aware that there were employees in the prison's system who were dissatisfied with T. Don Hutto's administration of prisons, particularly in regard to personnel. Billy Heard, a former parole supervisor, brought it to the attention of Nelson that Jack Grasinger, who had been appointed to head the prisons' education programs, had been convicted of a crime. Hutto responded that Grasinger had been convicted of statutory rape in California 25 years previously, but, in Hutto's opinion, the conviction did not affect his ability to perform in his present position. After having been fired from his position due to poor record keeping and other matters regarding the performance of his duties, Heard was found dead in his pick-up. His widow claimed that he had been killed because of what he knew about prison personnel. The coroner ruled that Heard died of a self-inflicted wound (Associated Press, 1974a).

The call for an investigation of the prison system and Hutto's administration by Senator Nelson was accompanied by a statement of support for Hutto by Governor Dale Bumpers, along with complaints by other disgruntled employees. Employees charged that Hutto, whose early career in prison work was at the Texas Department of Correction, was employing friends from Texas for positions in the Arkansas system and was even forcing some employees out of their positions so that he could bring in more people from Texas (Jordan, 1974). A survey of top positions indicated that nine of the top twenty positions were held by Texans ("Nine Texans in Top Jobs at Prisons," 1974). Some department employees resigned in protest of what they described as favoritism in hiring practices. Others claimed that there existed a termination list of persons who were to be fired from their positions. Neither the corrections board nor the legislature was convinced that the charges were substantiated or that they required action ("Queries on Prisons Answered," 1974; Associated Press, 1974b). A report of the legislative committee that looked into allegations indicated that there was no evidence to support the charges against Hutto's administration to include incompetence, favoritism, and continuing brutality ("Prison Officials Given Clean Bill," 1974).

The prison system continued to receive public attention as it was undergoing the transition into a more contemporary type of prison organization. Joseph Weston, an announced Republican candidate for governor in 1974, claimed that Governor Bumpers's neglect of the prison system was willful and shameful. He charged that the use of inmate trusties as tower guards was one of the horrible situations at the prisons that Bumpers had failed to correct. He cited an incident in which trusty inmates fired shots at escaping inmates (Associated Press, 1974c).

The new women's unit was under construction in Pine Bluff, although some feared that it would not have a large enough capacity to accommodate the expanding prison population of women. It was built in part from federal crime funds and was a dramatic improvement over the existing women's unit. Commissioner Hutto and his staff were also seeking funding for a diagnostic and classification center to be located adjacent to the women's unit in Pine Bluff. This center was to contain a central hospital and would serve as a reception center for male inmates. Correctional officials pointed out that substantial savings in constructions costs were possible if inmate labor was used. For the diagnostic unit to be contracted on the open market would require about $7 million, whereas the actual costs dropped to $3 million through the use of inmate labor ("Hutto Awaits Word on Diagnostic Unit," 1974).

Although there were many lawsuits filed against the prison system, an unusual one was filed in the U.S. District Court in 1974. An inmate claimed that the prison was unable to provide him with adequate treatment for his mental illness. Robert Finnegan, a 16-year-old inmate from Little Rock, had serious mental illness and charged that Tucker prison lacked facilities and staff to deal with such disorders. The suit asked that the state send Finnegan to a facility where he could receive proper care ("Teen-Age Inmate Files Suit, Claims Lack of Mental Care," 1974). There was little question that the resources for dealing with mentally ill inmates were limited. The psychologist who worked part time for the Department of Corrections testified in court that the treatment provided for Finnegan was to assign him to the hoe squad and to place him in isolation if he had a crisis such as a schizophrenic episode (Terrell, 1975a, b, and c). Judge Henley dismissed the suit without prejudice, explaining that the suit could be introduced in the future and that Finnegan may be entitled to relief under other litigation regarding prison conditions (Associated Press, 1975).

Although the department had employed its own guards to replace inmate trusty guards, little training was available for the new guards and the pay was low. Several incidents raised the question of security at the prisons. Apparently, board members were frustrated that there were still problems of security and order after spending so much money to hire guards. Commissioner Hutto sought to convince the board that the security staff was doing a good job under less than perfect conditions and that security was always a problem in prisons. It was apparent that resources were severely limited for either training or for increasing pay (Zimmer, 1974).

Impact of 8th Circuit Reversal

The celebration of being released from the federal court supervision by the district court was short-lived. A few months after Judge Henley's decision to terminate the case, the 8th U.S. Circuit Court of Appeals determined that the prisons were still unconstitutional and reinstated the case. The appellate court indicated that major constitutional deficiencies still existed, citing evidence of physical and mental brutality, torture, racial discrimination, lack of rehabilitative programs, abuses of solitary confinement, and inadequate food and clothing. This ruling, which resulted from appeals filed by attorneys on behalf of the inmates, remanded the case back to the district court level (Armbrust, 1974; *Finney v. Arkansas Board of Correction*, 1974).

In elaborating its concerns, the court of appeals noted that there still existed a continuing failure by the correctional authorities to provide a constitutional, and in some respects, even a humane environment within their institutions. Although some improvements had taken place, serious deficiencies such as overcrowding, inmate assaults, excessive force, verbal abuse, and inhumane punishment still were in place according to the court. The court ordered the lower court to address the lack of rehabilitation, racial discrimination, medical and dental care, solitary confinement, and the disciplinary process. Additionally the court ruled that the entire trusty guard system must be eliminated (Armbrust, 1974; *Finney v. Arkansas Board of Correction*, 1974).

The state Board of Correction and Commissioner Hutto were caught off guard by the reversal. In response they requested that the Court of Appeals rehear the case, claiming that the court ruled on the system as it existed several years ago without taking into account the changes that were already in place, as well as those which were then being implemented. The board members admitted that overcrowding was still a problem but denied that other deficiencies still existed, pointing to substantial progress on all other points raised by the court. As an example, Hutto stated that the only remaining inmate guards were tower guards who were scheduled to be replaced in the next few months. Hutto offered his opinion that if the Arkansas system was unconstitutional at that time, then there is simply not one prison system in the United States that is constitutional (Husted, 1974).

The 8th Circuit Court denied the petition requesting a rehearing of their decision to reinstate the Arkansas prison case ("Court Denies Prisons Plea," 1974). The only alternatives at that point were to continue efforts to adapt the prisons to the requirements of the court or to appeal to the U.S. Supreme Court. After considerable debate and recommendation from the legislative council to appeal to the Supreme Court the board decided, upon advice of the state attorney general, not to make such an appeal (Associated Press, 1974d; *Finney v. Arkansas Board of Correction*, 1974).

Continuing Court Supervision

Thus, prison officials continued to operate under the scrutiny of the federal court. They were required to give attention not only to making improvements to the system but also to convince the court that the improvements fulfilled constitutional requirements. The first order of business was to develop a strategy to alleviate overcrowding. The board approved plans to develop work release and prerelease programs, to develop temporary housing outside of existing prisons, to increase the use of parole, and to convert space that had been used for other purposes to inmates housing ("Prison Plans Approved," 1974). Additionally, the board approved plans to construct new inmate living quarters at Tucker (Dean, 1975). This interest in finding alternative housing was motivated by the federal appellate court's statement that it might become necessary to enjoin the state from accepting any more prisoners or even reducing the current numbers ("Hearings Open Next Week on Prisons' Conditions," 1975; *Finney v. Arkansas Board of Correction*, 1974).

Legislators also joined in the search for reducing overcrowding by proposing alternatives to incarceration. One bill was passed that allowed convicted felons to serve their time in alternative service. Thus, the person would still be in custody but would be in the community working under supervision ("Plan Would Provide Alternative to Prison," 1975). Also, the parole board stepped up its efforts to alleviate overcrowding. In December 1975, the board approved parole for 134 persons ("State Board Gives Paroles to 134," 1975).

Finney v. Hutto I (1976)

Judge J. Smith Henley indicated that his last lengthy written opinion in the Arkansas prison reform saga would be *Holt v. Hutto* (*Holt III*) in 1973. As noted, the 8th U.S. Circuit Court of Appeals did not agree and remanded the case back to the district court (*Finney v. Arkansas Board of Correction*, 1974). Since the Arkansas prisons were back in the trial-level federal courts it became necessary to participate in another round of hearings to determine if the prison had improved sufficiently to meet standards of the court. Judge Henley announced that hearings would begin in March of 1975. By that time Henley had been elevated to the 8th U.S. Circuit Court of Appeals and was assigned by designation back to the district court to preside over this specific Arkansas prison case (*Finney v. Hutto*, 1976; Terrell, 1975a).

Hearings were conducted by Judge Henley and by a federal magistrate, Robert Faulkner. The use of the magistrate was expeditious by the holding of some hearings at the prisons (Feeley, & Rubin 1998). The hearings included testimony, which by that time had become familiar. Inmates recited incidents of violence, poor security, inadequate facilities, lack of medical treatment, fights among inmates, homosexuality, unprofessional conduct of guards, and overcrowding (*Finney v. Hutto*, 1976; Kleinhauer, 1975; Terrell, 1975b).

Prison officials testified that much of what the inmates claimed was exaggerated or false. They also pointed out there was some truth in inmate claims and that conditions were being improved as quickly as possible with available resources. The Correction Department's information officer also pointed out that the cost of litigation was making it even more difficult to improve the system and provide needed care to the inmates (Terrell, 1975c).

In the summer of 1975, Hutto arranged for members of the legislature to tour prison facilities to show them the progress that had been made and to explain the needs that he hoped to address in the next legislative session. Having seen the current arrangement for visitation, Senator Knox Nelson noted the need for visitation facilities at Cummins. One legislator described the new small cell housing facility at Tucker as a motel. Also the legislators were shown the most recent acquisition designed to deal with crowding. Sixty house trailers had been purchased from the U.S. Department of Housing and Urban Development that were previously used to house persons displaced by natural disasters. In Arkansas 36 trailers were moved to Cummins and the rest to Tucker, each of which would be converted to house 10 to 12 inmates. In sum, the legislators were told that the system was operating well, including the farming operations, but that they could expect further funding requests to continue improvements to comply with the court (Tirey, 1975).

Judge Henley also toured the prisons along with the attorneys for each side and announced that overall he was very impressed. The major reservation he expressed on the tour regarded the overcrowding, which was apparent in all living areas he saw. He noted that the prisons were generally clean and orderly (Terrell, 1975d). It was obvious that Henley was seeing enormous improvements that had resulted from his orders of the last few years (Terrell, 1975d). The

Arkansas prison system had by this time expanded from the original Cummins (women's and men's units) and Tucker units to include a new reformatory for women that was about to open in Pine Bluff, Arkansas; the Alcoholic/Narcotic Rehabilitation Center; a work-release center and a pre-release center at the Benton State Hospital in Benton, Arkansas; another work release center in Blytheville, Arkansas; and the Department of Correction Livestock Production Center near Booneville, Arkansas (*Finney v. Hutto*, 1976). Judge Henley did not observe any constitutional or other issues of concern in the facilities other than Cummins and Tucker and the existing women's reformatory situated at the Cummins property.

Meanwhile, the struggle between available resources and prisons reform continued. The farms were profitable, but the funds they produced were far from filling the needs of the prison system. According to Hutto, the farms could be expected to raise about $2 to $2.5 million per year in addition to the $1 million in commodities consumed by the prison population each year (Tirey, 1975). Still, the corrections operations were increasingly becoming more dependent on state funds both for operating and for construction. The Correction Board in the fall of 1975 voted to ask the legislature for $13.17 million for construction projects. These funds were to be applied to living facilities at Cummins and Tucker, to the new women's unit at Pine Bluff, to the diagnostic unit at Pine Bluff, to a new unit for youthful offenders, and to visitation and medical facilities at Cummins ("Prison Buildings Sought," 1975).

In August of 1975 inmate Carl Joe Vaughn died in the Cummins infirmary after working in the fields. The preliminary indication was that he died of a heat stroke, but inmates disputed this ruling and claimed that Vaughn was beaten to death by free-world guards and other inmates. Vaughn had just been transported to Cummins from Tucker at his request and was immediately placed in the fields to work (Scudder, 1975a and b). The matter was brought to the U.S. District Court, which was hearing other matters related to the prisons, but was dismissed after the medical examiner's report became available. The autopsy report indicated that Vaughn died of natural causes and not from trauma or drugs as had been speculated. This ended the controversy (Scudder, 1975c).

A glimpse of the prisons from an inmate's perspective in the mid-1970s comes from a diary kept by Alvin Tyger during his 10 months at Cummins. Tyger describes the days of working in the fields and of the schemes devised to adjust to prison life on the Arkansas farms. For example, men would purposely injure themselves or have others do so in order to avoid the long hot workdays on the hoe squad. It was common, he wrote, for inmates who collapsed from the heat to be ridiculed and dealt with in a verbally and physically abusive manner. In some cases this was by free-world guards; in others it was by inmates with the approval, or even encouragement, of the guards ("Diary Details Inmate's Despair," 1975).

Henley's Order

Judge Henley's order has been referred to as *Finney I* (Feeley & Rubin, 1998) and lauded as "the 'most comprehensive, thorough examination' of a prison system ever undertaken by a court" (as cited in Feeley & Rubin, 1998, p. 71).

Overcrowding

Judge Henley first addressed the issue of overcrowding. In February of 1976, an order was entered that required that the old women's reformatory at Cummins be closed and inmates be transferred to the new women's reformatory in Pine Bluff by June 30. Commissioner Hutto advised the court that this would be accomplished (*Finney v. Hutto*, 1976; Terrell, 1976a). The inmate population continued to increase by the time of the court remand hearings in 1975 for the reason that admissions of inmates began outpacing discharges. Even with the construction of new housing units and the addition of mobile homes, inmates were being housed in a gymnasium and the infirmary was not limited to the sick (*Finney v. Hutto*, 1976).

In response to the crowding problems, Judge Henley ordered that the inmate population be limited to no more than 1,650 at Cummins and 550 at Tucker. At the time of the order there were 1,518 at Cummins and 501 at Tucker. Prison officials estimated the total capacity of the two units was a little over the 2,200 set by the court. The court allowed these maximums to be exceeded on a temporary basis in emergency situations. Further, Henley ordered that isolation cells hold no more than two inmates at a time, prohibited the department from sentencing inmates to punitive isolation for indefinite periods, and ordered that food and other conditions such as provision of bunks and mattresses in the isolation unit be improved (*Finney v. Hutto*, 1976; Terrell, 1976a).

Health Care

The court observed that the quality of medical facilities and care had improved significantly and included a full-time physician who was assisted by paramedics and two part-time dentists. The court did note that eye care was limited to provision of glasses. The prison system had a contract for services from a hospital in Pine Bluff near the prisons. However, a new hospital was being built in conjunction with the new women's reformatory in Pine Bluff.

In addition, the court's new ruling required the Department of Correction to provide professional services for inmates with mental disorders. Judge Henley accepted the department's program for group therapy for mental cases that had previously been implemented but also ordered the department to hire one or more full-time psychiatrists or psychologists to be available to provide the therapy needed by inmates (*Finney v. Hutto*, 1976; Hays, 1976). Judge Henley recognized that some inmates would resort to malingering in order to avoid work and that it was necessary for steps to be taken in order to minimize the number of cases of malingering. The court's solution to this problem was to ensure that any disciplinary action against an inmate include evidence from the inmate's treating physician as to the nature of the inmate's diagnosis (*Finney v. Hutto*, 1976).

Rehabilitation

The court noted substantial improvements in the rehabilitation programs that had been implemented in the Arkansas prison system since the last round of district court hearings. The drug and alcohol treatment unit, the pre-release unit, and the two work-release centers were all started in 1975. The Department of Correction also established a state-sanctioned school district for all inmates who lacked high school education. College-level courses were also available for qualified and "trustworthy inmate[s]" (*Finney v. Hutto*, 1976, p. 262). The department was also found to have created meaningful vocational training programs in areas including auto and farm equipment repair, welding, woodworking, graphic arts, and upholstering (*Finney v. Hutto*, 1976).

Mail and Visitors

Judge Henley found that the prison system's regulations regarding inmate mail and visitation had been revised so as to comply with the requirements of *Procunier v. Martinez* (1974). Judge Henley noted that the old regulations that concerned the 8th Circuit had predated the *Martinez* decision (*Finney v. Hutto*, 1976).

Legal Assistance

The Department of Correction had hired a licensed attorney as a full-time state employee to serve with the title "legal advisor to inmates." The attorney could not represent inmates in Section 1983 cases against the state or state officials but could represent inmates in other civil cases, including post-conviction relief actions in state and federal courts. Judge Henley stated that the 8th Circuit Court of Appeals might not have fully understood the role of the legal advisor when considering *Finney v. Arkansas Board of Correction* (1974). It was also held that the inmate "writ writers" who often assisted other inmates with legal matters were allowed to function in a manner that is consistent with the U.S. Supreme Court ruling in *Johnson v. Avery* (1969). These writ writers were also known as "jailhouse lawyers" and were prisoners who lacked formal legal training or licensure, but by personal experience and study gained at least a modicum of expertise in legal matters of interest to many inmates (Palmer, 2010, p. 169). Many states had restrictions on the activities of jailhouse lawyers until the U.S. Supreme Court held that states could not prohibit such legal assistance if inmates did not have the ability to represent themselves and the state was not providing other legal services (*Johnson v. Avery*, 1969). The Arkansas procedures had been compliant with *Johnson* for years, contrary to the 8th Circuit findings in *Finney v. Arkansas Department of Correction* (1974). Furthermore, the state had also set up law libraries at Cummins and Tucker for the use of inmates and the writ writers (*Finney v. Hutto*, 1976).

Inmate Safety

Inmate safety and the exposure to assault by staff and other inmates was a concern in all of the previous litigation surrounding the Arkansas prisons. Judge Henley took up the issue of inmate safety by pointing out "it may be doubted that any prison is a 'safe' place for an inmate to live" (*Finney v. Hutto*, 1976, p. 263).

His discussion contrasted the former and then current conditions and practices that bear on the safety of prisoners in the Arkansas system. Henley described the old:

> In years past an ordinary inmate of the Department, referred to then as a "ranker," was in almost constant danger from other rankers, and he was also in danger of being killed by armed inmate guards. His danger of attack from other rankers was enhanced by the fact that the trusty guards would do little or nothing to protect him, and that the inmate floorwalkers assigned to patrol the barracks at night were of little, if any, value as far as inmate safety was concerned (*Finney v. Hutto*, 1976, p. 264).

Judge Henley explained the evolution of the trusty system from the almost total reliance on largely unrestricted armed trusty guards to limiting armed trusties, to guard towers under the supervision of free-world civilian guards, to the current system with no armed inmates acting in the capacity of guards.

Judge Henley resolved a remaining controversy over the continued use of inmates in security roles as "floorwalkers" to patrol the barracks at night. The floorwalkers were not armed and posed no risk to the other inmates in the barracks. Henley did state that while he had "doubt that the floorwalkers are of much protection to inmates, they [we]re not a source of danger to inmates" and may have had some deterrent impact on the "creepers and crawlers" mentioned in *Holt II* (*Finney v. Hutto*, 1976, p. 264). The court concluded that

> all in all officers and employees of the Department have done a reasonably good job in the field of inmate safety over the past three or four years, and the court does not find that the Department is failing to use ordinary care for inmate safety, or that either Cummins or Tucker is today such a dangerous place for an inmate to live as to raise a constitutional problem as far as inmate safety in itself is concerned (*Finney v. Hutto*, 1976, pp. 264–265).

Race Relations

The court noted that while there had been improvements, racial relations at Cummins and Tucker were still "bad" (*Finney v. Hutto*, 1976, p. 265). Reasons were posited to be from the lack of Black prison officials in the upper levels of administrative hierarchy, witting and unwitting racial prejudices of staff and inmates, and substandard and unprofessional correctional officers. Judge Henley struck something of a defeatist tone with his view that

> although in candor the court doubts that race relations, as such, will ever be any better in the Department than they are in the free world; and that observation is as applicable to any prison in the country as it is to the Arkansas prisons (*Finney v. Hutto*, 1976, p. 266).

But the state was making a concerted effort developing an "affirmative action plan" in hiring and promoting more Black officers. Judge Henley found fault with the plan in that it relied primarily on use of the Arkansas Employment Security Division (ESD) as the conduit for employee applications. The ESD used forms and made referrals that did not address race. The court viewed this racially neutral plan as being insufficient to correct the racial imbalance in employment of staff from minority populations. Judge Henley was not opposed to the use of ESD for employee searches but was critical of that agency being the exclusive method of hiring. He suggested exploring the use of alternative resources such as the Urban League, the NAACP, and the University of Arkansas at Pine Bluff, a historically Black college that is near to the primary Arkansas prison system facilities (*Finney v. Hutto*, 1976).

Black Muslim Issues

Judge Henley here, as in *Holt III*, took up issues raised by Black Muslim inmates and claims of First Amendment free exercise violations. The court specifically found that

> Muslims are not unduly restricted in the exercise of their religion. They can hold meetings as can members of other religious sects, the services of Muslim clergymen are not denied to them, and they are free to receive generally circulating Muslim publications (*Finney v. Hutto*, 1976, p. 270).

The greatest problem alleged by the inmates was related to dietary requirements of the Muslim religion. This issue appeared to be more problematic than by other First Amendment free exercise of religion challenges. Muslims are not permitted to eat pork or foods that have been contaminated by pork. Pork is a regular item on prison menus and vegetables are often cooked in pork grease. It was found that the department was making a good faith effort to accommodate the dietary restrictions of these inmates. The more difficult problem was that the Muslim inmates did not trust the non-Muslim kitchen staff to properly prepare their food. The court noted probable futility in further injunctive relief on this issue but made the largely symbolic gesture of enjoining the department from exposing Muslim inmates to pork or pork-contaminated foods. It was not ordered, but was suggested that Commissioner Hutto arrange for outside Muslims to inspect the kitchen and provide feedback for proper food handling (*Finney v. Hutto*, 1976).

Grievance Procedure

The state had instituted policies and procedures for the filing and handling of grievances by inmates. There is no requirement that state prisons have such procedures, but the court did point out the fact that such programs can do much to resolve disputes without the need for a prisoner to file a lawsuit to seek relief.

However, Judge Henley observed that to be effective, grievance procedures must be perceived by prisoners to be fair. The Prison Litigation Reform Act that was enacted in 1996 required prisoners to exhaust all state administrative remedies before pursuing litigation in the federal courts (Palmer, 2010).

Brutality

The Arkansas prison litigation started with complaints of brutality perpetrated against inmates by other inmates and the few free-world staff. These complaints persisted throughout the ensuing cases and produced injunctive relief in various forms in many of the cases, including *Holt I, II,* and *III.* Judge Henley noted that not all acts of violence are impermissible:

> It should always be kept in mind that the reasonable use of force by prison authorities is not only permissible but positively required on occasions. Hence, every incident of violence involving an inmate and a prison employee is not necessarily an incident of brutality (*Finney v. Hutto*, 1976, p. 271).

It was found that prison policy forbids brutality and excessive force. Officers who violate this policy had been terminated. Nonetheless, the court did "enjoin all Department personnel from verbally abusing or cursing inmates, and from employing racial slurs or epithets when addressing or talking with inmates" (*Finney v. Hutto*, 1976, p. 272).

Disciplinary Procedures

As discussed previously, the procedures for handling disciplinary matters were addressed with approval in *Holt III.* By the time the matter reached the 8th Circuit, the Supreme Court handed down *Wolff v. McDonnell* (1974), providing more guidance for lower courts in their review of such matters. Following *McDonnell,* the Board of Correction adopted new disciplinary procedures that they believed complied with the new case law. The Arkansas procedures went beyond *McDonnell* and set up two different disciplinary tracks for minor and major infractions. Henley found the procedures satisfied the due process requirements of *McDonnell,* including notice, decision maker, record, and review. Confrontation and cross-examination of witnesses by the inmate is limited, also as permitted by *McDonnell.* Inmates do not have the right to counsel at a disciplinary hearing but may have the assistance of a staff member appointed by the committee chair if the accused inmate is unable to fairly present his case (*Finney v. Hutto*, 1976).

Isolation (Administrative and Punitive) Units

Punitive isolation is a punishment for more serious disciplinary violations. Judge Henley found that "there is no question that the punishment that is one of the most dreaded by the inmates and that creates a serious constitutional problem is confinement in punitive isolation" (*Finney v. Hutto*, 1976, p. 275). Similarly situated are those inmates in "administrative segregation" who are held pending the disposition of their disciplinary matter. Contrary to the findings of the Court in *Holt I* and *III*, the court of appeals found that the conditions of confinement and grue diet were unconstitutional. On remand, Judge Henley also concluded that, based on testimony of witnesses and the judge's personal inspection of the facilities, conditions in punitive isolation and administrative segregation were unconstitutional. Henley explained "that either conditions were not as good in 1973 as the court thought they were or that the conditions have deteriorated since 1973" (*Finney v. Hutto*, 1976, p. 275). Conditions included housing up to four men in a single cell with some having to sleep on the floor; the grue diet not being nutritiously adequate; common violence; and inmates harming each other with the physical contents of the cells. The court specifically found "punitive isolation as it exists at Cummins today serves no rehabilitative purpose, and that it is counterproductive. It makes bad men worse. It must be changed" (*Finney v. Hutto*, 1976, p. 277). The order of the court was that no more than two men be confined in a cell, each man must have a bunk, and the grue diet must be discontinued. The court did allow continuation of the practice of removing mattresses from cells during the day for the reason that inmates would often act out their displeasure using mattresses by burning, tearing them up, and clogging up toilets with pieces of the mattresses. The court also set the maximum time that an inmate could be held in punitive isolation at 30 days. That was an increase from the 14-day period that was in use at the time. The increase was allowed because the conditions were to be greatly improved (*Finney v. Hutto*, 1976).

A related housing unit was the East Building at Cummins that was a maximum security unit used for protective custody of certain inmates who were at great risk of harm at the hands of other inmates, inmates deemed an escape risk, and inmates at risk for other reasons. Other institutions use the term "administrative segregation" for similar units. These inmates have better conditions than do those in punitive isolation, are released to work in specific areas of the prison, and have the same visitation and mail privileges as inmates in the general population. Judge Henley required that the procedures for evaluation and continued placement in this wing be reviewed at intervals not to exceed 60 days. Overcrowding in the punitive isolation and administrative segregations units was ordered to be reduced within a reasonable period (*Finney v. Hutto*, 1976).

Attorney Fees

The court pointed out that attorneys appointed in the initial Arkansas prison cases did not request and were not awarded any fees for their substantial services. In *Holt III*, attorneys Jack Holt and Phillip Kaplan were awarded attorney fees in the amount of $8,000 and were reimbursed for certain costs. It was observed that while the Department of Correction had made great strides in the improvement of conditions and practices, they had also demonstrated resistance to doing any more than necessary to satisfy the court. Judge Henley sought an incentive for a greater level of focus by the department and awarded additional attorney fees in the amount of $20,000 to be paid by the Department of Correction. The court explained, "Not only are the attorneys entitled to such a fee, but also the allowance thereof may incline the Department to act in such a manner that further protracted litigation about the prisons will not be necessary" (*Finney v. Hutto*, 1976, p. 285).

Supreme Court Weigh In

Finney I was subsequently affirmed by the 8th U.S. Circuit Court of Appeals (*Finney v. Hutto*, 1977) and by the Supreme Court of the United States (SCOTUS) (*Hutto v. Finney*, 1978). The 8th Circuit, in its order affirming the trial court, described the case as "the seemingly endless litigation involving the constitutionality of the Arkansas prisons" (*Finney v. Hutto*, 1977, p. 741). The issues before the appellate courts were conditions in the isolation unit and the award of fees for the inmates' attorneys. The Supreme Court held that conditions in the isolation unit as a whole, including the grue diet, filthy conditions, ongoing problems with overcrowding, violence, length of time in isolation by some inmates, and unprofessional conduct of the prison staff, constituted a violation of the Eighth Amendment prohibition against cruel and unusual punishment. The 30-day limit for confinement in isolation was found to be reasonable (*Hutto v. Finney*, 1978).

SCOTUS also upheld the award of fees and costs for the attorneys representing the inmates. The determination of the Court was that the Department of Correction had acted in bad faith regarding its efforts to comply with previous court orders. The additional fees awarded by the court of appeals were justified under the Civil Rights Attorney's Fees Awards Act of 1976 (42 U.S.C. § 1988) (*Hutto v. Finney*, 1978).

Conclusion

As stated, Judge J. Smith Henley hoped he was finished with the extended litigation and lengthy written opinions associated with the Arkansas prisons by his decision in *Holt III*. But it was not to be. Even Judge Henley's elevation to the 8th Circuit Court of Appeals did not keep him from being assigned back to the district court for the legal work required by the remand of *Holt III* in *Finney v. Arkansas Board of Correction* (1974). Following the extensive hearings after the remand, Judge Henley provided the Arkansas Department of Correction with detailed directions and requirements for further changes and improvements. The additional attorneys' fees awarded also served as an incentive to the department to get things done to the satisfaction of the court. Finally, the federal court decision announced that it would retain jurisdiction over the prisons indefinitely in order to bring the state prison system into compliance with the Constitution and the law (*Finney v. Hutto*, 1976).

The 8th Circuit provided substantial direction to the district court for continuing hearings and monitoring in the *Finney v. Arkansas Department of Correction* (1974) decision. The federal court "push" was given extra power to continue momentum in reforms to the state and the Department of Correction by the detailed decision by Judge J. Smith Henley in *Finney I* regarding overcrowding, rehabilitation programs, mail and visitation, legal assistance, inmate safety, race, and religion (*Finney v. Hutto*, 1976). The "push" was further accelerated by the opinion of the U.S. Supreme Court in affirming the trial court and appellate court decisions. But the effort to bring the Arkansas prison system into the 20th century was not complete. Continued litigation, including the first and only consent decree in the lengthy process and an outside person to observe and comment on compliance, would be necessary to bring the matter to a close.

REFERENCES

Armbrust, R. (1974, October 11). Prisons still ruled unacceptable. *Arkansas Democrat.*

Associated Press. (1974a, January 11). Senator will ask probe of prison. *Arkansas Democrat.*

Associated Press. (1974b, March 4). Prison board member denies retaliation charges. *Arkansas Democrat.*

Associated Press. (1974c, May 5). Weston accuses Bumpers of neglecting prison system. *Arkansas Democrat.*

Associated Press. (1974d, November 8). Opinion given on prisons. *Arkansas Democrat.*

Associated Press. (1975, May 25). Suit filed by Tucker inmate dismissed. *Arkansas Democrat.*

Correction board sets desegregation of cells. (1973, August 26). *Arkansas Democrat.*

Dean, J. (1973, August 13). Henley relinquishes prison case but cites administrative problems. *Arkansas Democrat.*

Dean, J. (1975, March 22). Architects are chose for project at prison. *Arkansas Democrat.*

Diary details inmate's despair. (1975, November 2). *Arkansas Democrat.*

Dudley, S., & Harris, M. K. (1977). *After decision: Implementation of judicial decrees in correctional settings.* American Bar Association.

Ex-inmate is awarded $43,250. (1972, April 5). *Arkansas Democrat.*

Feeley, M. M., & Rubin, E. L. (1998). *Judicial policy making and the modern state: How the courts reformed America's prisons.* Cambridge University Press.

Finney v. Arkansas Board of Correction, 505 F.2d 194 (8th Cir.1974)

Finney v. Hutto, 410 F. Supp. 251 (E.D. Ark. 1976)

Finney v. Hutto, 548 F.2d 740 (8th Cir. 1977)

Former inmate, shot accidentally, files $200,000 suit. (1973, September 7). *Arkansas Democrat.*

Hays, S. (1976, March 20). Ruling requires psychiatric care for prisoners. *Arkansas Democrat.*

Hearings open next week on prisons' conditions. (1975, March 22). *Arkansas Democrat.*

Holt v. Hutto, 363 F. Supp. 194 (E.D. Ark 1973)

Husted, B. (1974, October 19). Prison rehearing sought. *Arkansas Democrat.*

Hutto awaits word on diagnostic unit. (1974, May 26). *Arkansas Democrat.*

Hutto v. Finney, 437 U.S. 678 (1978)

Johnson v. Avery, 393 U.S. 483 (1969)

Jordan, T. (1974, January 16). Bumpers backs Hutto's work. *Arkansas Democrat.*

Kleinhauer, S. (1975, March 29). Cummins inmates allege beatings. *Arkansas Democrat.*

Morrissey v. Brewer, 408 U.S. 471 (1972)

Nine Texans in top jobs at prisons. (1974, February 6). *Arkansas Democrat.*

Palmer, J. (2010). *Constitutional rights of prisoners* (9th ed.). Matthew Bender & Company.

Plan would provide alternative to prison. (1975, January 19). *Arkansas Democrat.*

Prison buildings sought. (1975, September 14). *Arkansas Democrat.*

Prison plans approved. (1974, November 24). *Arkansas Democrat.*

Prison officials given clean bill. (1974, April 5). *Arkansas Democrat.*

Procunier v. Martinez, 416 U.S. 396 (1974)

Queries on prisons answered. (1974, February 24). *Arkansas Democrat.*

Scudder, J. (1975a, October 2). Motion request lie detector tests in inmate's death. *Arkansas Democrat.*

Scudder, J. (1975b, October 4). Inmate in isolation 3 days before death. *Arkansas Democrat.*

Scudder, J. (1975c, October 11). Autopsy says heat caused inmate's death. *Arkansas Democrat.*

State board gives paroles to 134. (1975, December 5). *Arkansas Democrat.*

Teen-age inmate files suit, claims lack of mental care. (1974, June 1). *Arkansas Democrat.*

Terrell, D. (1975a, March 22). Inmate entitled to medical care? *Arkansas Democrat.*

Terrell, D. (1975b, March 27). Prison inmate tells of beatings. *Arkansas Democrat.*

Terrell, D. (1975c, May 5). Prison hearings to curtail services. *Arkansas Democrat.*

Terrell, D. (1975d, August 20). Henley tours state's prisons; "He's impressed." *Arkansas Democrat.*

Terrell, D. (1976a, March 19). Court limits number in Arkansas prisons. *Arkansas Democrat.*

Terrell, D. (1976b, March 26). Inmate receiving adequate care for mental illness, doctors testify. *Arkansas Democrat.*

Tirey, B. (1975, August 8). Legislators get tour of state prisons. *Arkansas Democrat.*

Wolff v. McDonnell, 418 U.S. 539 (1974)

Zimmer, L. (1974, July 20). Laxity among guards at prison criticized by board. *Arkansas Democrat.*

KEY TERMS

Alternative service	Jail house lawyers
Floorwalkers	

QUESTIONS

1. Identify and discuss the growing pains associated with transitioning from the old to new prison system.

2. What is "alternative service," and why was it implemented to provide a constitutional, and in some respects, humane environment within the institutions?

3. In *Finney I*, Judge Henley's court order was lauded as "the 'most comprehensive, thorough examination' of a prison system ever undertaken by a court." Explain the court's rulings relative to prison overcrowding, health care, rehabilitation, and mail and visitors.

4. In *Finney I*, jailhouse lawyers were addressed. Describe a jailhouse lawyer and explain whether they were being used in the Arkansas system consistent with *Johnson v. Avery*.

5. What is a floorwalker? Compare the former and current conditions and practices of floorwalkers with the safety of prisoners in the Arkansas system.

6. The procedures for handling disciplinary matters were addressed with *Wolff v. McDonnell* (1974), providing more guidance for lower courts in their review of such matters. How did the Arkansas Board of Correction adopt new disciplinary procedures that addressed the new case law?

7. What was Judge Henley's rationale for awarding additional attorney fees in the amount of $20,000 to be paid by the Department of Correction? Do you believe it was justified?

11 | Final Orders

Introduction

The federal court litigation over the Arkansas prison system that began in 1968 was now in its final phases. The state was continuing to make progress through the federal court litigation process that had even reached the U.S. Supreme Court in *Hutto v. Finney* (1978). The Arkansas case would see a new judge, effort at consensus and agreement between the parties through a consent decree, and the appointment of an independent compliance coordinator to assist with supervision of the prison system. The court and the public would also see the state make significant investments through legislative appropriations.

State Response

Following the trial court decision in *Finney I*, it appeared that the time was at hand to get even more serious about complying with the courts in order for Arkansas to get the prison scandals behind them (*Finncy v. Hutto*, 1976). Top state officials recognized that the current reform efforts were not adequate and that changes required by the courts were going to be very expensive. Early in 1976, Governor Pryor estimated that the cost of prison improvements would be between $23 and 30 million. Shortly after the federal courts' most recent rulings, the governor's estimate had increased to between $25 and 50 million. Both estimates were shocking to the legislators, who found themselves in the position of providing still more funding for a prison system that had already required enormous expenditures in recent years (Associated Press, 1976).

Additionally, it was in the mid-1970s that public opinion in the nation, and in Arkansas, began to shift away from favoring rehabilitation toward a more punitive stance toward crime and criminals. Policymakers began to adopt the "nothing works" attitude toward rehabilitation of theorists such as Andrew Von Hirsch (1976). One of the first proposals for Arkansas prisons to get tougher on crime was to abolish good time (time off for good behavior). The object was to have inmates spend more time in prison to discourage future criminality. Hutto argued that such a law would have limited effect on deterrence and would greatly increase prison costs over the next few years. Good time had the effect of moving current inmates out of the prison to make room for the new admissions. At the time when the courts had placed a ceiling on prison populations, the removal of good time provisions, along with normal growth of the prison population, could, by Hutto's estimate, easily double the prison population from its current level below 2,500 to more than 5,000 by 1980. Hutto projected that if good time credit was abolished, the current $10 million figure anticipated for construction from 1976–1979 would expand to over $48 million ("Act Would Hike Prison Costs, Hutto Claims," 1976).

Another tactic for getting more restrictive on inmates was to have persons serve a given proportion of their sentence before becoming eligible for parole. The bill that came before the legislature, and was eventually passed, required that first offenders serve at least one-third of their sentence minus good time before being eligible for parole. Second offenders would have to serve one-half of their sentences, while third offenders would have to serve three-fourths of their sentences prior to becoming eligible for parole; fourth offenders would not be eligible for parole ("Hutto Almost Backs Glover's Proposal," 1976).

Another approach for dealing with prison crowding and with the population caps set by the courts was to let convicted inmates remain in the county jails for a longer period before transporting them to the state prisons. By having inmates serving the first part of their sentences in jail, the jails could help relieve prison crowding. This idea was implemented, but not without limitations and misgivings. The state Criminal Detention Facilities Board passed minimum standards for jails, which very few of the state's jails met. Many speculated that if the state began using county jails to house part of the prison population and many of these jails were substandard, it was likely that the federal courts would soon focus attention on jails, as they had already done with prisons. In addition, the increased number of inmates and expenses created a hardship for counties and for the sheriffs who administered the jails (Oswald, 1976a).

In the summer of 1976, women inmates were transferred from the woefully inadequate facilities on Cummins prison farm to the new women's reformatory at Pine Bluff. The transfer took place before construction was complete in order to comply with an order from Judge Henley who set a specific date for the old facility to be closed. Among other problems identified by the federal courts, Henley described the women's prison as hopelessly and unconstitutionally overcrowded. The new prison was dramatically different from the old one. The Pine Bluff prison looked like a modern office building or school. The buildings contained many windows and faced a courtyard. The new facility had a gym, a sewing room, a classroom, and areas for worship and recreation. There were no bars on the new prison, which had a capacity for 126 inmates. It was built at a cost of $1.4 million using inmate labor (Oswald, 1976, June 29b).

In the fall of 1976, T. Don Hutto resigned from his position of state corrections commissioner to become the deputy director of Corrections in Virginia. Hutto had served the Arkansas prison system for 5 years, following Robert Sarver as commissioner. During his tenure as commissioner Hutto orchestrated the changes required by the courts and sought the funds needed to do so from the state. Hutto placed a premium on changing behavior of inmates so that they could be returned to society as normal citizens with a reasonable chance of success. Under his direction the old trusty system was dismantled and replaced by an organization of state employees who operated the prison system (Oswald, 1976c).

At the end of the 5 years Hutto served as correctional commissioner, the state of Arkansas reached another level of prison reform. While it was still under the scrutiny of the federal court and it was far from a model prison system, the state had made giant leaps in changing the system that had stirred up controversy for more than 10 years. Arkansas had finally turned its back on the corrupt and abusive plantations of inmates secured and run by inmates, which placed a premium on saving or making money for the state while ignoring the need for a modern system based on law and policy. As Hutto stated at the announcement of his resignation, Arkansas doesn't have to take a back seat to anybody as far as prisons go at this time (Oswald, 1976c). Yet, there was still more to be done in order to emerge from federal court supervision.

Additional Litigation and a New Judge

Following the appeal of *Finney I*, Judge Henley withdrew from further trial level work on the continuing Arkansas prison litigation. The matter was then assigned to Judge G. Thomas Eisele, chief judge of the U.S. District Court for the Eastern District of Arkansas. Eisele was appointed to the federal bench by President Richard Nixon after having served as campaign manager for Winthrop Rockefeller's race for Arkansas governor and serving as Governor Rockefeller's chief of staff. His work as chief of staff between 1967 and 1969 made Eisele very familiar with the Arkansas prison system and its efforts at reform (Feeley & Rubin, 1998). Judge Eisele continued Henley's practice of using the services of Magistrate Robert Faulkner to conduct evidentiary hearings, along with conducting his own hearings.

FIGURE 11.1. Judge G. Thomas Eisele.

Finney v. Mabry (1978a), also referred to as *Finney II*, was a class action suit seeking relief for the inmates in the Arkansas Department of Correction. Judge Eisele took steps to facilitate complete and unvarnished testimony of inmates free from fear of reprisal by prison officials. These steps included limited discovery and withholding the identity of witnesses until the time of their testimony (*Feeley v. Rubin*, 1998). In order to ensure that the respondents had the opportunity for fair and adequate cross-examination of petitioners' witnesses, the respondents' attorneys were allowed to recall witnesses at a later time for additional questioning if that was deemed necessary (*Finney v. Mabry*, 1978a).

Finney II focused on disciplinary procedures in the Arkansas prison system, including those that had previously been approved by Judge Henley in *Finney I* and affirmed by the 8th Circuit Court of Appeals. So, Judge Eisele's decision finding the department's procedures inadequate was unexpected and controversial. Judge Eisele found that the department's disciplinary proceedings were constitutional on their face, but that "there are further unaddressed aspects of the process that have come to light in this Court's hearings, and disturbing interpretations and applications of Judge Henley's opinion by prison officials which require a new examination of the hearing process" (*Finney v. Mabry*, 1978a, p. 759). In particular, Judge Eisele found that much of the published procedures were not followed, with many cases decided with no witness statements being considered. Cases involving informants often did not even reveal the name of the informant, or even the full statement of the informant to the committee. Eisele observed, "The Court is convinced, from all the testimony, that this procedure invites, and has in fact permitted, correctional officers to obtain disciplinary sanctions against unsubstantiated and, indeed, fabricated charges" (*Finney v. Mabry*, 1978a, p. 765).

FIGURE 11.2. Arkansas Department of Corrections Director, James Mabry.

The disciplinary committee did maintain tape recordings of the hearing, but only kept the tapes for a period of 6 months. There was also evidence that prison officials sometimes ignored the policies and procedures and simply ordered the committee to render a decision and the punishment. These practices and procedures do not satisfy the due process requirements of *Wolff v. McDonnell* (1974).

The *McDonnell* case recognizes that the due process clause of the 14th Amendment does not afford prisoners the same protections that are available to a person facing trial for a criminal charge. Nor does a prisoner facing a disciplinary charge have the same due process protections as a probationer or parolee facing revocation and possible incarceration. However, the prisoner in a disciplinary proceeding does have a liberty interest in not losing good time credits or parole eligibility as considered in *Morrissey v. Brewer* (1972). The question becomes, "How much process is due?" The process must not be arbitrary and must promote a fair method of fact-finding and adjudication. Judge Eisele ruled that the disciplinary process must consider evidence in the form of written or oral statements of witnesses. If physical evidence exists, it should be considered (*Finney v. Mabry*, 1978a).

Disciplinary hearings in prison settings bring the opportunity for reprisal by an unhappy inmate. For this reason, it is often necessary to shield the identity of staff or other inmates as witnesses. However, the committee must take steps to consider the credibility of these witnesses. The witnesses must be identified to the committee and their testimony taken either orally or by written statements. The Court's ruling had the effect that due process in prison disciplinary hearings does not reach as far as the right to confront witnesses at a trial as required by the Sixth Amendment (*Finney v. Mabry*, 1978a). Judge Eisele also directed the department to maintain records, including tape recordings, of hearings indefinitely, pending further orders of the Court.

Finney II thus found that due process is as important in prison disciplinary hearings as it is in other more formal settings. Efforts by the State of Arkansas at prison reform are stifled by taking short cuts around processes to fairly address violation of institutional rules by inmates. Judge Eisele astutely noted "arbitrary treatment of inmates gives rise to the same (or greater) disorder and discontent as that which occurs whenever human beings are unfairly treated" (*Finney v. Mabry*, 1978a, p. 777). If inmates have faith that the disciplinary process is fair, outcomes on all levels will be improved for inmates and staff. It was essential that a fair and impartial process for resolution of alleged disciplinary violations be implemented and followed.

Consent Decree 1978

Soon after the decision in *Finney II* was entered, the U.S. Supreme Court handed down its decision in the appeal of *Finney I*. These two decisions together gave Judge Eisele additional leverage that he used to encourage the inmates and the department to work out a resolution of the remaining issues (Feeley & Rubin, 1998). A consent decree was negotiated by the parties and approved by Judge Eisele on October 5, 1978 (*Finney v. Mabry*, 1978b). The consent decree appears to have incorporated long-time and more current matters of dispute, including 39 provisions covering matters such as use of force, verbal abuse, medical, dental, and mental health care, the grievance procedure, conditions in housing units, elimination of the grue diet in the isolation unit, a maximum of 30 days in isolation, disciplinary hearing procedures, access to legal services and the law library, free exercise of religion by Muslim inmates, inmate population limits at Cummins and Tucker, personal hygiene items for inmates, and department staffing and personnel issues (*Finney v. Mabry*, 1978b).

The consent decree also included an agreement by the department to employ a compliance coordinator "with suitable legal, administrative and humanistic skills" to ensure that the department complies with all court orders (*Finney v. Mabry*, 1978b, p. 724). This person was given broad powers and authority. The compliance coordinator was to be provided adequate offices and staff and "unlimited access to any facilities, buildings, or premises under the control of ADC" (*Finney v. Mabry*, 1978b, p. 724). The compliance coordinator could attend institutional meetings, receive written reports, and meet with staff and inmates at his discretion. He was directed to file quarterly reports with the commissioner of correction, the Board of Correction, the attorney general, counsel for the inmates, and the clerk of the court. Reports were to cover the matters listed in the consent decree, whether the department was in compliance, and the degree of cooperation by the department. The order also set out a timeline within which the court intended that the department be in full compliance and jurisdiction of the court ended (*Finney v. Mabry*, 1978b).

Stephen LaPlante was appointed to serve as the compliance coordinator. LaPlante was recommended by the director of the National Institute of Corrections, Allan Breed (Feeley & Rubin, 1998). A position such as this is authorized under the Federal Rules of Civil Procedure, Rule 53(b). The official term in the rules for the position is "Master," but it was not used in this appointment for the reason that the word "master" could carry a negative association for Black prisoners (Feeley & Rubin, 1998). LaPlante served in this capacity for 3 years during which he gave great attention to the department and its operations and provided lengthy and detailed reports. He was frequently highly critical of the department, with his criticisms often being made public. Considering the past history of prisons and reform in Arkansas, the resulting conflict should not have been unexpected. The Board of Corrections announced that they would not renew LaPlante's contract when it expired on March 31, 1981. The attorneys for the inmates complained that LaPlante could not be fired because he was acting on behalf of the court even though his contract was with the state. Judge Eisele allowed the dismissal to stand but did extend LaPlante's contract for a few months to complete his reports. Eisele then resumed direct oversight of the case himself (Feeley & Rubin, 1998).

Seeing Daylight: *Finney III*

This matter was a hearing regarding compliance with previous orders of the court. The hearing was at the request of the inmate petitioners who had asserted that the state was no longer cooperating in good faith regarding the terms and conditions of the previous orders. Also under consideration were issues raised by an amended petition alleging other violations of the law and the Constitution. Judge Eisele found that the state was in compliance on many issues; will be in compliance on some issues following full implementation of new policies and procedures; but was still not in compliance on other issues (*Finney v. Mabry*, 1982a). It was found that most of the remaining violations were at Cummins, with some at Tucker, and no problems at the other units of the prison system.

Those planned but not yet fully implemented reforms included hiring 128 new correctional officers to remove all inmates from any positions of control or authority. Inmates had previously been removed from any position that would involve any use of force, but some inmates were still used as unarmed "floor-walkers," who assist guards at night in the barracks, and "turnkeys," who open and close mechanical doors under direct supervision of correctional officers and had no control over other inmates. The court's order and injunction included directions that those inmate positions be eliminated by April 12, 1982. It was stressed that inadequate professional staffing levels were a primary cause of the problems of the old system and would not be tolerated in the current system.

Judge Eisele ordered that the proposed staffing levels be completed and directed that "no return to the status quo ante is constitutionally permissible" (*Finney v. Mabry*, 1982a, p. 1038).

The court did find several areas in which the respondents had not yet complied with the Constitution or previous orders. These areas of concern included the continued use of open barracks for housing, overcrowding, inadequate numbers of minorities as staff, continued use of two segregated barracks, and the unacceptable use of racial slurs by staff to minority inmates (*Finney v. Mabry*, 1982a). The open barracks practice employed in eight of the Cummins 100-man housing units resulted in a security problem in that bunk beds are used in some areas of the barracks. This obstructed the view of correctional officers into certain areas. The visual observation problem was made worse by allowing inmates to hang sheets off the bunks to provide visual screening and privacy. These open barracks also had other areas that are difficult to monitor at night due to lighting and the distances involved. The prison officials claimed insufficient resources with which to reduce the number of inmates in these barracks. The court ruled that "limited resources cannot be considered an excuse for not maintaining the institution according to at least minimum constitutional standards" (*Finney v. Mabry*, 1982a, p. 1041). The court gave the respondents 30 days to offer proposals to resolve this issue of inmate security in the large open barracks (*Finney v. Mabry*, 1982a).

Race was a concern in the remaining issues still before the court. The court observed that the prison had been fully desegregated with the exception of cells in the maximum security unit. Judge Eisele ordered the prison officials to stop the general practice of using racially segregated cells in the maximum security unit. It was found that some cases might justify placing certain inmates in segregated cells. Similar to the security issue, respondents were given 30 days to submit proposals for accomplishing complete integration of the maximum security unit and methods for determining when separating certain inmates by race would be appropriate (*Finney v. Mabry*, 1982a). Officials were directed to take a more aggressive posture toward staff in stopping the use of racial slurs to inmates. The state was also ordered to redouble efforts to hire and retain minority members in staff positions (*Finney v. Mabry*, 1982a).

The court denied the petitioners' request that a "monitor" be appointed to ensure that required steps are taken by the state and prison officials. The state had demonstrated sufficient progress thus far without the need for an independent monitor to be appointed for the final phases of this litigation. It should be remembered, however, that the prisons were under the watchful eye of a compliance coordinator for 3 years pursuant to the terms of the 1978 consent decree that followed *Finney II*. The respondents were ordered to submit regular interim reports on their progress and a final report by June 14, 1982. The court found "great progress in improving conditions for inmates" but more was yet required, and "respondents must continue directly on the path they have charted to achieve success" (*Finney v. Mabry*, 1982a, p. 1046). The court received additional reports and conducted several hearings from 1981 to 1982 addressing the remaining concerns raised by the final reports of the compliance coordinator and Judge Eisele's hearings following the coordinator's departure (Feeley & Rubin, 1998).

Final Order

Judge Eisele conducted the final hearing in the class action matter on August 9, 1982. On August 20, 1982, Judge Eisele entered the final order in what he described as the "long, and at times turbulent, history" of the federal court supervision of the Arkansas prison system (*Finney v. Mabry*, 1982b, p. 629). The court noted with approval what was then a then relatively new and much improved version of the old 19th-century practice of privatization of correctional services. The lack of meaningful medical services was one of the original failings of the Arkansas prison system, and the Department of Correction had, without success, found an effective way to deliver healthcare services to inmates "in house." The department had recently contracted with an outside firm to provide medical care for inmates. The court noted the "medical services contract has met all expectations concerning its effectiveness and will very likely serve as a model for use in other institutional settings throughout the nation" (*Finney v. Mabry*, 1982b, p. 631).

The revised grievance procedures were also found to be in compliance with the consent decree and the Constitution. The disciplinary policies and procedures were also found to be reasonable and in compliance with the consent decree, the Constitution, and previous orders of the court. Similarly, the court found that procedures to be followed in a transfer to and confinement in administrative segregation were satisfactory and complied with the consent decree, the Constitution, and prior court orders (*Finney v. Mabry*, 1982b).

The lack of mental health services was a problem from the beginning of this litigation when there were no such services available to inmates. In 1981, the department opened a new mental health facility for "the most severely mentally ill inmates" (*Finney v. Mabry*, 1982b, p. 635). Additional improvements and expansion of mental health services resulted in a final conclusion by the court that this aspect of the correctional program in the Arkansas system was in full compliance with the consent decree, the Constitution, and previous orders of the court (*Finney v. Mabry*, 1982b).

Finney III directed the department to phase out the use of floorwalkers and turnkeys within a stated time period. It was reported to the court that this had been completed. Inmates did still serve as unarmed tower guards at Cummins and Tucker, but this was allowed within the parameters set by the court in previous rulings. These inmates were under direct supervision of armed free-world guards and posed no risk to security. The department was also in full compliance with regard to the staffing of correctional officers and other free-world institutional positions necessary to ensure security in all facilities. The court also noted that great progress had been made in stopping the previously common practice of guards using racial epithets and slurs to or in the presence of inmates. This positive change in staff behavior was even noted with approval by the Inmate Council (*Finney v. Mabry*, 1982b).

Finney III (*Finney v. Mabry*, 1982a) also required complete integration of the maximum security units and a reasonable process for determining whether nothing other than segregation of specific inmates by race would resolve security concerns. The Court now found that this had been completed in all units with the exception of the two-man cells in two barracks that housed certain inmates assigned to punitive and administrative segregation. In approving the proposed policy, the Court stated,

> The procedure utilized to effectuate that policy is now more clearly directed at identifying those individual inmates who would indeed pose a bona fide threat to security or safety if required to cell with an inmate of another race. The policy and procedure of the Department to effectuate integration of the entire institution, and the attitude of the Department to achieve that goal as exhibited by the final report, are no longer objectionable (*Finney v. Mabry*, 1982b, p. 639).

It was found that the problems with complete integration should continue to improve over time. It was further noted that much of the resistance to integration came from the inmates (*Finney v. Mabry*, 1982b). One can question whether this practice approved by the Court would have withstood a constitutional challenge had *Johnson v. California* (2005) been in effect at that time.

In this, his long-sought final order regarding the Arkansas prison litigation, Judge Eisele stated,

> The conclusion of the Court is, therefore, that the respondents are in compliance with the requirements of the Constitution, the Consent Decree, and all prior orders of the Court on all issues concerning the conditions of confinement at the various units of the Arkansas Department of Correction (*Finney v. Mabry*, 1982b, p. 641).

Eisele noted the dramatic changes from the early 20th century when "state prisoners were simply 'sold' to the highest bidder as contract labor" through state assumption of prison operations, but that did so with "but a handful of paid free-world people operating the entire prison system," to the current regime that has "approximately 1,000 free-world employees" (*Finney v. Mabry*, 1982b, p. 642). Judge Eisele recognized the efforts of the attorneys for the inmates, Phillip Kaplan, Jack Holt, Jr., and Phillip McMath; governors, including Faubus, Rockefeller, Bumpers, Pryor, White, and Clinton; state legislators; Department of Correction administrators; board members; and "the lowest echelons of the staff—the 'C.O.-1s' and their immediate superiors ... and the heavily burdened taxpayers of Arkansas" (*Finney v. Mabry*, 1982b, p. 643).

Judge Eisele concluded with the following:

> The Court is genuinely pleased that the facts and circumstances mandate its relinquishment of further jurisdiction in this case.
>
> It is therefore further ordered that the attorneys appointed by the Court to represent the plaintiff class be, and they are hereby, relieved of all further obligations herein.
>
> Finally, it is ordered that this case be, and it is hereby, dismissed with prejudice (*Finney v. Mabry*, 1982b, p. 643).

Conclusion

What was different from 1966 when word of the abuses at Tucker and Cummins was first widely revealed to Judge Eisele's final order in 1982? Gone was the use of physical torture, including the Tucker telephone and the strap as methods of discipline; gone were the filthy conditions and starvation diets; gone was the complete absence of state funding for prisons and reliance on fear and violence at the hands of inmate trusty guards supervised by only a handful of paid free-world employees to operate the prisons; gone was the corruption by administrators and trusty guards that flourished in the absence of state supervision. Where inmates previously lived in what must be described as a state of nature where the strong dominated and the weak cowered in fear, prison operations and inmate life now functioned under standardized rules and procedures that were governed by the Constitution and the rule of law.

Judge Eisele appropriately gave credit to the political leaders, including several governors, state legislators, Department of Correction officials, and the public for this transformation. While political and social pressures were essential to change, the real engine for reform was the federal court. The transformation from a "dark and evil world" unknown and largely unknowable to ordinary citizens to a modern prison in 15 relatively short years could not have occurred without the power and authority of an independent judiciary.

REFERENCES

Act would hike prison costs, Hutto claims. (1976, April 30). *Arkansas Democrat.*

Associated Press. (1976, March 22). Upgrading of prisons is costly, Pryor says.

Feeley, M. M., & Rubin, E. L. (1998). *Judicial policy making and the modern state: How the courts reformed America's prisons.* Cambridge University Press.

Finney v. Hutto, 410 F. Supp. 251 (E.D. Ark. 1976)

Finney v. Mabry, 455 F. Supp. 756 (E.D. Ark. 1978a)

Finney v. Mabry, 458 F. Supp. 720 (E.D. Ark. 1978b)

Finney v. Mabry, 534 F. Supp. 1026 (E.D. Ark. 1982a)

Finney v. Mabry, 546 F. Supp. 628 (E.D. Ark. 1982b)

Hutto almost backs Glover's proposal. (1976, June 16). *Arkansas Democrat.*

Hutto v. Finney, 437 U.S. 678 (1978)

Johnson v. California, 543 U.S. 162 (2005)

Oswald, M. (1976a, April 30). Limited prison changes asked. *Arkansas Democrat.*

Oswald, M. (1976b, June 29). Women prisoners leave Cummins. *Arkansas Democrat.*

Oswald, M. (1976c, September 24). Hutto quits position as correction chief. *Arkansas Democrat.*

Von Hirsch, A. (1976). Doing justice: The choice of punishment. Hill & Wang.

Wolff v. McDonnell, 418 U.S. 539 (1974)

KEY TERMS

"Nothing works" attitude

Consent decree

G. Thomas Eisele

Finney III

Stephen LaPlante

QUESTIONS

1. How did Arkansas propose to change the system to be consistent with policymakers' "nothing works" attitude toward rehabilitation? What were the consequences of those changes for state and county correctional facilities?

2. In 1976, T. Don Hutto resigned from his position of state corrections commissioner to become the deputy director of Corrections in Virginia. How long had he served in that capacity? Discuss the various changes Hutto orchestrated during his tenure.

3. What was the focus of *Finney* II? Explain Judge Eisele's unexpected and controversial findings, especially as they relate to *Wolff v. McDonnell* (1974), *Morrissey v. Brewer* (1972), and prison disciplinary hearings.

4. The consent decree included an agreement by the department to employ a compliance coordinator. Who was hired, and what was the compliance coordinator's responsibility?

5. The hearing *Finney III* was at the request of the inmate petitioners who had asserted that the state was no longer cooperating in good faith regarding the terms and conditions of the previous orders. Discuss the issues raised by an amended petition, alleging other violations of the law and the constitution.

6. On August 20, 1982, Judge Eisele entered the final order in what he described as the "long, and at times turbulent, history" of the federal court supervision of the Arkansas prison system. What was his ruling concerning medical services, grievance procedures, mental health services, floorwalkers and turnkeys, and integration of the maximum security units?

FIGURE CREDITS

Epilogue

Arkansas Prisons in the 21st Century

From a "Dark and Evil World" to a Modern Prison

Introduction

More than a half century ago, in 1968, State Prison Board Chairman John Haley asserted that Arkansas prison reform would continue and the Arkansas prisons could become an example of successful prison reform ("Haley Asserts Prison System to be 'Finest,'" 1968). Where Thomas Murton described the Arkansas prison system as a vestigial reflection of the institution of slavery as recently as 1969 ("Transcript of Murton's Prison Testimony," 1969), the Arkansas correctional system has made great strides and now operates modern prison facilities.

From Evil World to Modern Prison

The transformation from essentially a 19th-century Southern prison to a modern correctional system could not have occurred without the power, influence, and persistence of the federal courts. While it may seem that the period of federal court oversight from the first injunctive relief ordered in *Jackson v. Bishop* in 1967 to the end of ongoing federal court supervision in 1982 was far too long, there was a total transformation of the archaic pre-Murton Arkansas prison system described by Judge Henley as "a dark and evil world completely alien to the free world" to that which was in place in 1982 (*Holt v. Sarver II*, 1970, p. 381). The Arkansas prison litigation has been described as "the first and, in many ways, the most significant of all the prison cases" (Feeley & Rubin, 1999, p. 89). Arkansas is the only state that had its prison system as a whole declared to be unconstitutional (Palmer, 2010). The courts held the state to fulfill its constitutional duty to provide correctional facilities that are humane and satisfy the Eighth Amendment prohibition against cruel and unusual punishment. The U.S. Supreme Court in *Hutto v. Finney* (1978) affirmed that the Eighth Amendment will not permit punishments found to "transgress today's 'broad and idealistic concepts of dignity, civilized standards, humanity and decency'" (p. 685, quoting *Jackson, v. Bishop*, 1968, p. 579). Considering the starting point of the squalid conditions, corruption, inmate trusty guards, the torture of the Tucker telephone, the strap, the other abuses discovered by the Arkansas State Police in 1966, and the intransigence of certain state officials, it could have taken even longer to reach the final order ending ongoing federal court oversight in *Finney v. Mabry* (1982).

ADC Now

The Arkansas Department of Correction is the home to 19 prison units, including the women's unit, two work release centers, one re-entry center, and special units, including the Barbara Ester Unit that houses substance abuse, educational, and vocational-technical programs.

Where the old Arkansas prison system managed approximately 1,200 inmates with a handful of free-world employees, the system now has over 4,000 paid staff positions to supervise and care for just over 18,000 inmates. The Arkansas Department of Correction annual report for fiscal year 2019 states the department had 4,619 assigned positions, including 3,502 of which are security positions providing around-the-clock-supervision of inmates. In addition, staff positions include 144 full-time equivalent psychologists, social workers, advisors, and substance abuse program leaders (Arkansas Department of Correction, 2019).

Gender and ethnic diversity within the ADC personnel is increasing. The gender breakdown is 53% male and 47% female. The male staff is 60% White, 39% Black. Female staff is 32% White and 67% Black. However, it has been reported that the department had 500 vacant positions as of April 2019 (Moritz, 2019).

A 47-year veteran of the Arkansas Department of Corrections, Chief Deputy Director, M.D. "Dale" Reed, attributed the vacant positions to a "dwindling work-force," an assertion that is corroborated by the Bureau of Labor Statistics (BLS, 2019). The size, composition, and characteristics of the U.S. labor force have changed significantly in the last 50 years. These simultaneous changes, including the entry of the baby boom generation into the labor force and the significant growth of the labor force participation rate of women in the 1970s and 1980s, produced a steady growth in the workforce. However, times have changed, and the conditions that were present a couple of decades ago and that helped the labor force grow robustly are not present anymore. As a result, a shortage of qualified applicants is expected to increase.

Studies have revealed that inadequate pay and benefits, burdensome hours and shift work, inmate-on-staff assaults, and undesirable location of correctional facilities are factors that also render recruiting difficult (BLS, 2019; Keena et al., 2018; Moritz, 2019). Chief Deputy Director Reed acknowledged that ADC competes with other criminal justice agencies, specifically state law enforcement, the federal government, and private sector agencies, that offer more attractive jobs, pay, and benefit packages for well-qualified potential correctional employee applicants. In most instances, however, the ADC correctional officer's pay is comparable to that of members of other local and regional protective service occupations (M.D. Reed, personal communication, August 14, 2019).

For most of the 20th century, the Arkansas prison system operated as Chief Deputy Director Reed described, a "battlefield," and as Judge Henley defined in 1970, a "dark and evil world." Now, the Arkansas Department of Correction is accredited by the American Correctional Association (ACA) and proudly displays the coveted ACA Golden Eagle award designation. ACA is the oldest, and largest, private association developed specifically for practitioners in the correctional profession. Since 1954, ACA has published operational standards designed to enhance correctional practices for the benefit of inmates, staff, administrators, and the public. ACA does not provide oversight or monitoring of an accredited facility. It only verifies whether a facility is compliant with ACA policies and ACA disseminated standards at the time of accreditation. According to ADC, each of the various correctional facilities and administrative areas within ADC undergo audits every 3 years by ACA, with accreditation currently extended to the following:

- All adult correctional facilities (accredited under performance-based standards and expected practices for adult correctional institutions)
- Work-release facilities (accredited under performance-based standards for adult community residential services)
- The Central Office/Administrative Annex East (accredited under standards for the administration of correctional agencies)
- Arkansas Correctional Industries (accredited under performance-based standards for correction industries)
- The Willis H. Sargent Training Academy (accredited under standards for correctional training academies)

The ACA Golden Eagle award is presented to state correctional agencies in recognition of accrediting every component within their area of responsibility. The Golden Eagle award represents the highest commitment to excellence in correctional operations and the dedication of these agencies to enhancing public safety and the well-being of incarcerated individuals. In 2009, the Cummins unit was the last ADC correctional facility to receive ACA accreditation.

FIGURE E.1. Tucker unit entrance building and tower.

The department reports an operational budget for fiscal year 2019 of $354,107,530. This amount does not include correctional industries, farm, and work release. The department reports per inmate expenditures in 2019 as being $63.18 per day and $23,062 per annum. On June 30, 2019, the department reported an average daily population of 17,876 (Arkansas Department of Correction, 2019). Recall that when the Arkansas State Police began its investigation into conditions at the Tucker Farm in 1966, the state spent nothing on corrections over and above what was generated from farming operations (Feeley & Rubin, 1998).

FIGURE E.2. Tucker unit main entrance building's interior.

FIGURE E.3. Tucker unit administration building.

FIGURE E.4. Tucker unit chow hall.

FIGURE E.5. Tucker unit commissary.

FIGURE E.6. Tucker unit housing barracks.

FIGURE E.7. Tucker unit inmate pod barracks.

FIGURE E.8. Tucker unit inmate cell.

FIGURE E.9. Tucker unit inmate library.

FIGURE E.10. "The Ghosts of Tucker Past" from the Tucker Inmate Council, 2016.

The Ghosts of Tucker Past

Tucker Prison Farm in 1947. There were 1,300 inmates and 21 paid employees.

Hoe squad at work near the Tucker farm in 1933.

Hoe squad at the Tucker Unit today.

Tucker Prison Farm
The First 100 Years
1916 – 2016
A Brief History

1916	Tucker Prison Farm opened in March.
1933	Governor James Futrell closed "The Walls," the old prison in Little Rock, and all inmates were moved to the Cummins and Tucker farms.
1943	Act 1 created the State Penitentiary Board. The use of striped uniforms for inmates was stopped.
1964	Charles Fields was the last inmate executed at Tucker before the death penalty was declared unconstitutional.
1970	Governor Winthrop Rockefeller commuted the sentences of 15 death row inmates, which was the entire population of death row at Tucker.
1972	The U.S. Supreme Court declared capital punishment unconstitutional under existing procedures. The first prison rodeo was held at the Cummins Unit.
1974	Death Row inmates were moved from the Tucker Unit to the Cummins Unit. Sixty-seven inmates received G.E.D. certificates at the Tucker Unit during the department's first G.E.D. graduation ceremony.
1976	The U.S. Supreme Court declared capital punishment to be constitutional
1982	The 120-bed Tucker Modular Unit (Barrack #10) opened.
1984	The annual prison rodeo was discontinued by the Board of Correction.
1993	Female inmates were transferred from the Pine Bluff Unit to the Tucker Unit, and Tucker became the new women's prison unit. Male inmates were transferred from the Tucker Unit to the Varner Unit. The first female hoe squad turned out for work June 16, 1993 at the Tucker Unit
2016	Tucker Prison Farm will mark its centennial.

Tucker Fast Facts

In 1969, Thomas O. Murton, a penologist best known for his wardenship of Arkansas' prisons, published an account of the endemic corruption in the Arkansas system. The account was popularized in a fictional version by the 1980 Robert Redford movie, *Brubaker*.

White Lightning, a 1973 action film starring Burt Reynolds as Gator McKlusky, was largely filmed in Arkansas. In fact, in one part of the film where Gator escapes from prison, the movie was shot at the Tucker Prison Farm. Some of Tucker's hoe squad riders — including former Field Major Eddie Bell — played cameo roles. The film also starred Ned Beatty and native Arkansan Jennifer Billingsley.

FIGURE E.11. Cummins unit main gate entrance.

FIGURE E.12. Cummins unit master control room.

FIGURE E.13. Cummins unit main entrance security check.

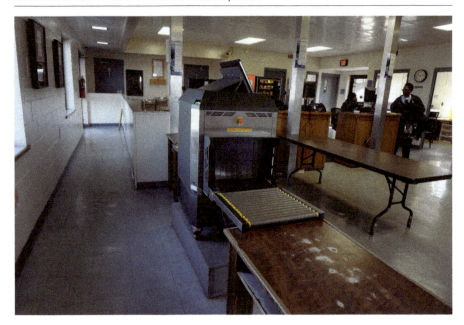

FIGURE E.14. Cummins unit open barracks.

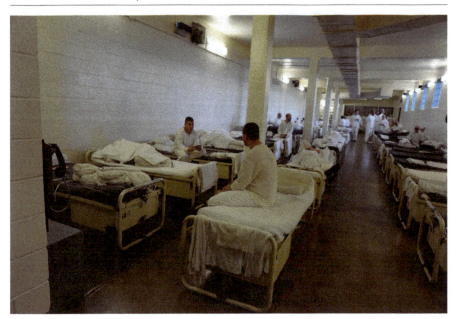

FIGURE E.15. Cummins unit barracks hallway.

FIGURE E.16. Cummins unit inmate dining hall.

FIGURE E.17. Cummins unit staff surveillance tower for the inmate chow hall.

FIGURE E.18. Cummins unit mailroom.

FIGURE E.19. Cummins unit chapel.

FIGURE E.20. Secretary of the Arkansas Department of Corrections, Wendy Kelley.

Education and Rehabilitation Programs

The mental health programs include sex offender treatment programs, a therapeutic community, a substance abuse treatment program, and self-study classes in anger management, stress management, parenting, communication, and other life skills (Arkansas Department of Correction, 2019). The demand appears to outpace the availability of the programs. The sex offender programs reported a total of 308 slots and a waiting list of 1,428 males and 11 females. The therapeutic community programs had a total of 239 slots with a waiting list of 1,039 males and 123 females. The substance abuse treatment program had 551 slots and a waiting list of 1,839 males and 203 females. This program also has a large group of over 3,000 on a wait list who are not eligible for various reasons (Arkansas Department of Correction, 2019). The self-study classes also report high levels of demand compared to available slots for inmate participation. These classes had, as of March 2019, a total of 1,938 participants and waiting lists of 5,358 (Arkansas Department of Correction, 2019). According to Chief Deputy Director Reed, ADC prioritizes and cycles the enrollment of its highest-risk and highest-need inmates to determine which inmates are (a) most likely to be released, (b) the highest risk to recidivate, and (c) have the highest need for rehabilitation programs to address those needs (M.D. Reed, personal communication, August 14, 2019).

Continuing Court Attention

With the entry of the final order in *Finney v. Mabry* (1982), the State of Arkansas was free of direct oversight of the federal courts by way of ongoing litigation, injunctive relief, frequent reporting, and court hearings. But the courts were still the ultimate remedy of choice for inmates with a complaint about conditions and treatment. As recently as 2015, the Arkansas Department of Corrections made it back to the U.S. Supreme Court where the department grooming policy was found to violate the protections of the Religious Land Use and Institutionalized Persons Act (RLUIPA) (*Holt v. Hobbs*, 2015). The department's grooming policy required inmates to be clean-shaven, unless an inmate had a medical condition that was aggravated by shaving facial hair. The petitioner requested an exemption from the policy to grow a one-half inch beard to comply with the dictates of his Muslim religion. This was a compromise suggested by the inmate. His religious belief was that he should not cut his beard at all but offered to trim the beard to the one-half inch limit allowed for those with qualifying skin conditions. The department took the position that institutional security justified the no-facial hair rule to prevent the ability to hide contraband and to ensure identification of inmates. The Supreme Court noted that the argument is weak in that such a short beard would not be able to hide contraband and the department did not have a corresponding rule requiring hair to be similarly short on the head. Also, the department could avoid identification problems by maintaining photographs of the inmate with and without facial hair. Security needs would not support the denial of the petitioner's requested accommodation of his religion (*Holt v. Hobbs*, 2015).

Inmate safety, while much improved, was still an issue that appeared in the federal courts. A 1995 incident in one of the open barracks at Cummins resulted in a suit for failure to protect (*Smith v. Arkansas Department of Correction*, 1996). The open barracks housing units have troubled the federal courts throughout the continuing Arkansas prison litigation from 1965 to 1982 (*Finney v. Mabry*, 1982a, 1982b). Smith (1996) sued the Arkansas Department of Correction for damages resulting from an attack by another inmate in an open Cummins barracks. Smith asserted that the department failed to provide adequate security in the barracks at night. One officer was assigned to supervise two adjoining barracks. The officer was positioned in the hallway between the two barracks. The department had long ceased the use of inmates in any positions related to security and had addressed the safety concerns resulting from inadequate sight lines for correctional officers to view activity in the barracks at night (*Finney v. Mabry*, 1982a, 1982b). But, it seems adequacy of staffing continued to be a problem not fully resolved by the *Finney* cases.

The petitioner in Smith cited the findings and recommendations of a study of the housing units at Cummins made at the request of the Arkansas General Assembly. Arthur Young & Company was retained to review the Arkansas Board of Correction and Department of Correction along with other state agencies. Their report was critical of the lack of adequate staffing and recommended that there be a minimum of two officers in each barracks (*Smith v. Arkansas Department of Correction*, 1996). Similarly, a 1991 U.S. Department of Justice report recommended two correctional officers for barracks during the night shift (*Smith v. Arkansas Department of Correction*, 1996). The district court in *Smith* entered an injunction requiring the additional officers for night shift security. The 8th Circuit Court of Appeals affirmed the district court's injunctive relief. The court was, at least in part, persuaded by the Arthur Young and Department of Justice reports suggesting the additional staffing requirements (*Smith v. Arkansas Department of Correction*, 1996). The role of the courts in ensuring continued adherence to constitutional standards is further illustrated by the *Smith* case. Even after the almost interminable litigation through the *Holt* and *Finney* cases, the department still had difficulty in taking positive action in response to recommendations by others. Less than 5 years after end of court supervision in *Finney v. Mabry* (1982a, 1982b), the department failed to act on the advice of Arthur Young & Company in 1986 regarding staffing in the open barracks during the night shift. This failure persisted even after a U.S. Department of Justice (DOJ) investigation in 1989 was settled following the DOJ report whereby the state agreed to increase the staffing levels as recommended by the DOJ. Even after these actions, it took the *Smith* (1996) lawsuit and another court order to get the agreed-on staff levels into compliance. The ACA accreditation process was also instrumental in getting the required staff positions approved for funding by the state (M.D. Reed, personal communication, August 14, 2019).

Recent Events

Inmate safety is of concern in any correctional facility. The reforms and improvements to the Arkansas prison system have not eliminated all risks of harm to inmates. The Arkansas Department of Correction reported four inmate suicides in a 2-month period at the Brickeys unit between March and April 2018. All four incidents were by hanging (Hardy, 2018). A Cummins unit inmate was found dead from self-inflicted wounds on May 21, 2019 (Turnage, 2019). The Arkansas prison system, like much of the rest of the country, is trying to come to grips with issues presented by the proliferation of social media. As part of the #FeelingCute social media challenge, female corrections officers were reported to have posted their photograph on a private Facebook correctional officers group with the caption, "Feeling cute. Those inmates wish they could have both of us. Meow" (Moritz, 2019). The posts were a violation of the Arkansas Department of Correction policy on social media and the individual officers were directed to cease such conduct (Moritz, 2019). Deputy Director Reed reports that this violation was quickly addressed and expects staff to comply in the future (M.D. Reed, personal communication, August 14, 2019).

The closed society and close living quarters of correctional facilities has proven to be an environment that is ripe for the spread of the COVID19 virus in the U.S. The Arkansas Department of Correction reported that as of July 2, 2020 there had been 1,884 positive tests among inmates who had recovered and 697 inmates positive and not yet recovered. Among staff, there were 184 positive/recovered tests and 57 who tested positive and not yet recovered (Arkansas Department of Correction, n.d.). The department has sought to limit the spread of the virus by hiring a private lab to conduct mass testing of inmates and quarantining those who test positive (ADC Secretary's Board Report, May 2020). The department further suspended visitation at all units (Arkansas Department of Correction, n.d.).

Impact of the Arkansas Prison Reform Saga

A search of the Thomson Reuters Westlaw (TM) database as of June 30, 2019, indicates that the 11 primary Arkansas prison cases[1] resulted in 3,300 federal case citations. The federal citations include 77 U.S. Supreme Court citations, 873 U.S. Circuit Court of Appeal citations, and 2,327 U.S. District Court citations. The U.S. Supreme Court citations include some of the most prominent cases in corrections law, including *Bell v. Wolfish* (1979), *Farmer v. Brennan* (1994), *Helling v. McKinney* (1993), *Hudson v. McMillian* (1992), *Rhodes v. Chapman* (1981), and *Wilson v. Seiter* (1991). *Hutto v. Finney* (1978) alone has been cited in 2,595 cases, including 48 U.S. Supreme Court decisions and 1,370 secondary sources such as law reviews and law journals.

---

1   *Holt v. Sarver* (1969); *Holt v. Sarver* (1970); *Holt v. Sarver* (1971); *Holt v. Hutto* (1973); *Finney v. Arkansas Board of Correction* (1974); *Finney v. Hutto* (1976); *Finney v. Hutto* (1977); *Finney v. Mabry* (1978); *Hutto v. Finney* (1978); *Finney v. Mabry* (1982); *Finney v. Mabry* (1982).

Conclusion

The Mission Statement of the Arkansas Department of Correction (2019), as published by the department, is the following:

> The Mission of the Arkansas Department of Correction is to provide public safety by carrying out the mandate of the courts; provide a safe, humane environment for staff and inmates; strengthen the work ethic through teaching of good habits; and provide opportunities for staff and inmates to improve spiritually, mentally, and physically.

The impact of court supervision on prison reform in Arkansas may be illustrated by the fact that "carrying out the mandate of the courts" is first in the listing of mission objectives.

Chief Deputy Director Reed gives credit for the successful transformation of the Arkansas prison system to a modern correctional system to multiple sources, including the federal courts, Governor Winthrop Rockefeller, the rigors of the ACA accreditation process, and dedicated and determined administrators such as Murton, Sarver, and Hutto. The influence of the courts cannot be overstated. Reed noted that the greatest hurdle to reform was reluctance of the legislature to provide money to address institutional needs. Continued court pressure was essential to overcome legislative inertia.

The reform process started in earnest with the scandals disclosed by the Arkansas State Police and the hiring of Thomas Murton. Reforms were continued under the dedicated efforts of administrators Sarver and Hutto. Judge Henley in *Holt II* (1970) said he would give a "reasonable" time: "[It] [wa]s going to have to be measured in months, not years" (p. 383). It took another 12 years. While not perfect, the Arkansas Department of Correction now operates a modern penal system that Deputy Director Reed says he "will hold up to anybody." It is a far cry from the horrific conditions and record keeping so bad that Thomas Murton initiated a contest to determine the actual and intended inmate population at the Cummins Farm (Murton & Hyams, 1969).

Deputy Director Reed noted that an old Delta expression is "you have to plow to the end of your row" (D. M. Reed, personal communication, August 14, 2019). From the Arkansas State Police investigation in 1966 to the final *Finney v. Mabry* orders in 1982, to the full ACA accreditation in 2009, the Arkansas Department of Correction made it "to the end of the row." But, the process does not end there. Diverse and sometimes violent populations, reluctant legislative funding sources, "get-tough" sentencing practices, inadequate staffing, and other issues will be ongoing challenges to be addressed by prison administrators in Arkansas and the nation. The continuing efforts to maintain a humane and effective system may be called the next row to be plowed.

REFERENCES

Arkansas Department of Correction, Coronavirus (COVID-19) updates. July 3, 2020. https://adc.arkansas.gov/coronavirus-covid-19-updates

Arkansas Department of Correction (2020). Secretary's Board Report, May, 2020. https://adc.arkansas.gov/images/uploads/DOC_Secretarys_Board_Report_May2020-FINAL.pdf

Arkansas Department of Correction. (2019). *Arkansas Department of Correction FY 2019 annual report.* https://adc.arkansas.gov/images/uploads/Division_of_Correction_FY19_Annual_Report_BOC_Approval-5272020.pdf

Arkansas State Police. (1966). Case report, Criminal Investigations Division (916-166-66). Report re Tucker State Prison Farm.

Bell v. Wolfish, 441 U.S. 520 (1979)

Bureau of Labor Statistics (2019). *Southwest information office: Labor force data.* https://www.bls.gov/regions/southwest/arkansas.htmFarmer v. Brennan, 511 U.S. 825 (1994)

Feeley, M. M., & Rubin, E. L. (1998). *Judicial policy making and the modern state: How the courts reformed America's prisons.* Cambridge University Press.

Finney v. Mabry, 534 F. Supp. 1026 (E.D. Ark. 1982a)

Finney v. Mabry, 546 F. Supp. 628 (E.D. Ark. 1982b)

Hardy, B. (2018, April 30). Brickeys prison reports fourth apparent suicide by hanging in two months. *Arkansas Times.*

Helling v. McKinney, 509 U.S. 25 (1993)

Holt v. Sarver II, 309 F. Supp. 362 (E.D. Arkansas 1970)

Holt v. Hobbs, 135 S.Ct. 853 (2015)

Hudson v. McMillian, 503 U.S. 1 (1992)

Hutto v. Finney, 437 U.S. 678 (1978)

Jackson v. Bishop, 268 F. Supp. 804 (E.D. Ark, 1967)

Jackson v. Bishop, 404 F.2d 571 (8th Cir., 1968)

Keena, L., Lambert, E., Haynes, S., May, D., & Buckner, Z. (2018). Examining the relationship between job characteristics and job satisfaction among southern prison staff. *Corrections: Policy, Practice, and Research, 5*(2), 109–129. https://www.tandfonline.com/doi/full/10.1080/23774657.2017.1421053

Moritz, J. (2019, May 5). "Feeling cute" posts by Arkansas corrections officers get noticed by prison officials. *Arkansas Democrat Gazette.*

Murton, T., & Hymas, J. (1969). *Accomplices to the crime: The Arkansas prison scandal.* Grove Press.

Palmer, J. (2010). *Constitutional rights of prisoners* (9th ed.). Matthew Bender & Company, Inc.

Rhodes v. Chapman, 452 U.S. 337 (1981)

Smith v. Arkansas Department of Correction, 103 F.3d 637 (8th Cir. 1996)

Turnage, C. (2019, May 22). Arkansas prison official: Inmate fatally wounded himself inside cell. *Arkansas Democrat Gazette.*

Wilson v. Seiter, 501 U.S. 294 (1991)

KEY TERMS

American Correctional Association

Chief Deputy Director M.D. "Dale" Reed

Golden Eagle award

QUESTIONS

1. It has been reported that ADC had 500 vacant positions as of April 2019. Chief Deputy Director Reed attributed the vacant positions to a "dwindling workforce." To what do you attribute the vacancies? Discuss the consequences of understaffing a prison.

2. In 2009, the Cummins unit was the last of the ADC correctional facilities to receive American Corrections Association accreditation. What are the advantages and disadvantages of ADC achieving ACA accreditation?

3. Despite being accredited by ACA, ADC has experienced significant continuing court attention since 1968 when Haley asserted that Arkansas prison reform could become an example of successful prison reform. The U.S. Supreme Court noted in *Bell v. Wolfish* (1979) that accreditation does not determine constitutionality. How might the court's view on accreditation affect the decisions in *Smith v. Arkansas Department of Correction* (1996) and *Holt v. Hobbs* (2015)?

4. While not a concern for the courts in 1969, in today's digital age, ADC has a social media policy. Is there an agency need for a social media policy for a correctional employee? How would you argue for or against the need for a correctional worker social media policy?

5. Chief Deputy Director Reed gives credit for the successful transformation of the Arkansas prison system to a modern correctional system to multiple sources, including the federal courts, Governor Winthrop Rockefeller, the rigors of the ACA accreditation process, and dedicated and determined administrators such as Murton, Sarver, and Hutto. To whom do you give the credit? Explain why.

FIGURE CREDITS

Fig. E.1: Copyright © by Arkansas Department of Corrections. Reprinted with permission.
Fig. E.2: Copyright © by Arkansas Department of Corrections. Reprinted with permission.
Fig. E.3: Copyright © by Arkansas Department of Corrections. Reprinted with permission.
Fig. E.4: Copyright © by Arkansas Department of Corrections. Reprinted with permission.
Fig. E.5: Copyright © by Arkansas Department of Corrections. Reprinted with permission.
Fig. E.6: Copyright © by Arkansas Department of Corrections. Reprinted with permission.
Fig. E.7: Copyright © by Arkansas Department of Corrections. Reprinted with permission.
Fig. E.8: Copyright © by Arkansas Department of Corrections. Reprinted with permission.
Fig. E.9: Copyright © by Arkansas Department of Corrections. Reprinted with permission.
Fig. E.10: Copyright © by Arkansas Department of Corrections. Reprinted with permission.
Fig. E.11: Copyright © by Arkansas Department of Corrections. Reprinted with permission.
Fig. E.12: Copyright © by Arkansas Department of Corrections. Reprinted with permission.
Fig. E.13: Copyright © by Arkansas Department of Corrections. Reprinted with permission.
Fig. E.14: Copyright © by Arkansas Department of Corrections. Reprinted with permission.

Printed in the USA
CPSIA information can be obtained
at www.ICGtesting.com
LVHW081459230224
772657LV00047B/1277

9 781516 581184